Brief Peeks Beyond

Critical essays on metaphysics, neuroscience, free will, skepticism and culture

WHAT PEOPLE ARE SAYING ABOUT

BRIEF PEEKS BEYOND

Better than any book I've come across, Bernardo Kastrup's collection of essays confronts two mysteries that must be urgently solved. The first is the mystery of reality. ... The second ... is the mystery of knowledge. ... To confront both mysteries at once ... requires courage, tenacity, a willingness to swim upstream, and thick skin. ... But if you have a persistent, acute mind like Bernardo's, an exciting journey opens up. (*From the Foreword*)
Deepak Chopra, M.D., pioneer in the field of mind-body medicine. Author of more than 75 books with 23 *New York Times* best sellers.

Some words, such as the collection of essays in *Brief Peeks Beyond,* have the ... power to evoke in the reader not just the concept of infinite Consciousness ... but the *experience* of it, a taste of its own essential reality. I have been touched by the profundity of these essays and know that they will imprint their healing intelligence in the broader medium of mind, from which humanity draws its knowledge and experience, for many years to come. (*From the Afterword*)
Rupert Spira, non-duality teacher and author.

In this pioneering, original and brilliantly written book Bernardo Kastrup is very critical of the still widely accepted materialist approach in science, while making use of many convincing rebuttals to materialist counterarguments. According to him all reality is in consciousness itself, because it is the only carrier of reality anyone ever knows for sure, but it is in a transpersonal mind-at-large, and not limited to our personal waking consciousness. His inevitable conclusion is that consciousness

must be fundamental in the universe. This important book is an excellent contribution to the growing awareness that the domination of materialism in science is irrefutably coming to an end, perhaps even in the next decade. Highly recommended.
Pim van Lommel, cardiologist, author of *Consciousness Beyond Life.*

Occam's Razor never cut so deep as in this penetrating critique of science, philosophy and the cultural cocoon we've constructed. Kastrup has followed up on his previous assault on dopey scientific materialism with a knockout punch.
Alex Tsakiris, author of *Why Science is Wrong... About Almost Everything* and host of the *Skeptiko* podcast.

Bernardo has the ability to communicate with the readers, through challenging them, in order to help our human consciousness to (re-)merge with the Whole of Consciousness, the 'Infinite Womb' of all that expresses Itself in time/space. For the open-minded and openhearted seekers of truth, this is great stuff to read.
Fred Matser, humanitarian, philanthropist, author of *Rediscover Your Heart.*

Brief Peeks Beyond

Critical essays on metaphysics, neuroscience, free will, skepticism and culture

Bernardo Kastrup

BOOKS

Winchester, UK
Washington, USA

First published by iff Books, 2015
iff Books is an imprint of John Hunt Publishing Ltd., No. 3 East Street, Alresford,
Hampshire SO24 9EE, UK
office1@jhpbooks.net
www.johnhuntpublishing.com
www.iff-books.com

For distributor details and how to order please visit the 'Ordering' section on our website.

ISBN: 978 1 78535 018 4
978 1 78535 019 1 (ebook)
Library of Congress Control Number: 2015930443

A CIP catalogue record for this book is available from the British Library.

Design: Stuart Davies

UK: Printed and bound by CPI Group (UK) Ltd, Croydon, CR0 4YY
US: Printed and bound by Thomson Shore, 7300 West Joy Road, Dexter, MI 48130

We operate a distinctive and ethical publishing philosophy in
all areas of our business, from our global network of authors to
production and worldwide distribution.

Contents

Other books by Bernardo Kastrup

Rationalist Spirituality: An exploration of the meaning of life and existence informed by logic and science

Dreamed up Reality: Diving into mind to uncover the astonishing hidden tale of nature

Meaning in Absurdity: What bizarre phenomena can tell us about the nature of reality

Why Materialism Is Baloney: How true skeptics know there is no death and fathom answers to life, the universe, and everything

More Than Allegory: On religious myth, truth and belief

Coming March 2019
The Idea of the World: A multi-disciplinary argument for the mental nature of reality

Ideally, what should be said to every child, repeatedly, throughout his or her school life is something like this: 'You are in the process of being indoctrinated. ... What you are being taught here is an amalgam of current prejudice and the choices of this particular culture. The slightest look at history will show how impermanent these must be. You are being taught by people who have been able to accommodate themselves to a regime of thought laid down by their predecessors. It is a self-perpetuating system.'[1]
Doris Lessing

Disentrenchment of formative contexts provides societies with a range of material and intangible advantages ... In fact, all the varieties of individual and collective empowerment seem to be connected in one way or another with the mastery the concept of disentrenchment ... describes.[2]
Roberto Unger

Acknowledgments

The inspiration, insights and intuitions behind a book never arise in a vacuum. Indeed, I am indebted to many who, directly and indirectly, have helped in the development of the ideas expressed here.

The many free-flowing, openhearted conversations I've had with my friends Rob van der Werf, Paul Stuyvenberg, Guiba Guimarães, Natalia Vorontsova, Fred Matser and Rick Stuart, about the nature of life and reality, have helped open me up to myriad aspects of my own humanity and the world. These people are no longer lost in the trance of our society's usual games. Instead, they are willing to engage with truth whatever it may entail. I gratefully acknowledge their influence on me. I am also grateful to my friend Alex Tsakiris and Niclas Thörn for the sharp discussions that helped shape some of the more critically incisive essays in this book. Finally, the subtle encouragement I was given by Pim van Lommel and Henry Stapp – two people I greatly respect and admire – have strengthened my resolve to complete this work.

I am thankful to the participants of my online discussion forum[3] for their help with this project, particularly in its initial stages, when their suggestions influenced its directions most clearly. With the risk of leaving equally important names out, I'd like to explicitly acknowledge the contributions of Don Salmon, Bob Clark, Saajan Patel, Peter Jones, Neil Creamer, Paul Middleton and Stewart Lynch. I am also grateful to Robin Carhart-Harris and Enzo Tagliazucchi, researchers at Imperial College, London, for their willingness to engage with me in an in-depth email discussion regarding the effects of psychedelics in the human brain.

I am indebted to Deepak Chopra for his continuing support in promoting my work and for the wonderful foreword he wrote for this book. While I may have some skill in logically explaining aspects of the truth, Deepak has the exceptional ability to *make them alive* to those with the eyes to see. Having come to know him and his ideas more closely than through the occasional TV show or debate, I've developed great respect for Deepak. Likewise, the generous validation I've received from Rupert Spira, someone who knows more intimately and profoundly than me much of what is written here, has been crucially encouraging. The masterful afterword he wrote captures the spirit of this book in a manner I couldn't hope to emulate.

Finally, this work may have never seen the light of day. As I wrote my earlier book, *Why Materialism Is Baloney,* a very dark and difficult period of my life was unfolding. Only a strange yet irresistible – even compulsive – sense of duty kept me going. Once the manuscript was duly complete, however, the compulsion had nothing left to attach itself to. An incongruous mixture of relief and emptiness overtook me. I was done; there was nothing else to achieve or aim for. Life had lost its *felt* meaning. It's hard to describe how dark that mental space is, or how strong its gravitational pull. Had I stayed there much longer, I don't know how things would have turned out. Yet here I am, with a new book imbued with more fighting spirit than any of my previous ones. It was the serendipitous appearance in my life of Claudia Damian, who embodied and radiated the very meaning I could no longer *feel* in being alive, that enabled this revival. Her love, affection and living example of how to relate to life simply and authentically, helped me escape the cage of my thoughts and reconnect with *immediate experience,* source of all true meaning. Her entrance into my story – timed to perfection – was palpable evidence, if any were needed, of something I already knew: *nothing really happens just by chance.* I am grateful to her, as well as to whatever organizing principles or agencies placed her in my world, for my new lease of life. With this book, I am trying to make it count.

Foreword by Deepak Chopra

Better than any book I've come across, Bernardo Kastrup's collection of essays confronts two mysteries that must be urgently solved. The first is the mystery of reality. Holding this book in your hands, or any physical object, you are being unwittingly tricked. The object feels secure and stable. It occupies three dimensions. You can feel its weight in your hands. Yet none of these facts are reliable or even valid. They slip through our fingers like sand once we take seriously the quantum revolution that occurred over a century ago. The solid, stable, reliable world vanished into clouds of invisible energy, and in a stroke everything we took for granted in everyday life was returned to its true state, as a profound mystery.

Even a quantum physicist would feel shaken to accept that he is driving a cloud of energy to work instead of a Honda, and so the mystery of reality has been pushed aside. Science is about things that can be measured and data that can be collected. With a shrug, most of us believe that this is enough. Only a sliver of thought is given to the 'real' reality that lies beyond the world's appearance.

The second mystery to be solved is wrapped up in the first. This is the mystery of knowledge. How do we know what we know? The obvious answer is 'through the brain.' But the human brain is a physical object like a bicycle, tree, or block of granite. It has no privileged position in Nature. The glucose that serves as your brain's primary nourishment can't think, any more than the sugar in a sugar cube can think. Besides, the brain vanished into a cloud of invisible energy along with everything else in Nature after the quantum revolution. Relying on it for true knowledge is shaky at best.

If only a sliver of thought is devoted to the first mystery – finding the 'real' reality – even less is devoted to the second

1

– discovering where knowledge comes from. To confront both mysteries at once, as Bernardo Kastrup does, requires courage, tenacity, a willingness to swim upstream, and thick skin. Science disparages and dismisses metaphysics, even though 99% of scientists haven't actually investigated what it is. History isn't just written by the victors; it's thought about by the victors. Science in our time feels supremely victorious, and the door to metaphysics is padlocked with a sign reading 'Don't Bother to Enter.'

But if you have a persistent, acute mind like Bernardo's, an exciting journey opens up. You get to think your way to the truth, and when thinking falters, you can 'peek beyond' by means of insight, intuition, and self-awareness. This is what separates physics from metaphysics (and why the ancient Greeks placed metaphysics higher). If the 'real' reality is accessible at all, it must be knowable through the mind. Beyond space, time, matter, and energy, nothing can be measured scientifically. There is no data to collect. There is no time before time came into the picture via the Big Bang. What does exist is the pre-created state of the universe. To explore it requires an Einstein of consciousness – as Einstein himself realized. Having theorized relativity strictly through mental work (so-called thought experiments), he declared that he was astonished when Nature turned out to confirm his theory.

Why should Nature conform to what we think about it? If you stand back, there's no compelling reason for it to. Nature could conform instead to a cat's perception of reality or a snail's or perhaps any nervous system at all, including those we can't conceive of. There's no reason to give the human mind access to the 'real' reality except for one possibility. Nature and the human mind could be intimately connected in the 'beyond' that metaphysics points to. The cosmos may be conscious, as some physicists are beginning to speculate. The human mind could be a reflection of God's mind, a religious notion that can be translated into non-religious terms. Or, if you want to be truly radical, creation may be a single thought expressing itself across the canvas of the universe in countless ways, including our individual thoughts. When you think the word 'rhinoceros,' you could be going to the same creative source where stars are born.

What saves these possibilities from being mere fancy is that for thousands of years there have been sages, seers, mystics, and philosophers who undertook the journey into consciousness that is the primary – indeed, the only – tool of metaphysics. Their findings are just as valid about reality as colliding electrons in a high-speed particle accelerator. The field in which they are valid, however, isn't materialistic. There are two fields, actually. One is the field of existence, or ontology, which looks into what 'real' means at the most basic level of being. The other is the field of knowledge, or epistemology, which looks into how it happens that reality allows itself to be known in the first place.

Bernardo isn't fortunate by the standards of mass media, which breathlessly announces the discovery of the Higgs boson but remains silent about metaphysics. But he's very fortunate to discover many cutting-edge topics that push the envelope of both science and philosophy. To be frank, unless a philosopher can satisfy the demands of science, meeting it halfway about the brain, the nature of time, the existence of multiple universes, dark matter and energy, etc., the whole enterprise will just be zombie philosophy. It will move around as if alive but actually be dead.

Fortunately, this is a fruitful time for 'peeking beyond,' because the accepted worldview of science, locked in its materialistic assumptions, has failed to show where time and space came from, what consciousness is, how deterministic laws of nature can be reconciled with free will, whether the brain can think or only parallels the mind's invisible processes, and a host of related questions. These 'meta' issues will never be resolved, Bernardo holds, unless we investigate the two areas that are his passion: ontology and epistemology. Do you know where your next thought is coming from? Do you know where any thought comes from? Neither does science with all its confidence and research findings. *Brief Peeks Beyond* is as much a book of questions as of answers, but it has the enormous advantage that its author knows which questions to ask and where to go to find the answers.

Deepak Chopra
Carlsbad, California
November 2014

1. Introduction

This is probably the most important book I've written. The original idea for it seemed easy enough: my publisher and I discussed creating an anthology of essays I had previously written for webzines, blogs and magazines. The intent was to update the essays and organize them into a coherent structure. Once I embarked on the project, however, something within me saw an opportunity and I became determined to take it way beyond its original scope. The result, which you now hold in your hands, could no longer be honestly described as just an anthology. *It has turned into an experiment in 'nonlinear philosophy,'* with a new, unifying message of its own. Allow me to elaborate.

As I reviewed my original essays, I noticed for the first time that they were pieces of a larger jigsaw puzzle. Only with the benefit of hindsight did I realize this; the overall picture in the puzzle had eluded me up to that moment. It became clear that much of the material consisted in explorations of different angles of a single motif: *an idea gestalt – an organized cognitive whole beyond the mere sum of its parts – about the human condition as it is presently manifested.* It has various facets related to science, philosophy of mind, the underlying nature of reality, the state of our society and culture, the influence of the mainstream media, etc. Because of this apparent disparity of facets, the gestalt that links them together can't be conveyed through a linear narrative. There are just too many important nuances to capture that way. *It can only be conveyed by tackling each of its facets within its own context so that you, dear reader, can combine the pieces of the puzzle and reconstruct the gestalt in your own mind.* This is precisely what this book attempts to achieve. The essay format turns out to have been critical in that it allowed me to approach the target motif through several different angles, helping you build an overall picture of it facet by facet. If the book succeeds in its endeavor,

5

at the end of it you will be looking upon the present nexus of the human story in a very different way.

I've attempted to make each essay in this book suggestive of, and conducive to, this global cognitive gestalt. Each contributes an important angle to it. Yet, when putting the original material together, it became clear to me that there were gaps; important pieces of the puzzle were missing. For this reason, many of the essays here are entirely new, having never before been published. They are meant to cover the gaps. All previously published material was also updated and in many ways improved. Several essays were largely rewritten to reflect new, more complete insights I've had since I first wrote them, or to make their message crisper and clearer. Most were also adapted so as to complement each other in suggesting the subtleties and nuances of the global motif that is the message of this book. Even among the essays that were least changed in terms of the number of words edited, the importance of the changes is disproportionate to the space they occupy.

Overall, this work is characterized by a new readiness on my part to go all out with my points of view. In my previous works, I've held myself back in the interest of striking a more moderate note with broader appeal. It is, however, unclear whether that was effective. What is sure is that it pruned the full expression of my views. Now, having turned 40 and witnessed my life take turns I'd never expected, I feel less motivated to compromise on my discourse. Life is just too short for that. Therefore, this book tackles, head-on, subjects I have hitherto kept out of bounds: God, 'conspiracies,' the obvious flaws of science as practiced today, the often insidious role of the media and a number of other polemical topics. You be the judge of whether my uncensored views still hold up to reason and the available evidence.

This book can be read in two ways: in sequence, from beginning to end; or by picking a different essay at each sitting. The essays have been organized in a logical and coherent sequence, optimized for insinuating the subtle bridges and relationships between the various different topics. This way, readers who are willing to read this book from cover to cover will probably develop a better grasp of the ideas in it. That said, I am well aware that many readers will prefer to pick their favorite topic from the table of contents, depending on their mood and disposition of the day, and go straight to it. I confess to often preferring this approach myself, especially when reading in bed before sleep. Therefore, I also made sure that each essay is self-contained and can be read independently of the others. The majority can be read in well under an hour. When appropriate, I refer to other essays where certain topics mentioned are covered in more depth. The price for this modularity, however, is some redundancy: many of the essays contain summaries of my metaphysics, which is necessary to give context to the ideas they express. I've endeavored to strike an optimal balance between redundancy and modularity, so readers neither feel bored with repeated content, nor miss essential context for understanding each essay.

Whichever way you prefer to read this book, I do suggest that you always start with essays 2.1 and 2.2. They provide context that underlies what is discussed in most other essays. Although the key contextual points are, as mentioned above, repeated each time, readers will derive more value from the rest of the book if they have more extensive prior grasp of those two initial texts.

A couple of observations should be made at this point. This is largely a critical work: it criticizes today's science, philosophy, media, culture and society. It is *also* largely a body of – hopefully well-substantiated – *opinions*. Yet, the criticisms it contains are not always preceded by a disclaimer asserting that what follows is an expression of opinion. Doing so would be highly detrimental to flow and readability. Let this be the general disclaimer, thus: unless stated otherwise, you should assume that what you will find in the following pages is an expression of my opinions. The extensive substantiation of my arguments does not change this fact.

Another important observation: I use the words 'mind' and 'consciousness' interchangeably. The meaning I lend to the word 'consciousness' – and thus 'mind' – is defined early in essay 2.1. I use the term 'psyche' when I mean *personal* consciousness, or *personal* mind. This terminology may be confusing to some: in non-duality circles, the word 'mind' has come to be associated with 'thoughts;' that is, with a particular type of contents of consciousness. Yet, my use of the terms is more consistent with their traditional meaning in Western philosophy.

Finally, this book contains a high concentration of ideas. Very few words are wasted. I go quickly to the point and don't ramble around. While this will probably feed the enthusiasm of some readers, it may prove a little too intense to others. I apologize to the latter: my approach here reflects my surrender to what comes more naturally to me, rather than a deliberate attempt to favor a particular segment of my readership.

So if you're ready, buckle up and join me in a multi-faceted, fast-paced, nonlinear exploration of the human condition in the early 21st century. Here we go!

2. On metaphysics and cosmology

Our culture takes for granted that the empirical world exists 'out there' and is fundamentally independent of consciousness. This postulate seems to explain a number of things that we, otherwise, would allegedly be unable to make sense of: the continuity of events while we are asleep, the undeniable correlations between brain states and experience, the fact that we all seem to inhabit the same world, etc. For this reason, we've allowed our values, economic and political systems, ways of relating to nature and each other, psychology, medicine, social dynamics, etc., to be all subtly colored – if not outright *determined* – by such a postulate. But does it stand to reason and evidence? In this chapter, we will explore the underlying nature of reality and our condition as conscious entities within it.

Essay 2.1 summarizes the metaphysics more extensively described in my earlier book *Why Materialism Is Baloney*. But beyond a mere summary, it also *extends* and *refines* that metaphysics, elaborating on it in a more direct, less metaphor-loaded manner. Essay 2.2 then lists and addresses each of the key materialist counter-arguments against the ideas in essay 2.1, refuting them one by one. It is not only the longest essay of this book, but probably one of its most important and original contributions as well. Essay 2.3 takes the form of a short story. It seeks to illustrate a different *way of seeing* and interpreting the ancient ideas of an immortal soul and an afterlife from the perspective of the metaphysics described in essay 2.1. Essay 2.4 discusses how the survival of consciousness beyond physical death is, in fact, a direct implication of our most basic common sense. Essay 2.5 confronts a distinction that materialism has difficulties with: the obvious difference between living beings and inanimate objects. It also explains why the notion that all reality is in consciousness does *not* imply that inanimate objects are themselves individually conscious. Essay 2.6 then bites a big bullet: God. It argues that the existence of a conscious, omniscient, omnipresent and omnipotent agency is, surprisingly, a direct implication of metaphysical *parsimony*. This is profoundly counterintuitive from a materialist perspective, which holds precisely that the existence of a deity *defies* parsimony. The essay further maintains that evidence for God is literally all around us. Finally, essay 2.7 grapples with one of the biggest mysteries in science today: the measurement problem of quantum mechanics. It argues that the explanation for that conundrum is, in fact, the very same phenomenon that explains how our ordinary awareness arises from seemingly unconscious mental activity. In the process of making its case, the essay ends up bringing together the Copenhagen and the Many-Worlds interpretations of quantum mechanics, which materialism deems irreconcilable.

2.1. A more parsimonious, logical, non-materialist worldview

The mainstream metaphysics of our culture – materialism – posits that the empirical world is fundamentally outside consciousness. The world supposedly consists of an unfathomably complex assemblage of stand-alone material particles, all of which would still exist in the absence of any subjective experience. It's not difficult to see why so many of us buy into this view: the environment we live in is clearly outside our heads and different individuals undoubtedly agree on what its salient aspects look like, so we all seem to share the same environment. When I go to a stadium to watch a football match, the other thousands of people in the stadium apparently experience the same match. The obvious explanation for this sharing of experience is that the match exists outside the personal consciousness of the spectators, so they can all simultaneously observe it. If the world were just a kind of subjective dream, how could separate people share the same dream? Moreover, there are correlations between the material activity of brains and subjective experience: through brain-imaging technology, neuroscientists have demonstrated these correlations beyond any doubt.[4] Therefore, materialism seems to be entirely justified in extracting one additional conclusion: not only does matter exist outside consciousness, specific arrangements of matter in the form of active brains *generate* consciousness. All this seems to make perfect sense.

There are, however, two major problems with it: first, the seemingly persuasive argument behind materialism is ridden with circular logic; second, since consciousness is the only carrier of reality anyone can ever know for sure, inferring an entire universe outside consciousness comes at a very steep price in terms of parsimony. Let us explore all this.

To begin with, we need to define more precisely what we mean by the word 'consciousness.' Although everybody has an intuitive understanding of it, the word itself is often overloaded with metaphysical assumptions. A materialist might define 'consciousness' as the result of certain types of brain activity, while a religious person might define it as the essential attribute of an immaterial soul. In both cases, the word is overloaded with a particular *explanation*. To avoid these explanatory biases, it's useful to define 'consciousness' in a purely operational manner. In this spirit, I use the following definition in this book: *consciousness is that whose excitations are subjective experiences.* In other words, every subjective experience is a particular excitation of consciousness – whatever consciousness may intrinsically be – just like ripples are excitations of water. This operational definition is precise and metaphysically neutral.

Now notice that, in exactly the same way that there is nothing to ripples but water, there is nothing to subjective experience but consciousness. There's nothing to an excitation but that which is excited. Therefore, there is a degree of equivalence between experience and consciousness, so we could perhaps also say that *consciousness is raw subjective experience itself.* This is an admittedly more restrictive version of the definition above: after all, we don't say that water *is* ripples; ripples are just a *behavior* of water. Water continues to exist even when it's not rippling. However, it is extremely difficult to find semantic room for the word 'consciousness' *without* experience. What sense is there in saying that one is conscious without being conscious *of* something? I am not saying that there can't be intrinsic consciousness without experience; in fact, my definition of consciousness in the previous paragraph implies precisely that there is. Eastern spiritual traditions have also spoken for centuries of 'pure consciousness' without experience. What I am trying to point out here is merely the impossibility to coherently *articulate* this pure consciousness in language. As such, whatever consciousness may intrinsically be in the absence of experience – in the absence of ripples – is fundamentally beyond our ability to talk about or make sense of. Hence, defining consciousness rather restrictively as its own behavior seems fair enough for discussion purposes, as long as we understand what we are doing.

With all this in mind, we can then assert that *consciousness* – whatever it may intrinsically be – *is the only carrier of reality anyone can ever know for sure.* It is the one undeniable empirical fact of existence. After all, what can we really know that isn't experienced in some form, even if only through instrumentation or the reports of others? If something is fundamentally beyond all forms of experience, direct or indirect, it might as well not exist. Because all knowledge resides in consciousness, we cannot *know* what is supposedly outside consciousness; we can only *infer* it through our capacity for abstraction.

Now, because of the principle of parsimony (which I elaborate upon in essay 4.7), we are only justified in inferring an abstract universe outside consciousness if this inference is *necessary* to make sense of things. For instance, if we cannot otherwise make sense of the fact that thousands of people can experience the same football match concurrently, then – and only then – we are justified in inferring that there is a match outside experience.

But notice what a great demand this is: it is enough that we find *one* coherent explanation for reality on the basis of excitations of consciousness alone for a postulated universe outside consciousness to become akin to the Flying Spaghetti Monster.[5] Like the Spaghetti Monster, we cannot *prove* it isn't there; but it would be entirely unnecessary – and flat-out ridiculous – to seriously propose its existence.

I claim that we do not need more than consciousness to explain reality: *all things and phenomena can be made sense of as excitations of consciousness itself.* According to this more parsimonious view, the ground of all reality is a transpersonal flow of subjective experiences that I metaphorically describe as a stream. Our personal awareness is simply a localization of this flow: a whirlpool in the stream. It is this localization that leads to the illusion of personal identity and separateness. The body-brain system is the *image* of the process of localization in the stream of consciousness, like a whirlpool is the image of a process of localization in a stream of water. There is nothing to a whirlpool but water. Yet, we can point at it and say: there's a whirlpool! Analogously, there is nothing to a body but consciousness. Yet, we can point at it and say: there's a body!

For exactly the same reason that a whirlpool doesn't generate water, the body-brain system doesn't generate consciousness. Yet, because the image of a process carries valid information about the inner dynamics of the process – just like the colors of flames carry valid information about the microscopic details of combustion – brain activity correlates with subjective experience. This is why neuroscientists find tight correspondences between a subject's conscious inner life and their measured brain activity: the latter is simply what the former *looks like* from the outside. We don't say that lightning is the *cause* of atmospheric electric discharge, do we? Lightning is simply what atmospheric electric discharge looks like from the outside. For exactly the same reason, it is absurd to say that neurons cause thoughts, emotions or perceptions. *Neurons are simply what our thoughts, emotions and perceptions look like when another person observes them.*

Still according to this more parsimonious interpretation of reality, *it is the body-brain system that is in consciousness, not consciousness in the body-brain system.* After all, it is the whirlpool that is in the stream, not the stream in the whirlpool. Think of the empirical world as a collective dream: in a dream, it is your dream character that is in consciousness, not consciousness in your dream character. This becomes obvious when you wake up and realize that the whole dream was your mind's creation. But it isn't obvious at all while you are asleep: during the dream, it is easy to implicitly assume that your consciousness is somehow inside your dream character. Can you be sure that the same illusion isn't taking place right now?

Moreover, if the body is in consciousness, as opposed to the other way around, then the fact that our bodies are separate does *not* imply that our personal psyches are fundamentally separate. Indeed, once you drop the notion that your consciousness is confined to your body, it becomes entirely plausible that our psyches are all united at the deepest, most obfuscated levels. Depth-psychology, despite erroneously calling it the 'collective unconscious,' has accumulated decades-worth of evidence for the existence of this obfuscated, collective part of consciousness.[6] Inferring that personal psyches share a common root does not entail postulating a new, abstract theoretical entity – namely, a universe outside consciousness – but merely *extrapolating* consciousness itself beyond its face-value personal limits. As such, to see the world as akin to a shared dream grounded in a collective, obfuscated part of consciousness is much more parsimonious than materialism.

But where is this collective part of consciousness? It's easy to see. As our personal psyches are like whirlpools in a broader stream, so the broader stream itself is a transpersonal form of consciousness that underlies all reality and unites all whirlpools. The broader stream *is* the 'collective unconscious.' Aldous Huxley ably called it 'mind-at-large,'[7] a more accurate terminology that I shall adopt from this point on. For the same reason that the experiences of another person appear to us as a seemingly objective phenomenon – namely, an active brain – the seemingly objective world around us is what experiences in mind-at-large look like from the outside. In other words: for the same reason that a neuroscientist can know that a person has conscious inner life merely by measuring the person's brain activity, we can know that mind-at-large exists merely by observing the world around us. *The empirical world itself is the overwhelming, concrete evidence for the existence of mind-at-large.*

Think about it for a moment: an active brain is a structured collection of so-called subatomic particles. Yet we know that an active brain is what conscious processes look like from the outside. Likewise, consensus reality is *also* a structured collection of subatomic particles. Therefore, it, as a whole, must *also* be the outside image of conscious processes. But whose conscious processes? Those of mind-at-large, of course; whose else could they be? Personal experiences are to brain activity as the transpersonal experiences of mind-at-large are to the world we observe around us. The correspondences that lead to this conclusion are clear: our consensus reality – that is, the empirical world – is the framework wherein active brains arise as local structures, just as the stream – that is, mind-at-large – is the framework wherein whirlpools arise as localized patterns of water flow; whirlpools are made of nothing but the stream's water, just as active brains are made of nothing but the subatomic particles of consensus reality; there is nothing to an active brain but those particles, just as there is nothing to a whirlpool but water; etc.

Interpreting reality as excitations of mind-at-large allows the physical world to be exactly what it seems to be: to have colors, flavors, smells, textures and melodies. It acknowledges that those colors, flavors, smells, textures and melodies exist *outside our head*. After all, it is our head that is in consciousness, not consciousness in our head. The materialist metaphysics, on the other hand, posits that all qualities of experience – all colors, flavors, smells, textures and melodies – are generated by our brain. Therefore, they can only exist inside our skull! *It is materialism that says the world we perceive is inside our head*. According to it, the actual world 'out there' is a purely abstract realm of *concepts* and associated *quantities*. Matter, as such, has no intrinsic *qualities:* it isn't hard or rough, or cold, or concrete; it's just an abstract *concept* to which we attach *numbers* in order to characterize it. We can't even visualize what this abstract world may be like, since visualization necessarily entails the qualities of experience.

Recently, physicist Max Tegmark acknowledged the awkwardness of this situation by deeming the metaphysical conceptualizations of materialism, like atoms and subatomic particles, to be unnecessary 'baggage.'[8] The obvious next step in this line of reasoning is to acknowledge the sufficiency of experience, but Tegmark isn't ready to go that far: he still insists on some form of reality outside consciousness. He drops the conceptual part of it but keeps the quantities. In other words, he postulates that *it is all just numbers out there;* no particles to attach the numbers to. At first sight, this seems to be just an extreme version of the materialist endeavor to replace reality with abstractions. But if you look carefully, you will notice that, by being so ready to embrace abstraction all the way, Tegmark comes full circle: *after all, mathematics – quantities and their relationships – is a mental construct.* 'The fool who persists in his folly will become wise,' said Blake. By positing that the physical world consists solely of mathematical entities, there is an important way in which Tegmark is at least flirting with the views expressed in this essay.

The key to the consciousness-only ontology I am proposing is the realization that there can potentially be two angles, or facets, to an experience: the necessary first-person but also a possible second-person perspective; the inside and the outside views. This way, what I feel when I watch erotic material is a first-person, inside perspective of the experience of arousal. But if I am placed in a brain scanner while watching erotic material, the neuroscientist operating the brain scanner will gain a second-person, outside perspective of my arousal in the form of patterns of brain activity. Notice that the second-person perspective is *also* an experience: the neuroscientist *sees* my brain activation patterns; he just doesn't feel arousal. Indeed, the first- and second-person perspectives, despite being correlated, are qualitatively *different* experiences: observing brain scans is anything but arousing! To say that there is a second-person perspective to an experience means only that valid information about it is carried by another experience in another part of the broader stream of consciousness. Naturally, there can be experiences in the stream that have no second-person perspective at all. An 'experience' without a first-person perspective, however, is a contradiction in terms.

It is the localization of flow in the broader stream of consciousness – the formation of whirlpools – that gives rise to a second-person perspective and, with it, the illusion of a world outside consciousness. Let's unpack this slowly, step-by-step.

Neuroscience has found out empirically that our *ordinary* awareness correlates with *reverberating* brain activity, involving back-and-forth communication between different brain areas.[9] Insofar as it is a phenomenon of the nervous system, this reverberation is a consequence of the localization of experiences. Now, just as it does with sound in a room, reverberation *amplifies* the localized mental contents caught in it. Analogously to how the stronger glare of the Sun obfuscates the stars at noon, the amplified, reverberating mental contents in the 'center' of the whirlpool obfuscate everything else, to the point of rendering it all *seemingly* unconscious. This is the reason why depth-psychology has come to adopt the misnomer 'unconscious.' What psychology and neuroscience mistakenly consider unconscious neural processes are merely the outside image of *obfuscated* mental contents in the periphery of the whirlpool, which don't get caught in the reverberation. They correspond to what analytical psychology calls the 'personal unconscious.' Of course, the amplification of reverberating mental contents in the 'center' of the whirlpool also obfuscates everything going on *outside the whirlpool* itself; that is, in mind-at-large. In the terminology of analytical psychology, the obfuscated processes in mind-at-large are called the 'collective unconscious.' All these obfuscated mental contents, both inside and outside the whirlpool, are still in consciousness – for the same reason that the stars are still in the sky at noon – but not in the field of *ordinary, lucid awareness.* As neuroscience has empirically determined, the latter only arises from reverberation.

There's no true unconscious, for all reality is in consciousness. But because the conscious activity unfolding in mind-at-large becomes *seemingly* unconscious from the point of view of a whirlpool, every human being effectively turns into a dissociated personality – an *alter* – of mind-at-large. People with Dissociative Identity Disorder, for instance, can exhibit multiple alters, each experiencing itself as separate from the rest of the psyche and having its own stream of thoughts, imagination, memory, skills, emotions, self-image, etc.[10] Alters arise because they become seemingly unconscious of the mental activity in the remaining parts of mind. This is easy to see when we turn it around: if I were lucidly aware of your entire inner life, and you of mine, we would be effectively the same conscious entity, wouldn't we? We feel that we are separate precisely because we are seemingly unconscious of each other's inner lives. It is thus easy to see that the reverberation/amplification of mental contents in the 'center' of their whirlpool can effectively dissociate human beings from the rest of mind-at-large. Mind-at-large suffers from 'Dissociative Identity Disorder' and we are its 'alters.'

Finally, the key point: *the formation of an alter delineates a boundary between mental activity inside and outside the alter.* This boundary is what creates the second-person perspective of experience and the illusion of a world outside mind: conscious activity unfolding outside the alter can only become accessible to it from a second-person perspective. The first-person perspective becomes obfuscated by the reverberation/amplification mechanism in the whirlpool.

How exactly does this process work? To visualize it, let's get back to the stream metaphor. Each whirlpool corresponds to a person and each person to at least one alter of mind-at-large. The rim of the whirlpool delineates the boundary between ourselves – including our thoughts, fantasies, emotions, bodily sensations, etc. – and the outer world, which we perceive through our five senses. The whirlpool's rim is our sense organs: skin, eyes, nose, ears and tongue. Let us now imagine that experiences are disturbances of the water flow in the stream – that is, excitations of consciousness. Dynamic processes creating disturbances *inside* a whirlpool can become amplified and lucid: these are our thoughts, fantasies and emotions, which all constantly arise within ourselves. However, because of obfuscation, we become seemingly unconscious of similar dynamic processes creating disturbances *outside* our respective whirlpools.

Very well. Now, *some of those outside disturbances create ripples that penetrate our whirlpools through their rim.* This is what our sense perceptions are. We call those incoming ripples 'photons,' 'sound waves,' 'scent molecules,' etc. Once they penetrate the whirlpool – that is, engage our sense organs – the incoming ripples may also become amplified, reaching our lucid awareness. But the ripples that penetrate a whirlpool are just *traces* of outside dynamic processes unfolding in mind-at-large; the wake of the ship, not the ship itself. While the original outside disturbances that generated the ripples correspond to the *first-person* perspective of experiences in mind-at-large, the incoming ripples correspond to a *second-person* perspective of those original experiences. Indeed, it is for this reason that the second-person perspective of an experience feels so qualitatively different from the first-person one: the incoming ripples *aren't* the outside disturbances that generated them in the first place; the wake isn't the ship, although it corresponds to the ship's movements. Active neurons aren't arousal, but merely the trace left by arousal.

The second-person perspective of an original experience is the result of amplification, within a whirlpool, of ripples generated by the outside disturbance of consciousness that is the original experience. The second-person perspective is always itself an experience *within* a whirlpool, which carries information about a disturbance of the stream of consciousness *outside* the whirlpool. When you see another person, what you perceive are the ripples that the whirlpool corresponding to that other person has generated. If you close your eyes, you can no longer see the person because you are making it impossible for these ripples to penetrate your own whirlpool.

In conclusion, we can explain personal awareness by a process of localization in the flow of a broader, transpersonal stream of experiences. We can explain the so-called 'unconscious' psyche by the obfuscation of mental contents that results from reverberation of experiences within localized awareness. We can explain the divide between thoughts, emotions and imagination on the one hand, and perceptions on the other hand, by the dissociation that accompanies this obfuscation. We can explain the correlations between brain activity and subjective experience by the first- and second-person perspectives of experience that result from the dissociation. And, finally, we can explain consensus reality as the shared second-person perspective of mental activity unfolding in a collective, obfuscated part of consciousness. In short, we can explain *all* reality without postulating anything but consciousness itself.

Philosophers call this worldview *idealism*. All we need to do to make idealism work is *extrapolate* consciousness beyond the limits of personal psyches. This is entirely reasonable for at least two reasons: first, there is significant empirical evidence for transpersonal states of consciousness;[11] second, regardless of any empirical evidence, inferring that the boundaries of a *known* ontological category extend beyond face-value limits is much more parsimonious than inferring a whole *new* ontological category, such as a universe outside consciousness. Even if there were no extra empirical evidence in its favor – though there is plenty – idealism would still trump materialism on grounds of parsimony alone.

This essay is an attempt to summarize a worldview described in detail, and substantiated rigorously, in my earlier book *Why Materialism Is Baloney*. Naturally, I can't really do justice to an argument originally laid out in 250 pages when squeezing it into only a few paragraphs. Many important points had to be left out. Therefore, I urge those interested in a more in-depth understanding of this worldview – as well as those inclined to dismiss it on the basis of what this essay fails to cover – to read that more complete work before final judgment. For understanding the views expressed in the remainder of this book, however, the present essay provides sufficient background.

2.2. Materialist arguments and why they are wrong

I am a proponent of the philosophy of idealism: the notion that all reality is grounded in a transpersonal form of consciousness of which we, as living beings, are merely dissociated complexes, or alters. I maintain that inferring a whole universe fundamentally outside consciousness is unnecessary: we can explain all reality purely as excitations of consciousness itself. Moreover, I also maintain that inferring this universe outside consciousness is *insufficient* to make sense of reality: it fails to explain consciousness itself, the most present – and arguably sole – fact of existence, as discussed in essay 3.1. My argument for idealism is summarized in essay 2.1. Here, I'd like to tackle some of the most common materialist counter-arguments to it.

This essay is organized as a series of criticisms and rebuttals, with interspersed commentary. The criticisms are the materialist counter-arguments to idealism. The rebuttals are my respective rejoinders. For ease of reference, criticisms and rebuttals are organized in numbered pairs.

There are different ways in which the materialist criticisms listed below are fallacious. A common fallacy is a kind of circular reasoning called 'begging the question.' One begs the question when one takes the conclusion of an argument as a premise of the argument. For instance, if one says: 'God exists because the Bible says so, and the Bible is true because it was written by God,' one is begging the question of God's existence. Although the circularity of the reasoning is obvious in this simplistic example, one often begs the question in an indirect and somewhat concealed manner. In the next five pairs of criticism and rebuttal, I explore common ways in which materialists beg the question, arguing for the validity of materialism by assuming materialism in the argument. The circularity of their reasoning becomes clear once it's pointed out, so it is rather surprising how often educated, otherwise intelligent materialists fall for it.

Criticism 1: Our sense perceptions provide direct evidence for a world outside consciousness.
Rebuttal 1: All we can assert with certainty about our sense perceptions is that they are a particular modality of experience. Other modalities are thoughts, emotions and imagination. The difference is that we often identify with our thoughts, emotions and imagination – that is, we think they form part of who we are – and seldom identify with the contents of our sense

perceptions. Indeed, we do not ordinarily believe that the world we see around us is part of us. Moreover, while we have some degree of direct volitional control of our thoughts, emotions and fantasies, we do not have any direct volitional control of the world we perceive around us. We cannot change the world by merely wishing it to be different. Therefore, all we can assert is that our sense perceptions represent *a modality of experience that we do not identify with or have direct volitional control of.* That's it; nothing more. When materialists assert that sense perceptions are direct evidence for a world outside consciousness, they are at best begging the question. If not, then they are necessarily concluding that experiences we do not identify with, or have direct volitional control of, can only originate in a world outside consciousness. Such a conclusion is, of course, illogical and betrays a surprising incapacity to see alternatives. See the next rebuttal.

Criticism 2: Because we cannot change reality by merely wishing it to be different, it's clear that reality is outside consciousness.

Rebuttal 2: This begs the question in roughly the same way as the previous criticism, but let us elaborate on the answer in a different way. The fact that certain contents of consciousness fall outside the control of our personal volition does not imply that they originate outside consciousness itself. After all, there are plenty of examples of undeniably mental phenomena that we do not identify with and cannot control: our nightmares, schizophrenic hallucinations, spontaneous visions, certain obsessions and compulsions, etc. Schizophrenics do not identify with and cannot control their hallucinations; they experience them as external phenomena. Yet, their hallucinations are entirely mental. Similarly, we do not identify with and cannot control the part of our psyches that generates our dreams and nightmares, otherwise we would never have the latter. We experience the scenarios of our dreams and nightmares as if they were external to us. Yet, they are entirely mental. Schizophrenic hallucinations and dreams clearly aren't perceptions of a strongly objective world outside mind. They are generated subjectively by and within mind. The only difference that can be empirically asserted between dreams and hallucinations on the one hand, and the ordinary waking world on the other hand, is that the latter is a shared experience, while the former are usually personal, idiosyncratic experiences. But they are all experiences in consciousness.

Criticism 3: Because we are separate beings inhabiting the same environment, the empirical world has to be outside consciousness.

Rebuttal 3: The idea here is that, if the world is a kind of collective dream, how can we all be sharing the same dream world, given that our psyches aren't connected? Naturally, this begs the question entirely: it is only under the notion that our psyches are generated by our bodies that we can say that they are disconnected; after all, our bodies are indeed separate. But if reality is in consciousness, then it is our bodies that are in consciousness, not consciousness in our bodies. The fact that our bodies are separate in the canvas of spacetime simply does not imply that our psyches are fundamentally disconnected. To say so is analogous to stating that, because one has two applications open in a computer screen, one must be using two separate computers! It is the application that is in the computer, not the computer in the application. Separate applications do not imply separate computers.

Criticism 4: It is untenable to maintain that there is no reality independent of consciousness, for there is plenty of evidence about what was going on in the universe before consciousness evolved.

Rebuttal 4: This, of course, assumes materialism – the notion that consciousness is generated by, and confined to, biological nervous systems – in a circular argument for materialism. Biological nervous systems indeed evolved at some point in time. But if the entire universe is in consciousness, then it is nervous systems that evolved in consciousness, not consciousness in nervous systems. Nervous systems are images of particular localization processes in consciousness, which could and did evolve later than other, earlier processes in consciousness. Those earlier processes weren't biology, but corresponded to everything that happened in the universe before life arose. A living being is like a whirlpool – a localization of flow – in a stream of transpersonal experiences, while non-biological phenomena are like ripples. As such, nothing in idealism precludes the possibility that there were plenty of ripples long before the first whirlpool ever formed (more on this in essay 2.5). The fact that there is evidence for the existence of the universe before nervous systems arose does not invalidate idealism. The circularity of this criticism should be self-evident enough. Yet, well-known biologist, author and militant materialist Jerry Coyne attacked my work precisely along these lines.[12]

Criticism 5: It is not parsimonious to say that the world is in consciousness, because this would require postulating an unfathomably complex entity to be imagining the world.

Rebuttal 5: The assumption here is that consciousness can only exist if it is generated by something else; by an entity outside consciousness, whose complexity must be proportional to the complexity of the mental contents being generated. This is a hardly disguised way to assume materialism in the first place: to assume that mind must be reducible to complex arrangements of something outside mind. Naturally, when one claims that the world is in consciousness, one is claiming precisely that consciousness is irreducible, primary, fundamental. Consciousness, as such, is not generated by complex entities or, for that matter, by anything outside consciousness: it is simply what is. To say that irreducible consciousness generates the world poses no more problems than to say that irreducible laws of physics generate the world. In fact, it poses less problems, since it avoids the so-called 'hard problem of consciousness' altogether (see essay 3.1). For the same reason that we accept that simple laws of physics generated the unfathomable complexity of today's universe, fairly simple 'laws of consciousness' could – and did – generate the phenomenality of all existence. In both cases, very simple rules generate unfathomable complexity, something well understood in complexity science.[13] The difference is that materialism postulates these complexity-creating rules to exist fundamentally outside consciousness and, in some totally non-understood way rather akin to magic, to generate consciousness. Idealism, on the other hand, sticks to the obvious: the complexity-generating rules are the intrinsic regularities of the unfolding of consciousness itself. This is not only much more parsimonious and empirically honest, it avoids the artificial and unsolvable 'hard problem of consciousness' altogether.

I personally believe that most materialists beg the question sincerely. They can't see the circularity of the ways in which they interpret, and then think to confirm their interpretations of, reality. This happens because we live in a culture that has completely lost objectivity: we can't see past the assumptions and beliefs we are immersed in, and indoctrinated into, since childhood. This is understandable, even though it remains one's personal responsibility to overcome it at some point.

However, when it comes to militant materialists – often

scientists – who make it their mission in life to promote the materialist metaphysics, the stakes are higher. When these people come to the mainstream media and beg the question of materialism so vocally, condescendingly and blatantly, they are going much beyond doing harm to themselves. It is your children, especially those still going through the educational system, who are listening to them with the openness characteristic of those who trust authority and aren't yet ready to evaluate more critically what's being said. Whether these militant materialists are genuinely confused in their question-begging or not is irrelevant: by choosing militancy, they take on the responsibility of knowing better. After all, ignorance of the law does not entitle anyone to commit the crime. Their actions are irresponsible. If it weren't for the damage they cause, it would be entertaining to watch these people promote idiocy with the hubris of an emperor with no clothes. However, the reality of the situation is rather serious.

And it doesn't stop at question-begging. Some of the most common arguments used by materialists contradict materialism itself! Indeed, these arguments seem to be made by people who completely fail to understand the internal logic and implications of materialism. Unfortunately, such confused individuals – who can often be found in so-called 'skeptics discussion fora' on the Internet – tend to be the most tireless champions of materialism. Oh, the irony. The following are two of their favorite lines.

Criticism 6: The world is clearly not inside our heads, therefore idealism is wrong.

Rebuttal 6: I blush to have to refute this point but, since it comes up so often, I felt I couldn't ignore it. You see, it is materialism that posits that the world you perceive is inside your head. After all, experience is supposedly the product of brain activity. Your *actual* skull is allegedly above the stars you see at night, a point acknowledged by materialists in a formal academic paper.[14]

The actual world outside your head purportedly has none of the qualities of experience – no color, flavor, melody, texture or odor. After all, if the qualities of experience are somehow squirted out by brains, there is absolutely no reason to believe that they exist anywhere else but inside skulls. On the other hand, idealism states that the world you perceive is indeed outside your head. It does entail that it's all in consciousness, but then it is your head – as a part of the world – that is in consciousness, not consciousness in your head. Remember: it is your dream character that is in your dreaming consciousness at night, not your consciousness in your dream character. Under idealism, your head occupies a tiny 'space' in the canvas of transpersonal consciousness, the rest of the world occupying other 'spaces' in it. As such, the world you see around you indeed exists outside your skull and has phenomenal qualities. Idealism does justice to our most concrete and visceral intuitions about reality, while materialism flies in their face.

Criticism 7: Idealism is too metaphysical.
Rebuttal 7: No ontology in the history of humankind has been or is more metaphysical than materialism. Unlike all spiritual and religious ontologies – which postulate transcendent realms comprising qualities that can presumably be experienced through meditation, ritual or, in the worst case, physical death – the strongly objective realm of materialism is, by definition, purely abstract. It can never be known – since knowledge exists only in consciousness – but only inferred. All the phenomenal qualities we attribute to the world – like solidity, palpability, concreteness – are qualities of experience and, as such, not applicable to the real world of materialism. Idealism, on the other hand, grants actual reality to the solidity, palpability and concreteness of matter. It doesn't postulate the felt concreteness of a rock to be a mere product of brain activity; instead, it posits that the rock really is concrete insofar as it exists. If anything,

idealism is the ultimate acknowledgement of the physicality of the world as known through experience. It embodies a sane return home from the mad abstractions with which materialists attempt to replace reality.

The majority of the materialist arguments against idealism simply reflect a partial or distorted understanding of idealism itself. Because materialism has attained the position of mainstream worldview, materialists seem to feel that they don't really need to properly understand what they are criticizing before they start shooting. Protected by the clout of the mainstream, some don't even seem to feel that they need to think straight: many materialist arguments reflect obvious misapprehensions of the empirical evidence or clear failures of simple logic.

Criticism 8: There are strong correlations between brain activity and subjective experience. Clearly, thus, the brain generates consciousness.

Rebuttal 8: There are strong correlations between the colors of flames and the microscopic details of combustion. Similarly, there are strong correlations between lightning and the patterns of atmospheric electric discharge. Does lightning cause atmospheric electric discharge? Or is it simply what atmospheric electric discharge *looks like* from a certain perspective? Aren't flames simply what combustion looks like from the outside? In exactly the same way, active neurons are simply what subjective experience looks like from the outside. An active brain is merely the image of a process of localization in the flow of transpersonal consciousness, like a whirlpool is the image of a process of localization in a stream of water. The brain doesn't generate consciousness for exactly the same reason that a whirlpool doesn't generate water.

Criticism 9: Unconscious brain activity precedes the awareness of certain decisions, showing a clear arrow of causation from purely material processes to experience.

Rebuttal 9: The idea here is that, in certain laboratory experiments, neuroscientists could predict the choice a person was going to make by measuring activity in the person's brain. Neuroscientists could make this prediction just before the person was lucidly aware of making the choice.[15] On this basis, materialists conclude that unconscious brain processes are the cause of the experience of making a choice. This seems reasonable at first sight, but only at first sight. Materialists mistake different degrees or modes of consciousness for a total absence of consciousness. Right now, for instance, you are lucidly aware of the letters on the page in front of you. But that doesn't mean that you are unconscious of your peripheral vision: of the things going on somewhat behind and around the book in your hands. You're just less conscious of them, or conscious of them in a different, non-lucid manner. Materialists unwarrantedly equate lack of lucid awareness – a particularly high degree, or sophisticated mode, of consciousness – with lack of consciousness. As I elaborate upon in essay 2.1, our lucid awareness results from a reverberation phenomenon that amplifies certain contents of consciousness. Neuroscience characterizes this reverberation as back-and-forth communication between different brain areas, which correlates well with lucidity.[16] The moment the reverberating contents of consciousness become amplified, they obfuscate all other contents, the way the Sun obfuscates the stars at noon. The stars are all still there at noon, their photons still hitting your retina. Technically, you are still seeing the stars. But you don't know *that* you are seeing them because they become obfuscated. Similarly, the contents of consciousness that become obfuscated by the 'glare' of reverberation are all still in consciousness, but you are not lucidly aware of them. Instead of conscious and unconscious neural processes, what we have are highly amplified and severely obfuscated contents of consciousness, respectively. There is no actual unconscious. What neuroscience today calls 'consciousness' is simply an amplified part of consciousness, a mode of experience. As such, the laboratory experiments in question reveal simply this: people first make a conscious choice in an obfuscated part of consciousness; later, that conscious choice becomes amplified through mental reverberation; only thereafter do people become lucidly aware of the earlier conscious choice and, thereby, capable of reporting it. There is no arrow of causation between unconscious processes and experience, because there are no unconscious processes to begin with.

Criticism 10: Because psychoactive drugs and brain trauma can markedly change subjective experience, it's clear that the brain generates consciousness.

Rebuttal 10: People who argue this tend to implicitly assume some form of mind-matter duality. Because drugs and trauma can clearly alter consciousness through physically interfering with the material brain, then – the argument goes – the brain must generate consciousness. But notice that the entire rationale assumes that drugs, trauma and brains – matter in general – are in some sense distinct from consciousness, which is precisely what idealism denies. You see, if the whole universe is in consciousness, then a pill or a well-placed knock to the head are simply the images of processes in consciousness. They are turbulent ripples in the stream, which can upset the ordinary balance and dynamics of a delicate whirlpool. As such, drugs and physical trauma are also in consciousness; where else could they be? What is a pill but what you see, touch and otherwise feel in your fingers? It has color, flavor and texture. It's a set of subjective perceptions with the qualities of experience. As far as you or anyone else can ever know for sure, a pill is in consciousness. Therefore, that a pill or physical trauma to the head can alter one's state of consciousness is no more surprising than the fact that your thoughts can change your emotions. Thoughts and emotions are both in consciousness, so we are perfectly comfortable with the fact that they can influence each another. For that exact same reason, we should be perfectly comfortable with the fact that drugs and physical trauma also influence our phenomenal states. As there is nothing to the brain but consciousness, so there is nothing to a pill and physical action but consciousness.

Criticism 11: During dreamless sleep, or under general anesthesia, we are clearly unconscious. Yet, we don't cease to exist because we become temporarily unconscious. Obviously, then, our body cannot be in consciousness.

Rebuttal 11: The best one can assert upon waking up is that one cannot recall any experience during the preceding hours; not that experiences were absent. Indeed, it is impossible to distinguish between the absence of recall of an experience and the absence of the experience itself. What we refer to as periods of 'unconsciousness' – be them related to sleep, general anesthesia, fainting, etc. – are simply periods in which the formation of memory access paths is impaired. The very disruption of waking mental processes induced by anesthetics or sleep compromises our ability to form coherent associative links to the corresponding memories. As a result, later recall becomes difficult or impossible, since the links aren't available (see essay 3.3). For all we know, we may wander into rich phenomenal landscapes during sleep and narcosis, but be unable to remember any of it upon returning to a lucid state. Think of how elusive dreams can be: at the moment you wake up, you may still remember an early morning dream; five seconds later, you already forgot it, but still remember that you had a dream; by the time you stand on your feet, you can't even remember that you dreamed at all. Or reciprocally: you may remember nothing when you wake up – declaring yourself to have been unconscious all night – and then suddenly recall, hours later, that you actually had a very intense dream. How can you know that you are ever truly unconscious? One could claim that the absence of dream-related brain activity in several periods during the night, as measured by electroencephalography, proves that there are phases of true unconsciousness during sleep. But this fails to notice that there are always plenty of other types of activity in a sleeping – or otherwise 'unconscious' – brain, which may well correlate with non-recallable experiences different from ordinary dreams. In fact, materialists themselves appeal to the explanatory power of subtler types of brain activity when trying to make sense of near-death experiences.[17]

Criticism 12: The stability and consistency of the laws of physics show that the empirical world is outside consciousness.

Rebuttal 12: The hidden assumption here seems to be that all conscious processes must necessarily be capricious and erratic. This could be true in some sense only if all conscious processes were tied to neural activity, for neural activity tends to be somewhat unstable and unpredictable. But this is an implication only of materialism. There is nothing in idealism requiring it. There is nothing in idealism that precludes the possibility that processes in the collective, transpersonal but obfuscated levels of consciousness – mind-at-large – unfold according to very stable, strict patterns and regularities, which we've come to call the 'laws of nature.' To say that all nature is grounded in consciousness does not imply that all nature is grounded in the whimsical segments of consciousness that we call our personal psyches.

Criticism 13: To postulate a collective and obfuscated part of consciousness as source of consensus reality is equivalent to postulating a world outside consciousness.

Rebuttal 13: From a strict philosophical perspective, this is outright incorrect. When we say that our personal psyches are merely parts of a broader mind-at-large, all we are doing is extrapolating a known and empirically undeniable ontological category – namely, consciousness itself – beyond the spacetime boundaries we ordinarily associate with it. But when we say that there is a whole universe outside consciousness, we are inferring a whole new ontological category. These two things aren't equivalent by any stretch of the imagination. Here is a rather dramatic analogy to help you gain some intuition about it: in order to model the early universe, physicists also extrapolate across space and time the validity of the laws of physics known on Earth today. Doing so is obviously different, and much more reasonable and parsimonious, than inferring an unprovable Flying Spaghetti Monster to be the hidden cause of all things. Now, in addition to this philosophical point, the practical implications of these two ontologies are also totally different. This is explored in details in essay 8.2, but let me anticipate a couple of points elaborated upon there: if the universe is a transpersonal stream of consciousness and we are merely localizations of flow – whirlpools – in the stream, than physical death is a *de*-localization, or *de*-clenching, of consciousness, not its demise. Moreover, if the body is merely the outside image of a localization of experience, then mind and body are fundamentally the same thing. This may open new avenues for our quest to understand memory (see essay 3.3) and validates a richer form of healthcare: integrative mind-body medicine (see essay 8.3). Finally, there are other psychological, social and cultural implications explored in essay 8.2.

Criticism 14: Why would consciousness deceive us by simulating a materialist world?

Rebuttal 14: Was planet Earth deceiving us until a few hundred years ago, by simulating a flat world? Was the Sun deceiving us by pretending to move around the Earth? Consciousness is not simulating anything. Just like the Sun, from the very beginning it's simply been doing what it does, which is a reflection of what it inherently is. It's us, human beings, who misinterpret the activity of transpersonal consciousness and assume it to correspond to a universe outside consciousness. To suggest that the natural activity of consciousness is some kind of purposeful and deceitful simulation of our own delusions is astonishingly anthropocentric.

Criticism 15: Idealism is solipsistic and, as such, unfalsifiable.

Rebuttal 15: Solipsism is the notion that the whole world is an individual's private dream; that other people don't have inner life, but are merely shells projected by the individual's own dreaming mind. Since there is only one person's dream going on, the person can arbitrarily dream up empirical evidence for any explanatory model she wishes to entertain within the dream; her explanations of reality can't be falsified by comparison to observations or the testimonials of other 'people.' Since Karl Popper made clear the arbitrariness of unfalsifiable explanations,[18] we've known that they can't be taken seriously. For instance, some creationists assert that the fossil record was placed on Earth purposefully by God, in order to deceive gullible souls with the idea of evolution and distinguish the faithful from the sinful. Such an assertion is unfalsifiable and, for obvious reasons, cannot be taken seriously. By equating idealism with solipsism, this criticism attempts to label it equally unfalsifiable. The problem, however, is obvious: idealism is totally different from solipsism. Under idealism, other people do have inner life; they do have their own personal streams of experience and their testimonials carry weight. Moreover, still under idealism, consensus reality arises from a part of consciousness – mind-at-large – that transcends personal psyches; it isn't merely a personal dream. Although it's still entirely in consciousness, the world isn't produced by your personal imagination alone. Therefore, unlike solipsism, idealism can be validated or falsified by comparison to observations and the testimonies of other individuals.

Criticism 16: One cannot prove that idealism is true.
Rebuttal 16: I am tempted to answer this on the cheap and simply say: one can't prove materialism either! But let us be a little more patient and thoughtful here. The claim of idealism is that it can explain at least everything that materialism purportedly explains, but then with fewer postulates. Namely, idealism does not require postulating a whole universe outside consciousness itself. This way, if the claim holds true, then idealism already wins over materialism on grounds of parsimony alone. In other words, if we can indeed explain all nature purely in terms of excitations of consciousness, then idealism is better than materialism for the same reason that Darwinian evolution is better than the Flying Spaghetti Monster: both explain the evidence but the latter requires more postulates (namely, the Monster Himself, the realm where He supposedly exists, the mechanisms through which He interacts with material reality, etc.). So to attack idealism by claiming that it is unprovable reflects a basic misunderstanding of the issue: one does not need to prove idealism. Proof is a requirement for ontologies that postulate *extra* theoretical entities – which then need to be justified and substantiated – not for an ontology that postulates *less.* The proper way to attack idealism is to try to show that it cannot satisfactorily explain what materialism purportedly explains. In other words, materialists should focus on the

explanatory power of idealism. That said, they should also keep in mind that the entire body of my work, including this book, lays out an extensive case precisely for the strong and broad explanatory power of idealism.

As of this writing, I am not aware of any better materialist counter-argument than those listed and refuted above.

2.3. Finding truth within the dream

Imagine that you are lying on your couch one lazy Sunday afternoon, relaxed and unworried. Your life isn't perfect, but everything seems to be going fine lately. There are no oppressive thoughts in your mind demanding your attention. You surrender fully to the moment and find yourself closing your eyes, even though you aren't tired.

Slowly, you begin to drift into a strange world of fleeting hypnagogic images. Even one wrong thought could cause the whole thing to collapse, but you deliberately and carefully allow yourself to slide further in. A subtle, delicate transition in awareness gradually takes place. You realize in amazement that you are now dreaming, even though you still retain awareness of the couch you're lying on.[19] The phenomenon is as interesting as it is surreal: the old reality seems to have been replaced with a parallel timeline in a parallel realm. Despite your bewilderment, the dream continues to pull you deeper in, like the entrancing, irresistible song of a mermaid. You fight to remain lucid but it's no use. Soon, you completely forget about the couch, the Sunday afternoon and even who you are. You're now fully entranced; fully in the dream. Connections with your real life are severed.

Except that a nagging feeling remains in the back of your mind: deep within, in a way that isn't self-reflective, there is that intuition that you aren't really from this land where you now find yourself; that you aren't really this character you seem to be playing in this story. You can't pin it down; you can't define or articulate what it means. It's just a hazy, diffuse and slippery feeling. And since you quickly conclude that there's nothing you can do about it, you decide to simply go on with your life.

But what's your life about again? You look around and find yourself sitting at the shore of a beautiful lake. Tall mountains surround it. A warm summer breeze caresses your skin. Someone is sitting next to you, to your left, but you can't really remember who she is. You just know that the situation is perfectly ordinary. Whoever she is, she belongs right there with you. As she stares out to the lake, apparently lost in thoughts, she asks:

— What do you think will happen when you die?

Strangely, her question doesn't surprise you. What does is that the answer seems to flow autonomously out of you, as if someone else were speaking through your mouth:

— I know that I have a soul and that, after I die, my soul will simply return to where it came from, which is another world.

— But where is this otherworld you speak of? Where is your soul right now? Why can't I see or touch it?

You know intuitively that your friend is asking the wrong questions.

— You think of my soul as a kind of ghost that inhabits my body and, after I die, floats out in space like a gas cloud. This isn't how it works.

— How come not? If your soul exists it must be somewhere. And this otherworld you speak of, where your soul is supposed to go after you die, must also be somewhere. Where is it? Is it behind those mountains? Is it up in the sky?

— No, it's in none of those places. It's nowhere. And you will never be able to see, touch or measure my soul. Can't you see that you are thinking about it in the wrong way?

— How so? You're beginning to sound very flaky with all this woo. It's very simple: if we can't find or measure the soul anywhere, it isn't there; it doesn't exist. If we can't find this otherworld of yours anywhere, it doesn't exist. It's just as simple.

Beginning to lose your patience, you take a deep breath and

manage to carry on:

— You are assuming that my soul is inside this body. *But it is this body and this place that are inside my soul.* So you could never find my soul anywhere here. It's the wrong place to look.

— Are you saying that the lake, the valley and all those enormous mountains around us right now are all inside your soul?!

Before you can reply, she giggles sarcastically and continues:

— You must have a mighty big soul then!

— You don't understand. Our notions of space and time are entirely relative to this realm. They only exist within it. It makes no sense to speak of the size or age of my soul, because my soul is not inside space or time.

— You make no sense to me. If you say that your soul *goes to* another world after you die, that requires movement in space and time...

You know in your heart that you will never be able to explain in words what you mean. The very structure of language *presupposes* the notions of space and time intrinsic to this realm. Nouns *presuppose* the existence of things within this realm. How to explain the soul if it isn't a thing? How to explain the otherworld if it isn't in space and time? 'I can't make sense of this even to myself,' you admit. Indeed, everything you said came from intuition, not from a linear or logical grasp of what it all entails. *You realize that even you don't really understand what you've been talking about.* The irony is rather cruel.

Almost imperceptibly, you sigh and stare out to the lake in resignation. The breeze causes the water to ripple gently, forming intricate and rather beautiful interference patterns. To the right, where a stream drains into the lake, eddies form and dissolve in a beautifully choreographed dance. For a moment you drift away...

Then you hear your friend say abruptly, in a firm but benevolent voice:

— Here, let me help you understand what you've been trying to say.

As you turn to face her, you freeze: she is holding a gun pointed straight at your face. Before you can even ask yourself what's happening, she smiles... and fires. Time slows to a crawl as you watch the bullet emerge from the barrel, travel through the air and finally hit you right between the eyes. Your entire body shudders and propels itself upward...

...But you land safely on your couch. Startled, you sit up and look around. It's a lazy Sunday afternoon and there's nothing to worry about. While you're still halfway between the dream and real life, it dawns upon you with crystalline clarity: 'Of course! This is what I meant to explain to her! *Her trying to find my soul and the otherworld in her frame of reality was like looking for my real body and this living room inside my dream...*'

2.4. Survival of consciousness beyond death: an implication of common sense

This essay is about a surprising but direct implication of our common sense about the nature of reality; an implication that you are probably unaware of. Becoming aware of this implication has the potential to change your life.

Our common sense asserts that the colors we see, the sounds we hear, the smells we feel, the textures we sense, constitute the actual physical world. We take it for granted that they all exist outside our head. On the other hand, the mainstream materialist metaphysics asserts that death is the end of our consciousness. Even if we don't acknowledge this intellectually or spiritually, most of us fear the end of consciousness with enough sincerity to betray our belief in its possibility.

Now, the point of this essay is quite simple: these two assertions are mutually exclusive. They cannot be both true. Either your common sense is utterly wrong and everything you sense around you right now, including the book in front of you, is a kind of 'hallucination' inside your head, or your consciousness doesn't end upon physical death.

For the sake of argument, let's start with the postulate that bodily dissolution – death – indeed implies the end of consciousness. Such belief is entirely based on the idea that your body, particularly your brain, generates all your experiences. After all, what other reason could we have to believe that consciousness ends if the brain stops working? But if the belief is true, then all of your subjective experiences and their qualities – colors, sounds, flavors, textures, warmth, etc. – are merely representations created within your head. The 'real world out there' has none of the qualities of experience. Supposedly, it is a purely abstract realm of quantities akin to mathematical equations. It cannot even be visualized, for visualization always entails qualities. In essence, if this is true, your entire life unfolds inside your skull. Your *actual* skull is somewhere beyond the room where you are sitting, enveloping it from all sides. After all, the room you are experiencing right now is supposedly within your head.

But what if all this is baloney? What if the colors, sounds and smells you are experiencing right now constitute the *real* reality – the *actual* physical world – not 'hallucinated' copies of it within your skull? Then the necessary implication is that the physical world is in consciousness, for it is then *made of* the qualities of subjective experience. But if so, then it is your body that is in consciousness, not consciousness in your body. After all, your body is in the physical world, not the physical world in your body. Hence, the dissolution of your body cannot imply the end of consciousness; not any more than the death of your character in a nightly dream can imply your physical death. It is the character that is in your dreaming consciousness, not your consciousness in the character. Do you see the point?

As such, either the entire world you experience is a kind of 'hallucination' inside your skull, or we have absolutely no reason to believe that physical death entails the end of consciousness. It's one thing or the other. You take your pick: Which alternative is crazier? I've taken mine: I am unable to deny the reality of my immediate experience of the world, which far precedes the models and abstractions of our mad materialist culture.

So let us dare entertain the possibility that the physical world is exactly what it seems to be: that it has *qualities*, not just quantities. Let us acknowledge what every civilization before Western rationalism always took for granted: that colors, smells, sounds, and flavors aren't just inside our heads. How do we then explain the big questions that materialists claim to require an abstract reality fundamentally outside consciousness in order to be made sense of? This is the subject of essay 2.2. That essay shows that all questions that lead materialists astray can be logically and empirically made sense of under the rigorous and parsimonious view that the entire universe is a phenomenon of consciousness, in consciousness. Your intuition that the environment of qualities you experience around you right now, with all its colors, sounds, smells, and textures, is the *actual* physical world – as opposed to a kind of hallucinated copy inside your head – is entirely correct. The implication of this, however, is that your consciousness – your subjective experience of being – will not cease to exist upon your physical death. This is an inescapable conclusion derived from logic, clear thinking and empirical honesty. It so happens to *also* be a hopeful conclusion for many.

2.5. The actual difference between living beings and inanimate objects

In July of 2014, I gave a long and engaging interview to Rick Archer, host of *Buddha at the Gas Pump*, an Internet talk show.[20] Rick pressed me on the distinction I make between idealism and panpsychism; that is, between the notions that everything is *in consciousness* and that everything is *conscious*. As my readers know, I reject panpsychism: I reject the idea that inanimate objects, such as subatomic particles or home thermostats, are conscious. But I strongly endorse the notion that everything is *in consciousness* and exists only insofar as it is in consciousness. To Rick, such a distinction wasn't clear. Therefore, I'd like now to clarify this point.

As discussed in my earlier book *Why Materialism Is Baloney*, summarized in essay 2.1, I acknowledge a fundamental distinction between inanimate objects and living beings. It is true that the distinction may be difficult to recognize at microscopic levels – are viruses alive? – but that doesn't change the fact that a teddy bear and a polar bear are very different bears.

I maintain that inanimate objects are excitations of consciousness, like vibrations are excitations of a guitar string or ripples excitations of water. There is nothing to a vibrating guitar string other than the string itself, yet the string manifests a discernible behavior that we call 'vibration.' Analogously, there is nothing to a ripple other than water, yet water manifests a discernible behavior that we call 'rippling.' In this exact same way, inanimate objects are simply 'ripples' of a transpersonal stream of consciousness that I call mind-at-large. Ultimately, they are nothing but consciousness itself; images in mind of excitations of mind.

Living beings, on the other hand, are images of processes of *self-localization* in mind-at-large, like a whirlpool is the image of a process of self-localization in a stream of water. Again, as there is nothing to a whirlpool but water, there is nothing to a living being but consciousness. In summary:

Inanimate objects: ripples in mind-at-large.
Living beings: whirlpools in mind-at-large.

Very well. My claim is that the formation of whirlpools in mind-at-large corresponds to what psychiatrists call *dissociation*. The localized, self-reinforcing vortex of experiences begins to reverberate in the center of the whirlpool, in a phenomenon that neuroscience has characterized as back-and-forth communication between different brain areas.[21] Remember: the brain is what the center of the whirlpool looks like. So it is entirely natural that we should find an image of this reverberation process in the brain. And as is the case with any reverberation process, the reverberating mental contents become amplified and end up obfuscating all other mental contents outside the whirlpool. This corresponds effectively to a dissociation of the whirlpool from the rest of mind-at-large. To help you gain some intuition, here is how the International Society for the Study of Trauma and Dissociation describes a psychological condition called Dissociative Identity Disorder:

> [It] is the most severe and chronic manifestation of dissociation, characterized by the presence of two or more distinct identities or personality states ... accompanied by an *inability to recall* important personal information ... The *amnesia* typically associated with Dissociative Identity Disorder is asymmetrical, with *different identity states remembering different aspects of autobiographical information.* There is usually a host personality who identifies with the client's real name. Typically, the host personality *is not aware* of the presence of other alters.[22]

Clearly, dissociation corresponds to a loss of lucid awareness – 'amnesia' or an 'inability to recall' – by one part of mind of what's going on in the rest of mind. *I maintain that the obfuscation of outside mental contents by the reverberation process inside a whirlpool causes this.* Indeed, it causes the illusion that we, human beings, are separate from each other and from the rest of the universe. As such, each living creature is akin to a dissociated 'alter' of mind-at-large. The *outside image* of the alter is a biological body.

Now, inanimate objects, being mere ripples in mind-at-large, do not entail the localization of flow that leads to reverberation. There is thus no obfuscation or dissociation. Inanimate objects aren't alters of mind-at-large, but merely the outside image of other processes unfolding in mind-at-large.

Here is an analogy to help you visualize this: the outside image of conscious processes unfolding in your psyche is neural activity in your brain. If you daydream about a tropical holiday location with trees, waterfalls and singing birds, all those images will correlate with particular, measurable patterns of activated neurons in your head. Theoretically, a neuroscientist could identify different groups of neurons in your brain and say: group A correlates with a tree; group B with a waterfall; group C with a singing bird; etc. But, based on your direct experience of what it feels like to imagine this scenario, is there anything it is like to be group A in isolation? Is there anything it is like to be group C in and of itself? Or is there *only* something it is like to be *the whole daydreaming you* – your whole brain – imagining trees, waterfalls and birds as component parts of an integrated scenario? Do you experience multiple separate streams of imagination – one for trees, another for waterfalls and another for birds – or only one stream wherein trees, waterfalls and birds are all together? Do you see the point? Unless there is dissociation, there is nothing it's like to be separate groups of neurons in a person's brain. We can only speak of the holistic stream of imagination of the person as a whole.

For exactly the same reason that there is nothing it is like to be an isolated group of neurons in a person's brain, there is nothing it is like to be an inanimate object. An inanimate object is simply what a segment of a global, holistic stream of imagination in mind-at-large looks like from the point-of-view of a whirlpool. There is indeed something it's like to be mind-at-large as a whole (see essay 2.6), but not an inanimate object in and of itself.

All right, let's now take another step in this line of reasoning. In the same way that a whirlpool causes disturbances in the flow of water surrounding it, the formation of an alter in mind-at-large also causes ripples of consciousness in its surroundings. These ripples are like the wake left by the whirlpool's rotation, which propagate beyond the boundaries of the whirlpool itself. It is because of this wake that we can perceive other living beings in much the same way that we perceive inanimate objects: when we see and hear another person, what we perceive are the ripples that the whirlpool corresponding to this other person has imprinted onto mind-at-large, and which ended up penetrating our own whirlpool through our sense organs. We call these ripples 'photons' and 'air vibrations,' respectively.

While alters cause ripples in mind-at-large, not all ripples arise because of alters. In other words, while living beings can be perceived as images in consciousness, not all images in consciousness are of living beings. Some ripples arise spontaneously in mind-at-large itself, as a direct result of its own stream of imagination. Though both whirlpools and ripples are nothing but water in movement, ripples aren't whirlpools. Idealism holds, not panpsychism.

2.6. Finding God in metaphysical parsimony

Theology has been the subject of much bashing by neo-atheists over the past several years. A blog post by militant materialist Jerry Coyne, in September of 2014, seems to encapsulate the essence of their grievance: 'What good is a discipline that tries to tell us about the qualities of a nonexistent object?' Coyne asks rhetorically. 'It's as useful as a bunch of scholars trying to tell us about the characteristics of the Loch Ness Monster, or Paul Bunyan.'[23] Any counter-argument to this is delicate, since it necessarily requires defining the most overloaded word in the history of language – 'God' – in some particular way that many are bound to disagree with. Yet, there are some common attributes almost always associated with God, and God alone: *omniscience, omnipresence* and *omnipotence*. Thus, it is fair to say that if one can identify a subject of study for which there is concrete evidence and which incorporates the three attributes just listed, then one will have refuted Coyne's argument against theology. This is precisely what I intend to do in this essay. But in order to make my argument, I first need to take you on a brief tour of a more parsimonious, logical way of interpreting the facts of reality than the materialist metaphysics entails. Bear with me.

Consciousness is the only carrier of reality anyone can ever know for sure. As I elaborate more extensively upon in essay 2.1, all things and phenomena can be explained as excitations of consciousness itself. As such, reality consists of a transpersonal flow of experiences, while our personal awareness is simply a localization of this flow – a whirlpool in the stream. *The body-brain system is merely what the whirlpool looks like from the outside.* It is no surprise, then, that brain activity correlates with subjective experience. Yet, for exactly the same reason that a whirlpool doesn't generate water, the body-brain system doesn't generate consciousness.

This worldview entails that the brain we can see and measure is simply how the first-person perspective of personal experience looks from the outside; that is, from a second-person perspective. In other words, neurons are what our thoughts, emotions and perceptions look like when another person experiences them. They aren't the *cause* of subjective experience, but simply the *outside image* of it. A neuroscientist might put a volunteer in a functional brain scanner and measure the patterns of her brain activity while the volunteer watches pictures of her loved ones. The neuroscientist would have precise measurements showing a pattern of activity in the volunteer's brain, which could be printed out on slides and shared with the volunteer herself. The patterns on those slides would represent what the volunteer's first-person experience of love looks like from the outside. In other words, they would be the image of subjective processes in the volunteer's personal consciousness; the footprints of love.

But if the neuroscientist were to point at the slides and say to the volunteer: 'This is what you felt when you looked at the pictures of your loves ones,' the volunteer would vehemently, and correctly, deny the assertion. The first-person experience of love doesn't feel at all like watching neurons activate, or 'fire.' You see, the image *correlates with the process* and carries valid information about it – like footprints correlate with the gait and carry valid information about it – but it *isn't the process*, for the same reason that footprints aren't the gait. Looking at patterns of brain activity certainly feels very different from love.

As our personal psyches are like whirlpools in a broader stream, so the broader stream itself is a transpersonal form of consciousness that underlies all reality. I call it 'mind-at-large.' Now, for the same reason that the experiences of another person appear to us as a seemingly objective image – namely, an active brain – the seemingly objective world around us is the image of experiences in mind-at-large. Moreover, for exactly the same reason that feeling love is completely different from watching the brain activity of someone in love, the first-person experience of mind-at-large will feel completely different from your watching the world around you right now. The world is the image of experiences in mind-at-large, but mind-at-large doesn't experience the world the way we do, for the same reason that our volunteer inside the brain scanner doesn't experience patterns of firing neurons! The volunteer experiences love, not firing neurons. When we look at the world around us, we do see the footprints of experience, but not the gait. And this is why theology not only has a concrete and worthy subject of study and speculation, but perhaps the ultimate one. Allow me to elaborate.

George Berkeley posited that the empirical world is an experience in the 'mind of God,' his term for mind-at-large.[24] The term, although admittedly old-fashioned and ambiguous, was and remains appropriate: if the empirical world consists of ripples (that is, inanimate objects) and whirlpools (living creatures) in the stream of mind-at-large, then the attributes omnipresent, omniscient, and omnipotent apply to the stream. Just think about it: *all reality* is excitations of mind-at-large, analogously to how quantum field theorists say that all reality is excitations of a postulated quantum field.[25] Therefore, mind-at-large is omnipresent. Unlike the quantum field, however, mind-at-large is, by definition, conscious. Therefore, it is omniscient. Finally, whatever else we may want to say about it, the world is certainly the *manifestation* of mind-at-large. What else could it be? There is, thus, a strong sense in which mind-at-large is also omnipotent, since it has operational control over the world (whether this operational control entails libertarian free will is a different question, explored in Chapter 7).

We can then say that *empirical reality consists entirely of outside images of ideas in the mind of God.* We cannot know how the world is felt by God simply by looking at the world, for the same reason that a neuroscientist cannot know what love feels like just by looking at brain scans. Yet, *when we contemplate the magnificence and incomprehensible magnitude of the stars and galaxies through our telescopes, we are essentially looking at a 'scan of God's brain.'* Indeed, a detailed study has found that the structure of the universe at the largest scales is very similar, clustering- and interconnect-wise, to the structure of a brain.[26] A striking image comparison published by the *New York Times* on 14 August 2006 illustrates the similarity very powerfully.[27] All nature – from atoms to galaxy clusters – is an outside image of God's conscious activity, in exactly the same way that a brain scan is an outside image of a person's subjective experiences. Theologians themselves have explained this in their own language as, for instance, a careful read of Henry Corbin will reveal.[28] This way, *God is literally all around you.* When you die, you're quite literally reabsorbed into God, as religious scripture has insisted upon throughout the ages. Your personal psyche – a whirlpool in the stream of God's thoughts and feelings – dissolves back into its original matrix. The outside image of this reabsorption process is your physical body losing its integrity and melting back into the Earth. How the process feels like from *within*, however, is a mystery for which our only clues are the reports of near-death experiences (see essay 6.1). As such, *the mystery of death consists in the shift of our experience of the world from second- to first-person perspective.*

Clearly, theology does have a very concrete subject: mind-at-large, or God. And theology also has concrete data to make inferences about this subject: nature itself. If one denies the validity of nature as data for the study of God, one must deny the validity of brain scans as neuroscientific data. What theologians call Creation is the 'scan' – the outside image, symbol, metaphor, icon – of God's ongoing, conscious, creative activity. Creation is an act of thought, the icon of an evolving idea in the mind of God. 'All the world an icon,' as Tom Cheetham summarized it.[29] Goethe, in *Faust,* preferred the word 'symbol.' He wrote: 'All that doth pass away / Is but a symbol.'[30] What in nature doesn't pass away?

This understanding touches on many currents of religious, philosophical and even scientific thought. For instance, French physicist Olivier Costa de Beauregard once concluded that the measurable universe we see is simply the passive, obverse side of an active *mental* universe, which he called *'infrapsychisme.'*[31] Physicist David Bohm's notions of *implicate* and *explicate order* also echo important aspects of this understanding: the explicate order is the world we can measure, while the implicate order is the reverse, hidden, primary reality whence the explicate order springs as a projected image.[32] 'Measurement is an externalization of that which can be known from within,' says my friend Fred Matser in a display of profound intuition.[33] The core idea in these and other analogous systems of thought is that reality has two sides: an inner side (direct experience, implicate order, *'infrapsychisme'*) and an outer side (the outside image of direct experience, explicate order, obverse side). Even renowned contemporary physicist Lee Smolin seemed to acknowledge this when he wrote:

> Perhaps everything has external and internal aspects. The *external properties* are those that science can capture and describe – through interactions, in terms of relationships. The *internal aspect* is the intrinsic essence, it is the reality that is not expressible in the language of interactions and relations.[34]

He went on to identify the 'internal aspect' with direct subjective experience: 'Consciousness, whatever it is, is an aspect of the intrinsic essence of brains.'[35] Notice that the duality I am suggesting here is merely one of points of view, not of substance: *the outside image of an experience is itself also an experience.*

Furthermore, if we look at how cultures throughout history have used the words 'soul' and 'body,' it is easy to see that 'soul' corresponds to direct experience and 'body' to what the experience looks like from the outside. As such, our own soul comprises our direct experience of life – our inner life – whose obverse side is our body. What Plato called the 'world soul'[36] is simply God's direct subjective perspective; the reverse side of the measurable universe. The measurable universe, in turn, is the obverse side of God's soul. *The Universe, thus, is God's body.* As such, nature is a perfectly valid subject of study for theology, in exactly the same way that the human nervous system is a perfectly valid subject of study for psychiatry.

Coyne could try to counter all this by saying that we already have the natural sciences for studying nature, and that the scientific method is much better suited for this purpose. This is as strictly correct as it misses the point entirely: theology is an attempt to see *past* the mere images and make inferences about the subjective, phenomenal processes behind those images; it is an attempt to see *past* the 'brain scan' and infer how it 'feels to feel' love in a direct way; it is an attempt to see *past* the footprints and understand where the hiker wants to go, as well as why he wants to go there. In this sense, theology and the natural sciences are entirely complementary.

And this isn't all. If we are whirlpools in the broader stream of mind-at-large, then the implication is clear: at bottom, our personal psyches are not only one with each other, but also one with mind-at-large. After all, there is nothing to a whirlpool but the stream itself. This way, we are merely *alters* of mind-at-large, analogous to the dissociated personalities presented by people with Dissociative Identity Disorder.[37] It follows that the deepest, most obfuscated regions of the human psyche – which depth-psychology has come to erroneously call the 'unconscious' – are transpersonal and entail the direct subjective perspective of mind-at-large itself. And here is the key point: people express their 'unconscious' perspectives through symbols and metaphors, which then form the basis of religious myths. Indeed, religious texts are the symbolic expression of the 'unconscious.' Carl Jung's masterpieces *Aion*[38] and *Answer to Job*[39] make this abundantly clear. Therefore, insofar as theology offers a way to interpret and make sense of the symbols and metaphors in religious texts – expressions of the 'unconscious' psyche, God's own subjective perspective – it also has a valid subject of study and a valid source of data.

In conclusion, both nature itself and religious texts are expressions of a mysterious divine perspective and, as such, valid sources of concrete data for theological study. Theology has a clear, concrete subject, as well as a clear and concrete challenge: to decode the divine mystery behind the images – both 'unconscious' and empirical – that we experience during life. Coyne is simply wrong. Whereas the natural sciences attempt to model and predict the patterns and regularities of nature, theology attempts to *interpret* these patterns and regularities so to make some sense of their first-person perspective; that is, God's perspective. Theology also attempts to interpret the symbols and metaphors in religious literature so to reveal the 'unconscious' psychic processes behind them, which betray something about the inner-workings of God's mind. In both cases, theology represents a legitimate attempt to provide a hermeneutics of texts and nature. This is essential, because a life worth living isn't only about practical applications, but also about meaning and purpose.

2.7. Quantum physics: a parsimonious solution to the measurement problem

In essay 2.1, I argue that we do not need to postulate a whole universe outside consciousness – outside subjective experience – in order to make sense of empirical reality. The implication is that the universe, including our bodies and brains, is in consciousness, not consciousness in our bodies and brains. This ontology, called idealism, is entirely compatible with a classical view of nature: it doesn't exclude the possibility that objects may exist in definite states and locations even if no living creature is observing them. Indeed, idealism entails the existence of a transpersonal form of consciousness underlying all nature, in which transpersonal experiences corresponding to objects with definite outlines can unfold, even when not observed by personal psyches. The latest experiments in quantum mechanics, however, seem to contradict this classical view of empirical reality.[40] They seem to show that, when not observed by individual psyches, reality exists in a fuzzy state, as waves of probabilities. This seeming implication of quantum mechanics isn't incompatible with idealism either. Indeed, there is a harmonious – even natural and synergistic – relationship between the two.

Before we jump into it, let me briefly recapitulate the core ideas in essay 2.1. Consciousness is the only carrier of reality anyone can ever know for sure. I maintain that we do not need more than this one undeniable fact to explain reality: all things and phenomena can be explained as excitations of consciousness itself. As such, underlying all reality is a stream of experiences that

I metaphorically describe as a stream of water. Experiences are represented by the movements – excitations – of water. As such, inanimate objects are like ripples experienced subjectively by the stream itself, which I call 'mind-at-large.' Living creatures are localizations of the flow of experiences in the stream: whirlpools. This way, the body-brain system is simply what a whirlpool in mind-at-large looks like from the outside. It doesn't generate consciousness for exactly the same reason that a whirlpool doesn't generate water. And since there is nothing to a stream full of ripples and whirlpools but water in movement, all reality is simply consciousness in movement.

Because of a natural mechanism of reverberation and amplification of mental contents that I discuss in essay 2.1, movements of water within each whirlpool obfuscate all movements outside the whirlpool. Therefore, a living creature can only be lucidly aware of the ripples that penetrate the rim of its own whirlpool – in our case, our skin, eyes, ears, tongue, and nose – but becomes seemingly unaware of everything else going on in the stream. This is the reason why we can't see when we close our eyes: the ripples from the broader stream that we call photons can no longer penetrate the rim of our whirlpool and get amplified within it. And since our thoughts, emotions and other forms of perception still get amplified inside, the outside ripples end up becoming obfuscated like the stars are obfuscated by the Sun at noon. Yet, those outside ripples are still in consciousness, for the same reason that the stars are still in the sky at noon. They just aren't in our personal awareness; they don't penetrate our whirlpool. As such, all nature is in consciousness in the form of ripples (inanimate objects) and whirlpools (living creatures) in the stream. But only certain aspects of nature enter personal awareness, in the form of ripples that penetrate a whirlpool and get caught and amplified within its central vortex.

This worldview is entirely compatible with classical physics: it does not exclude the possibility that the ripples of the broader stream that never penetrate a whirlpool can still exist in definite form, corresponding to a definite spacetime locus. They can still exist as unambiguous experiences in mind-at-large; that is, the stream itself. But quantum mechanics has been showing that such a view is untenable: when not observed by individual, localized consciousness – that is, when not penetrating a whirlpool – the empirical world isn't definite.[41] Instead, it exists only as fuzzy waves of probabilities. How to reconcile this with the worldview just described?

Clearly, *the ripples in the broader stream – mind-at-large – must be ripples of probabilities, governed by Schrödinger's equation.*[42] *They are subjectively experienced by mind-at-large as fuzzy possibilities, not definite storylines.* This isn't at all difficult to visualize: when we ponder our own uncertain future, we know exactly what it feels like to experience reality as fuzzy possibilities. Now, we know from direct experience that, when a ripple of probabilities penetrates a whirlpool, the many possibilities superposed in it seemingly collapse into one well-defined, classical storyline. After all, we see well-defined tables and chairs in definite locations, not gaseous clouds of possibilities. How this seeming collapse happens is not understood, an issue known in physics as the 'measurement problem.'

Idealism offers a promising new avenue to make sense of it. Because the seeming collapse apparently happens only within a whirlpool, it is reasonable to infer that whatever causes it has to do with the reverberation/amplification process inherent to the whirlpool. I will go further and speculate that the mechanism of seeming collapse *is* the amplification: *only one of the possibilities superposed on the ripple gets amplified, obfuscating all others in the same way that all excitations of mind-at-large external to the whirlpool are obfuscated.* In other words, the apparent collapse happens for the same reason that you can't see when you close your eyes. This is quite parsimonious, because both collapse and obfuscation are then explained by one and the same mechanism in the whirlpool. In fact, with that one mechanism of mental amplification – which, in the case of humans, neuroscientists identified as back-and-forth communication between different brain regions[43] – we get rid of an abstract world outside consciousness, the so-called 'unconscious' *and* of inflationary explanations for quantum collapse; all in one fell swoop.

Now, as it turns out, the particular storyline amplified by one whirlpool happens to be always consistent with the storylines amplified by all other whirlpools, since we all seem to share the same empirical world. How exactly this synchronization happens is an open question. But *that* it happens isn't at all implausible, since all whirlpools are part of one and the same mind. It is intuitively reasonable to expect that one consistent storyline should prevail in the 'dream' of this one mind-at-large.

Even more interestingly, there is a sense in which this idea brings the so-called Copenhagen and Many-Worlds interpretations of quantum mechanics – which are irreconcilable under materialism – closer together. This requires some background, so bear with me. According to the Copenhagen Interpretation, a fundamental transition occurs during the collapse of the probability ripple: in one moment, reality is a fuzzy superposition of possibilities; in the next moment, it somehow becomes a definite, single storyline. What exactly causes this rather magical transition is unclear.[44] Whatever the case, the Copenhagen Interpretation always requires the world to fit into not one, but two very different ontological frameworks: superposition and classical; fuzzy and definite. This, plus the unexplained agency required to cause collapse, motivates many physicists to look for an alternative interpretation. And the most popular alternative is the so-called Many Worlds Interpretation.[45] According to it, no real collapse ever occurs; only an appearance of collapse. All superposed possibilities in the probability ripple do actually play themselves out classically, but each in a different, hypothetical parallel universe. Each parallel universe comprises a definite, classical storyline. You and I happen to inhabit one of these universes, where the storyline we experience is one of the countless possibilities in the probability ripple. Countless other versions of you and me supposedly inhabit other parallel universes, living out all the other possibilities in the probability ripple. If this sounds far-fetched, it's because it is. The Many-Worlds Interpretation is extremely inflationary in that it requires postulating not one, not one million, but *countless* extra universes.

Now let's get back to my speculation about mental amplification and collapse. According to it, a kind of 'collapse' does occur, in that only one out of the many possibilities superposed on the ripple is amplified and, thus, experienced in a classical sense. This clearly differentiates one storyline from all the others and avoids the highly inflationary need to postulate classical parallel universes. But this 'collapse' isn't a fundamental ontological transition: it consists simply in the amplification of one particular possibility, which then obfuscates all others. All possible storylines continue to be experienced as fuzzy, obfuscated possibilities in the stream of mind-at-large, but only one is amplified and lucidly experienced in a classical manner. Again, this is parsimonious in that it avoids the need to postulate different ontological categories for superposed ('fuzzy') and collapsed ('definite') storylines. It all becomes a matter of *degree,* not of a fundamental transition in nature. Finally, notice also that this interpretation is entirely compatible with quantum decoherence, for reasons that escape the scope of this brief essay, but which physicists will easily recognize.[46]

In summary, we may have an opportunity here to perform a handsome trade-off: in exchange for accepting the unanswered question of how whirlpools get synchronized on the particular storyline they amplify, we solve the following problems: we get rid of the need to postulate an unprovable universe outside consciousness; we get rid of the unconscious mind and its problematic ontological status; and we solve the issue of interpreting the measurement problem in quantum mechanics. All in all, I dare entertain the possibility that this may be a promising avenue for future work by physicists and philosophers.

3. On consciousness, neuroscience and the media

The most vexing aspect of nature from a materialist perspective happens to *also* be the only carrier of reality anyone can ever know: consciousness itself. Indeed, materialism would make a lot more sense if consciousness didn't exist at all; if the entire universe consisted simply in the mechanical unfolding of unconscious processes. Clearly, it doesn't. So how could a metaphysics that fails to explain – *even in principle* – the one obvious aspect of existence attain, *and maintain,* the status of reigning worldview? Many indications are provided in the essays in this chapter.

Essays 3.1 and 3.2 discuss how materialists, unable to make sense of consciousness, attempt to deny its very existence. The in-your-face absurdity of this position, and how it is tendentiously spun by many scientists, philosophers and the media alike, is examined. Essays 3.3 and 3.4 address a problem that materialist neuroscience has failed to solve for more than a century: the nature of memories. They expose the public relations charade responsible for the pervasive cultural illusion that neuroscience knows what memories are and where they are located. Finally, essay 3.5 discusses the effects of psychedelics on the human brain, as well as their implications for the materialist axiom that the brain generates all experience. This essay was the most unsettling for me to research and write, for reasons that will become clear to you after you've read it. For a while, in the interest of avoiding polemic, I considered not including it in this book. Yet, precisely for the reason it is so upsetting to me, essay 3.5 is probably one of the most illustrative of the overall message of this work.

3.1. Consciousness: an unsolvable anomaly under materialism

Nobody in science or philosophy has ever managed to explain, even in principle, how presumably unconscious matter could possibly give rise to subjective experience. This is known as the 'hard problem of consciousness' or the 'explanatory gap' in philosophy of mind.[47] The issue is so significant that, in 2005, *Science* magazine chose the 'hard problem' as the second most important unanswered question in science.[48] Indeed, since all we can know about reality is, ultimately, a content of consciousness, the fact that we can't explain consciousness itself is rather vexing for science.

Some neuroscientists and philosophers speculate that consciousness is an 'emergent' property of the brain. 'Emergence' happens when a higher-level property arises from complex interactions of lower-level entities. For instance, the fractal patterns of snowflakes are emergent properties of complex interactions of water molecules. But to merely state that consciousness is an emergent property of the brain is rather a cop-out. In all known cases of emergence, we can deduce the emergent property from the characteristics of the lower-level entities that give rise to it. For instance, we can deduce the fractal shape of snowflakes from the characteristics of water molecules. We can even accurately simulate the formation of snowflakes in a computer. However, we cannot – not even in principle – deduce what it feels to see red, to be disappointed or to love someone from the mass, charge or momentum of material particles making up the brain. As such, to consider consciousness an emergent property of brains is either an appeal to magic or the mere labeling of an unknown. In both cases, precisely *nothing* is actually explained. Consciousness remains an anomaly under materialism. It would be much better if it didn't exist.

And so it happens that, in a move that should give anyone pause for thought, some materialist philosophers[49] and neuroscientists[50] assert that consciousness, well, actually doesn't exist! This is a position generally known as 'eliminative materialism.'[51] If these people were right, it would mean that you, dear reader, presumably aren't aware of the book you're reading right now. You aren't aware of the chair you're sitting on, the aroma of coffee in the air, the love you feel for your children, etc. You're merely an unconscious biological mechanism that mistakenly believes itself to be conscious.

The motivation behind eliminative materialism is clear: if we deny the very existence of consciousness, presto, we no longer need to explain it! The 'hard problem' magically disappears; the anomaly dissolves into thin air. But, as philosopher Galen Strawson pointed out, 'This particular denial is the strangest thing that has ever happened in the whole history of human thought.'[52] It is an attempt to make facts conform to theory, as opposed to theory conform to facts (more on this in essay 3.2).

Eliminative materialists try to substantiate their bizarre notion by claiming that the existence of consciousness is merely the mistaken conclusion of a model engendered by the brain; a model that cannot be trusted.[53] In other words, you just *compute* that you are conscious, but you really aren't. The premise behind this is ludicrous. I can create a computer program that ultimately attributes the logical value 'true' to a variable labeled 'conscious,' but obviously that doesn't take the computer any closer to having inner life the way you and I have, no matter how complex the program. As philosopher John Searle demonstrated decades ago with his famous 'Chinese Room' thought experiment, the manipulation of variables is utterly unrelated to subjective experience.[54] Moreover, eliminative materialists fail to notice that their claim about the non-existence of consciousness is itself the output of their intellectual models; models that, according to their own logic, cannot be trusted. If I can't trust my brain when it tells me I am conscious, why should I trust it when it suggests I am not? The Gödelian self-defeat here is ironic.

If anything, the denial of consciousness is an admission of the impossible impasse that materialism has brought upon science and philosophy today. The danger it entails, however, is the willingness of eliminative materialists to replace the starting point and carrier of anyone's reality – our very consciousness – with convoluted systems of abstraction. Here we have consciousness trying to trick consciousness into believing that it doesn't exist! Yet, the incoherence of this position doesn't stop the mainstream media from routinely publishing eliminative materialist views.[55]

For the sake of preserving a minimum degree of empirical honesty in our culture, we must remain grounded in the primary datum of reality: experience itself. *Experience is what there is before we start theorizing about the world and ourselves.* It takes precedence over everything else. It is the departing point and necessary substrate of all theories. All knowledge resides in consciousness, the sole canvas of reality anyone can ever know for sure. Everything else – all abstractions, all conceptual frameworks – is provisional. We must never forget this, lest we totally lose our connection to reality.

There are other ways in which consciousness is an anomaly under materialism in general, not only its rather absurd eliminative formulation. For instance, today's scientific worldview requires that every property of a living system be explainable, at least in principle, by Darwinian evolution. In other words, if consciousness really exists – for instance, as an emergent property of the brain – it should play a role useful for survival. Otherwise, it is impossible to explain why it allegedly arose in the first place. The problem is that we can, *in principle,* explain the structure and function of every living being without requiring consciousness.

Indeed, *under the assumptions of materialism,* it's not difficult to imagine that computer technology could one day replicate human brains in all detail. It's also not difficult to imagine that robotics technology could one day perfectly replicate a human body. Put these two things together and you can coherently conceive, *under materialism,* of an entirely unconscious, purely mechanistic system that perfectly replicates the structure and function of a human being; a system wholly indistinguishable from a conscious person. Yet, there would be nothing it is like to *be* that system. It would have no inner life. It would perform functions and process information totally 'in the dark.'

This little thought experiment clearly illustrates that all conceivable structure and function of conscious beings can, *in principle, and under materialist assumptions,* be achieved without consciousness. Therefore, evolutionarily speaking, consciousness just shouldn't be there. Yet, materialists keep trying to argue otherwise. Case in point: neurologist and militant materialist Steven Novella, while implicitly acknowledging the existence of subjective experience, argued that there are at least three survival advantages for brains to have evolved it:[56]

1. The brain needs to pay attention to certain things and subjective experience is required for attention.
2. The brain needs a way to distinguish a memory from an active experience. Therefore, memories and active experiences must 'feel' different.
3. Behavior conducive to survival requires motivation and, therefore, conscious emotion.

All three are incoherent arguments within the framework and logic of materialism itself. Under materialism, attention has absolutely nothing to do with a need for consciousness. It is simply a mechanism by means of which an organism focuses its limited cognitive resources on priority tasks or functions. Computer operating systems do this all the time – using techniques like interrupts, queuing, task scheduling, etc. – in a purely algorithmic manner that doesn't require any of the associated computations to be accompanied by experience.[57] Regarding point 2, and still under the assumptions of materialism, there are countless ways to identify, classify and differentiate data without anything 'feeling' anything. Computers do this all the time as well, without being conscious. Does your home computer have trouble separating photos of last year's holidays from the live feed of your webcam? Information streams from memory and active experience can simply be tagged or routed in different ways so the brain – assumed to be akin to a computer under materialism – never mixes them up. What would be easier to evolve: mere data tagging or the inexplicable property of becoming conscious? Finally, point 3: motivation does not require emotion or any sort of subjective experience. Within the logic of materialism, motivation is simply a calculation; the output of an algorithm tasked with maximizing gain while minimizing risk. As any computation, it doesn't need to be accompanied by experience in order to be functionally efficacious. Novella's attempt to present consciousness as something 'natural' or 'advantageous' within the framework of Darwinian evolution fails internal logic.

You see, whichever way one looks at it, consciousness is an unsolvable anomaly under materialism: we can neither explain how it is generated, nor why it evolved. Unfortunately for materialists, this one anomaly is also the very matrix of all knowledge and the carrier of everyone's reality!

So you may now ask: 'How do *you*, Bernardo, solve the hard problem then?' My solution is simple: there is no 'hard problem' to begin with; it is merely a linguistic and conceptual construction. If you think that this is precisely what eliminative materialists say, you are right! But there is a twist: *I don't absurdly deny the existence of consciousness.* Allow me to elaborate.

An entire universe fundamentally outside consciousness is an inference – an explanatory model – not an empirical observation. Our failure to explain consciousness itself on the basis of this inference *is* the 'hard problem.' As such, the 'hard problem' is the result of our getting lost in conceptual labyrinths of our own making. It has no existence outside our own mentation. We, as a culture, find ourselves now in the strange position of having to explain how abstractions of consciousness generate consciousness. Such a circular problem, of course, can never be solved! We're just chasing our own tails at light speed.

Every theory of nature must grant at least one free miracle: a primary entity. This is so because we can't explain one thing in terms of another, and that in terms of another, and then another, forever. At some point, we hit rock-bottom and encounter one or more entities that we simply cannot explain, but *in terms of which* we can explain *all the rest* of reality. Thus, the best theories of nature postulate the smallest possible number of primary entities and then explain as much as possible on that basis. Materialism requires several primary entities, like the irreducible, abstract subatomic particles of the Standard Model of particle physics. It then succeeds in explaining many ancillary aspects of nature in terms of these abstract particles, but fundamentally fails to explain the most obvious and concrete one: consciousness itself. This is a double whammy that renders materialism highly problematic as a metaphysics. Despite requiring multiple primary entities, it still fails to explain consciousness, which for all we know is all there is.

I propose that *the self-evident alternative is to take consciousness itself as the sole primary entity* of nature. This has been staring us in the face from the moment we were born. Not only is it a parsimonious choice by requiring a single primary entity, it completely avoids the 'hard problem' without absurdly denying the very existence of consciousness. As discussed in essay 2.1, we can then explain all other aspects of reality solely in terms of excitations of consciousness, somewhat analogously to how quantum field theorists attempt to explain nature in terms of excitations of a postulated quantum field.[58] Even the leading-edge mathematical apparatus of physics can be ported straightforwardly onto this view by taking consciousness itself to be, for instance, the hyper-dimensional 'brane' of M-theory.[59]

Because the notion that the brain generates consciousness is so deeply inculcated in our culture, my proposal is bound to raise many questions. Many people may even consider it excessively counterintuitive, since the world at large seems to be so disconnected from our inner lives. All these questions, however, can be answered rationally, coherently and in an empirically honest manner, as done in essay 2.2. We, as a 21st century society, deserve better than the convoluted, mad systems of abstraction that keep materialism alive. We deserve to restore our connection to reality.

3.2. The incredible trick of disappearing consciousness

Explaining consciousness remains a vexing failure in science and philosophy today. How can the warmth of love, the bitterness of disappointment, the redness of an apple, the sweetness of strawberries be explained in terms of mass, momentum, charge or any of the properties of matter? How can *concrete qualities* be explained in terms of *abstract quantities and relationships*? Nobody has an answer to this, and not for lack of trying. Such failure to solve the so-called 'hard problem of consciousness' has led to a bizarre twist in philosophy of mind over the past three decades or so: the trick of disappearing consciousness. In a nutshell, it consists of this: since we cannot explain consciousness in terms of unconscious matter, it must be the case that consciousness is an *illusion*.

In a book inaccurately titled *Consciousness Explained,*[60] as well as in a talk titled *The Magic of Consciousness,* Philosopher Daniel Dennett shows that many of our perceptions and beliefs do not correspond to consensus facts. He parades a whole list of perceptual illusions to make his point. This, he suggests, chips away at what we call 'consciousness' and may eventually lead to the conclusion that there is nothing there; that the notion of consciousness will disappear once we understand all the tricks employed by the brain. It's difficult to see how illusions of and in consciousness can suggest the non-existence of consciousness – I tend to believe they suggest the opposite – but bear with me. Although Dennett claims explicitly that consciousness is an illusion,[61] he doesn't close his argument: he remains unable to actually explain how some perceptual illusions – particular contents of consciousness – could possibly imply the non-existence of consciousness itself.

Despite this, Dennett is far from alone in claiming that consciousness is an illusion. Other magicians suggest the same thing in mainstream video documentaries,[62] some of which provide a rather sobering peek into the surreal state of our culture. Indeed, I often wonder how the mainstream media can so consistently get away with in-your-face incoherence. I guess it has to do with the fact that people tend to get bewildered by authority figures telling them that their most fundamental intuitions about reality are wrong. There is some kind of dazzlingly 'wow' factor about this. Yet, sometimes, counter-intuitiveness is simply what it seems to be: a sign of utter intellectual confusion. The media seems to be filling the vacuum left by the incomprehensible wonder of religion with the incomprehensible wonder of scientific and philosophical folly. All the airtime dedicated to unprovable theories about parallel universes, as well as to all kinds of science fiction marketed as science possibility, seems to be part of this broader pattern. But I digress.

Let us try to remain lucid. If consciousness is indeed an illusion, who or what exactly is having the illusion? Where can the illusion reside if not in consciousness itself? After all, if the illusion weren't in consciousness, we couldn't be talking about it, could we? Moreover, the supposed non-existence of consciousness simply does not follow from the observation that certain perceptions or beliefs fail to correspond to consensus facts. If anything, what does follow is that there is such a thing as consciousness, where the illusions pointed out can reside. Dennett suggests that, if enough aspects of experience are found to lack any correspondence with consensus fact, consciousness will be shown to be inexistent. This is wholly illogical: even if we find one day that everything we experience fails to correspond to consensus fact, that will simply show that consciousness is populated with illusions. It will leave consciousness itself intact. We are still conscious of illusions, in exactly the same way that we are conscious of our dreams.

To try to escape the inescapable, magicians appeal to a kind of word dance that philosopher Galen Strawson called 'looking-glassing': to use the word 'consciousness' in such a way that, whatever one means by it, it isn't what the word actually denotes.[63] What could motivate this kind of semantic obscurantism? If we carefully deconstruct it, we find that what appears to be actually denied are just some of the face-value traits ordinarily attributed to consciousness, not consciousness itself. Consider this passage from a *New Scientist* article titled 'The grand illusion: Why consciousness exists only when you look for it':

> If consciousness seems to be a continuous stream of rich and detailed sights, sounds, feelings and thoughts, then I suggest this is the illusion. First we must be clear what is meant by the term 'illusion'. To say that consciousness is an illusion is not to say that it doesn't exist, but that it is not what it seems to be – more like a mirage or a visual illusion.[64]

Naturally, this completely empties the trick of any significance. Yes, it looks like consciousness isn't exactly what it seems to be at face value; so what? To refute some of the face-value traits ordinarily attributed to consciousness doesn't render consciousness itself – raw subjective experience – an illusion. To argue otherwise is entirely equivalent to proclaiming that, because the Earth isn't flat – as it appears to be at face value – then it must be an illusion; and to proclaim this while standing firmly on the Earth! Where is one 'standing' when one consciously proclaims consciousness to be an illusion?

Obviously, raw subjective experience isn't an illusion: it is the only carrier of reality anyone can ever know. It is the sole undeniable empirical fact of existence. Yet, magicians often choose their language so to still be able to state that 'consciousness is an illusion.' Consider this part of the quote above again: 'To say that consciousness is an illusion is not to say that it doesn't exist, but that it is not what it seems to be.' This usage of language is counterintuitive to me. When we say that the alien spaceship in the sky last night was an illusion, we mean that the spaceship wasn't there; that it didn't exist. Maybe an airplane existed there instead, but not the alien spaceship. When we say that the voice we just heard was an illusion, we mean that the voice wasn't there; that it didn't exist. But when it comes to consciousness, magicians depart from this intuitive usage of the term 'illusion.' Why? At the very least, this departure opens the door to misunderstandings, since the word 'illusion' clearly evokes non-existence. When we learned that the Earth was actually a spheroid, we didn't turn around and proclaim the Earth to be an illusion. We simply said that the Earth wasn't what it seemed to be. So why not just say: 'consciousness isn't what it seems to be' and stop there?

You see, if a magician were to acknowledge that the 'illusion' of consciousness is just a matter of false attributions – like we falsely attributed flatness to the Earth without the Earth becoming any less real because of it – then the magic trick would be revealed and lose its appeal. That some of the face-value traits ordinarily attributed to consciousness are false is trivial:

it means exactly nothing as far as solving the hard problem of consciousness. It leaves us exactly where we started: we cannot, even in principle, explain how raw subjective experience arises from mass, momentum or charge. But to acknowledge this would be tantamount to admitting that we are not making real progress in understanding consciousness; that the 'hard problem' is not becoming any more tractable despite the many promissory notes to the contrary and the huge amount of resources spent on researching it. Do you see the dilemma?

Other magicians don't go as far as denying consciousness as a whole, but buy into and promote the fundamental notion underlying the magic trick. Some claim that certain aspects of experience – such as beliefs – do not really exist,[65] even though something most of us would call a 'belief' is undeniably experienced by every living person. The magicians make such a claim because these aspects of experience appear to be structured along syntactical patterns that have no obvious correspondence in brain anatomy or function. Naturally, we could criticize their rationale by pointing out that we also cannot find the high-level structure of software in the gates and wires of a computer chip, but that obviously doesn't mean that the software structure is inexistent. Be it as it may, the point here is that these more limited eliminativist claims still contribute to the absurd notion that one can deny the existence of direct, felt experience on the basis of theoretical abstractions. Have your beliefs disappeared just because someone couldn't find anything directly corresponding to them in the brain? Even if it were correct to call these experiences illusions, the then-illusory experiences would still be facts as such. An experience isn't nothing.

All attempts to turn consciousness into some kind of illusion ultimately fail. It couldn't be any different, since the attempts themselves necessarily reside in consciousness. *It is consciousness that is trying to convince itself that it is an illusion.* How could this ever work?

Now, having rejected all these different avenues for tackling the 'hard problem,' you may be wondering how *I* would solve it. It may then come as a surprise to you that I think there is no such a thing: the 'hard problem' is merely a linguistic and conceptual construction of human beings. It only arises when we conceptualize a whole universe outside consciousness and then postulate that this conceptual universe somehow generates consciousness. So we end up in the position of having to explain how an abstraction of consciousness can generate consciousness. Instead of playing this hopeless circular game, I propose that we must bite the bullet and accept the obvious fact that nature presents to us the moment we are born: consciousness is the one fundamental aspect of reality; the canvas of existence. The universe is nothing but excitations of consciousness itself. For further details on how this simple idea can explain literally everything, see essays 2.1 and 2.2.

3.3. What are memories, after all?

Under the materialist metaphysics, memories are supposedly analogous to information stored in a computer. Everything you can potentially remember must be physically encoded somewhere in your brain, like a little computer file. While in storage, the file is supposedly outside consciousness. When you play it back, it somehow re-enters consciousness. This, in a nutshell, is the materialist hypothesis of memory. It is so pervasive that the media routinely and casually speaks of memories being 'stored in the brain,' as if the hypothesis were an established fact.

The problem is that, if the hypothesis were true, we should be able to find those little files in the form of material traces stored somewhere in the brain. Neuroscience has been looking for them for more than a century, but hasn't turned up anything conclusive. In 2012, *Science Daily* summarized the present status: 'Despite a century of research, memory encoding in the brain has remained mysterious. Neuronal synaptic connection strengths are involved, but synaptic components are short-lived while memories last lifetimes.'[66] What has been found are some neural correlates of memory formation – that is, brain activity that accompanies it – but not the information storage itself.[67]

The pressure to produce results confirming the materialist hypothesis seems to be immense. A 2008 study was reported to have finally revealed 'where in the brain a specific memory is stored.'[68] What the researchers in fact found was that the same subset of neurons in the hippocampus and entorhinal cortex – two areas of the brain – get activated during both recall and the original experience. Having had volunteers watch short video clips during the experiments, the researchers 'found that the neurons that responded during viewing of a particular clip also responded during recall of that clip. ... This recurrence of selective activity during recall was not an isolated observation found in a few neurons, but was also evident when the population of responsive [neurons] was examined as a whole.'[69] This isn't at all surprising: we know that particular subjective experiences correlate with particular patterns of neural activation. When we recall an event we are, in essence, *re-experiencing* that event lucidly, so it's entirely expectable that many of the same neurons should activate again. The *real* question, of course, is: *how does the brain know which neurons to re-activate during recall? Where is the information about the pattern of re-activations stored?* The study sheds no new light on this question, which is the only question that really matters when it comes to explaining where memories are stored. Provided that the headlines suggest a confirmation of the materialist hypothesis, it is surprising how much inaccuracy one can get away with. Society is very forgiving when the error is on the side of the reigning metaphysics; a virtuous cycle that tendentiously maintains its ruling status.

Further research on memory has been producing seemingly contradictory results in recent years. For instance, a 2009 experiment indicated that memory formation depends on interplay between synaptic activity and DNA transcription in the neuron's nucleus.[70] A much-talked-about 2012 study, on the other hand, suggested that memories are encoded digitally in microtubules in the neuron's cytoplasm; a completely different mechanism.[71] Again in 2012, yet another study suggested that memories may be stored as patterns of synaptic connections in the hippocampus;[72] this is an inter-neuron mechanism, in contrast to the intra-neuron mechanisms of the previous two studies. In conclusion, after more than a century, neuroscience seems to be still all over the map when it comes to explaining where memories are stored. Yet, if one were to go by the headlines, one would think we've validated the materialist hypothesis multiple times over: 'Reducing memory to a molecule,'[73] 'Scientists claim brain memory code cracked,'[74] and so on.

So where do I personally stand? To simply say that I consider the materialist hypothesis false would be as strictly correct as it would be misleading. My position is subtle and, to make sense of it, we first need some brief background. Bear with me for a moment.

As discussed in essay 2.1, I am a proponent of *idealism,* which holds that the brain is in consciousness, not consciousness in the brain. As such, the brain is the image of a process of localization in a stream of transpersonal experiences, like a whirlpool is the image of a process of localization in a stream of water. The brain doesn't generate consciousness for exactly the same reason that a whirlpool doesn't generate water. Active neurons are what experiences *look like* from the outside, this being the reason why brain function correlates tightly with subjective states. Moreover, I believe that lucid awareness consists of reverberating – and therefore amplified – mental contents in the 'center of the whirlpool,' so to speak. Neuroscience itself has amassed evidence for this reverberation.[75] Mental contents in the 'periphery of the whirlpool' do not reverberate and, therefore, become obfuscated like the stars at noon. This creates the illusion of unconscious mental processes, but there is no actual unconscious. Everything that happens in the brain is the outside image of either lucid or obfuscated experiences. *Memories are nothing but ongoing obfuscated experiences in the periphery of the psyche.*

Analytical psychology divides the psyche of an individual into two segments: the ego and the so-called 'personal unconscious.'[76] According to this division, the ego comprises everything that you are lucidly aware of at any given moment. The 'personal unconscious,' in turn, comprises everything that you can *potentially* remember, but of which you are currently not lucid. Since I deny the existence of a true unconscious, I prefer to call these two segments 'lucid awareness' and 'obfuscated psyche,' respectively. Lucid awareness includes the reverberating, amplified contents of the psyche. Its outside image is what neuroscience calls the Neural Correlates of Consciousness (NCC).[77] The obfuscated psyche, in turn, includes the obfuscated contents. Its outside image comprises all the other neural processes in the brain that aren't NCCs.

According to this idealist view, memory formation entails a movement of mental contents from lucid awareness to the obfuscated psyche. Recall, in turn, entails the reverse movement. To use the metaphor of the brain as a whirlpool of transpersonal experiences, lucid awareness comprises mental contents circulating in the central vortex of the whirlpool – which reverberates – while the obfuscated psyche comprises mental contents circulating in the periphery of the whirlpool. Contents of the obfuscated psyche remain thus localized; they don't flow away and become lost in the broader stream of transpersonal consciousness. Precisely for this reason, they can potentially re-enter the center of the whirlpool. When this happens, we say that we 'remembered' something.

So far, I've been simply putting forward a different way

to *interpret* memory and recall. You may have noticed that everything I've said above is operationally indistinguishable from the materialist hypothesis of memory. Nonetheless, if we push this alternative interpretation a little further, different predictions arise.

As discussed above, idealism entails that memories are ongoing but *obfuscated* experiences in the periphery of the psyche. If neurons were the *cause* of all experiences, we should be able to find all memories somewhere in the brain. But under idealism, neurons are merely an *outside image* of experience, not its cause. It is thus entirely conceivable that this image is *partial*. After all, the image of a process is seldom complete; it seldom comprises all there is to know about the process. Flames don't convey all there is to know about combustion. Lightning doesn't convey all there is to know about atmospheric electric discharge. Therefore, *not all mental contents of the obfuscated psyche need to be detectable – even in principle – as something in the brain, or anywhere in the body for that matter.* In fact, it's coherently conceivable that the vast majority isn't. For instance, as discussed in essay 8.3, one relatively popular scenario among those involved in the healing arts, due to empirical reasons, is that memories of *self-generated* experiences – buried emotions, repressed thoughts and fantasies, hidden beliefs, etc. – can be found in the body, but those of past external events not necessarily so.

That there can be memories – obfuscated experiences circulating in the periphery of the whirlpool – that aren't correlated with information in the brain or body isn't as counterintuitive as it may seem at first. Before the advent of microscopy, the entire realm of cellular and microbial activity integral to the body's functioning was not only unseen, but unimagined. Before the advent of electromagnetic measurement techniques, the entire realm of electromagnetic activity essential to a working body was equally undetected and unimagined. So there is simply no reason why we should – *even in principle* – be able to find all memories in the body.

Having said all this, for the sake of keeping the discussion as close as possible to current scientific and cultural expectations, let us assume that at least *most* memories *can* be detected in principle. In other words, let us assume that most contents of the obfuscated psyche correlate with measurable information in the organism. What then are the operational differences between the materialist hypothesis and idealism?

If the body is what a whirlpool in the stream of transpersonal experiences looks like, then *the entire body* – except, of course, for the NCCs – *corresponds to the obfuscated psyche*. It is the whole body that is the whirlpool, not just the brain. Indeed, unlike the materialist view of the body as an unconscious mechanism, under idealism the entire organism is an *image of experiences*. And what are memories but obfuscated experiences? This is a crucial shift in the way we look upon the body. In the terminology of analytical psychology, we can thus say that *the body is what the 'personal unconscious' looks like from the outside.* Hence, one should expect to find memories *anywhere* in the organism – except, again, for the NCCs – not only in the brain. This gives theoretical grounding to the empirically motivated notion of cellular memory: the hypothesis that memories may be associated with the various organs and tissues of the body. For instance, studies on flatworms – creatures capable of regenerating even their whole brain in case of injury – revealed that they retain long-term memories even after their head has been severed.[78] This suggests very strongly that their memories are associated with their whole body, not only their brain. There is also a significant amount of anecdotal evidence indicating that organ transplant recipients inherit some of the donors' memories.[79] This shouldn't be possible under the materialist hypothesis, but is entirely expectable if the body is what localized, personal experience looks like from the outside. If a 'part of a whirlpool' is severed and implanted into another 'whirlpool,' it is indeed to be expected that the respective experiences should mix. Finally, psychological therapy has shown significant evidence for a connection between the body and memories.[80]

Summarizing:

- Neural Correlates of Consciousness (NCCs) = Reverberating center of the whirlpool = Lucid awareness = Amplified experiences.
- Other neural processes = Non-reverberating, nearby periphery of the whirlpool = Superficial contents of the obfuscated psyche = Superficial memories.
- Metabolism in other bodily tissues = Non-reverberating, remote periphery of the whirlpool = Deeper contents of the obfuscated psyche = Deeper memories.

One could argue that, if memories are indeed associated with the body as a whole, amputation of an organ or general tissue loss should noticeably impair recall, which doesn't seem to be the case. The problem is: it isn't the case with the brain either. Memory lapses in Alzheimer's patients only become noticeable after 40% to 50% of brain cells are already dead.[81] Removal of large and various parts of the brain of rats has been found to leave their memory largely unaffected.[82] If anything, associating memory to the whole body makes these facts more intelligible: a large part of the brain represents a much smaller fraction of the body as a whole. The idea of holographic biological storage[83] – originally envisioned to explain how the brain could maintain memories even after so much of it is lost – could conceivably be applicable, in some form, to the whole body. If this is the case, no noticeable difference in recall will occur until a huge amount of the body is removed; an amount incompatible with the preservation of life given the limitations of current transplant technology. This may sound highly speculative – and it is – but keep in mind that non-speculative alternatives for explaining memory do not exist at this point. Finally, to say that memory is associated with the body as a whole doesn't imply that all parts of the body are *equally* involved in *episodic* memory – that is, memory of past events. Until we find out exactly what the correlates of obfuscated episodic experience are, it is entirely conceivable that different organs or types of tissue are involved to widely different degrees.

The precise opposite of the argument above could, ironically, also be used against my hypothesis: illnesses that affect only the brain, such as Alzheimer's, as well as localized physical trauma to the brain alone, *can* significantly impair recall *even when the rest of the body remains intact*. Notice, however, that this doesn't imply that memories are all in the brain. It suggests only that brain illness and trauma can impair our ability to *amplify* otherwise obfuscated experiences, wherever these experiences may reside. We know that the reverberation process that amplifies mental contents happens only in the brain, taking up relatively small amounts of neurons in specific areas. It's thus no surprise that, *if damage to key brain pathways prevents the flow of information into these specific areas,* lucid awareness of the corresponding experiences becomes impossible. The memories will still be there in the body, but the patient will report an inability to remember – that is, to become lucidly aware of – certain things; an inability that will grow as more access paths to the 'center of the whirlpool' become compromised.

Whether memory is holographic or not, the core suggestion of idealism is to look upon it as a *robust global phenomenon* of the body, entailing plenty of *redundancy*. Instead of simplistically reducing memory to discrete bits of information stored locally in the biological equivalents of computer latches, maybe we can find the corresponding information reflected holistically on the operation of the body as a whole; like a global interference pattern formed by interacting waves from various local sources. If this is how memory works, *it is critical that we look beyond the brain, otherwise we will continue to miss essential pieces of the puzzle.* We cannot find the information present in an interference pattern by considering only the individual wave sources in isolation.

Another way in which idealism differs radically from the materialist hypothesis is this: according to materialism, memories are only experienced when recalled. Otherwise, they are merely unconscious information stored somewhere as material traces. According to idealism, on the other hand, *these material traces are the (partial) outside image of ongoing experiences.* As such, *memories never cease to be experienced.* You are continuously experiencing all your memories at all times. It's just that the vast majority of these experiences are obfuscated, only a small subset being amplified.[84] Forgetting and recalling things mean simply that different ones among the *ongoing* experiences in the psyche become amplified at different moments. Some of these ongoing experiences correspond to consensus facts. Others are simply personal fantasies or confabulations. Yet others, a conflation of the previous two cases. Whatever the case, 'recall' and 'amnesia' are simply the names we give to a swap of the mental contents reverberating in the psyche.

This difference between materialism and idealism has huge implications when it comes to our understanding of death: since the body is the outside image of localization in the flow of transpersonal experiences, bodily death is simply a de-localization – a release – of those experiences; the dissolution of the whirlpool. This way, neither your consciousness nor your memories cease to exist upon death, for the same reason that the water in a whirlpool doesn't cease to exist when the whirlpool dissolves. The water is simply released into the larger flow of the stream. While materialism implies that death terminates any possibility that one's memories can be re-experienced, idealism implies that the *ongoing* experiences in memory are simply released into a larger context of consciousness.

Memory remains a profound scientific mystery. There is

nothing wrong with there being mysteries in science but, in this case, science's less-than-tacit adoption of materialism as a metaphysics – which I discuss further in essay 4.4 – is artificially restricting it. Indeed, memory may be one of the anomalies that will eventually compel science to reconsider its illegitimate and neurotic marriage to materialism. This is not to deny that powerful forces are at play to maintain the *status quo,* including a baffling willingness by the mainstream media to err on the side of materialist views. But, short of outright scientific and intellectual censorship, no human game can ultimately resist the truths of nature.

3.4. Misleading journalism and the notion of implanted memories

In the summer of 2013, several people sent me links to an article published on *Scientific American.* The title promised something extraordinary: 'The Era of Memory Engineering Has Arrived: How neuroscientists can call up and change a memory.'[85] This certainly sparked my curiosity. After having read it, however, I was indeed amused, but not for the reasons I thought I would be. Allow me to elaborate.

The article started with references to science fiction films in which the hero at some point realizes that his memories were implanted by evil scientists. None of the past he remembers actually happened, but was artificially synthesized and inserted into his head. I immediately thought of the movie *Total Recall,* where people could go to a shop called 'Recall' and order custom-made memories of holidays, adventures, heated romances and what not, without actually having to live through any of that. The article then went on to suggest that cutting edge work done at the Massachusetts Institute of Technology (MIT) was comparable to these amazing sci-fi scenarios:

Scientists have captured specific memories in mice, altered

them, and shown that the mice behave in accord with these new, false, implanted memories. The era of memory engineering is upon us, and naturally, there are big implications for basic science and, perhaps someday, human health and society.[86]

Wow, really? Have we been able to synthesize and implant episodic memories like in *Total Recall?* I mean, no need for entire narratives... if even a simple episodic memory – say, of switching on the lights – could have been synthesized and implanted, it would be very significant not only for science, but for philosophy as well. If it were possible to synthesize and implant memories that way, it would imply that we knew exactly what memories were, as well as where and how they were encoded in the brain. However, things weren't as they seemed...

When you read the original scientific report[87] critically, here is what you discover:

- No episodic memories were synthesized at all.
- What was actually done was this: they found a way to measure and record the pattern of brain activity in mice when the mice were placed in a first environment – say, environment A – and then they managed to 'reactivate' that same pattern of brain activity later on, after the mice had been relocated to another place – environment B.
- When they re-activated the original pattern of brain activity – the one corresponding to environment A – with the mice already located in environment B, they simultaneously gave the mice electric shocks.
- When they put the mice back in environment A, without the shocks, the mice still got paralyzed with fear.

That's it. Now, let's look at what this actually means.

Both the experiences of being in environment A and of the

electric shocks weren't 'implanted' memories. *They actually happened.* They actually shocked the mice. They actually placed the mice in environment A. All the experiment accomplished was to create an association between environment A and the electric shock without needing to actually make the two happen together, as in classical conditioning. So there is a sense in which one could perhaps say that the memory of the association was induced, but that's totally different from what the article suggests in the beginning. No episodic memory was synthesized at all; not even a very tiny simple one. All experiences involved were actual experiences of the mice. They just tricked the mice into linking one real experience to another real experience. This is rather a cognitive link than a memory. They induced association, conditioning; they didn't implant episodic memories.

You might say that, by reactivating a certain pattern of brain activity, the scientists artificially created recall. This is true, but it doesn't address the important question of what memory is or where it's stored. You see, experiences correlate with brain activation patterns; we know that. So, if you induce a certain brain activation pattern in mice and associate that with a shock, it's no surprise that the shock will be cognitively linked to any future experience that triggers the same brain activation pattern. But that's not the question. The question is, *when I close my eyes and remember my dead father, how do I know what exact pattern of brain activity to bring back to my brain? Where is the information stored that allows me to reconstruct that pattern?*

In the MIT experiment, *the scientists created their own storage mechanism:* they genetically modified the mice to grow light-sensitive switches in each neuron that got activated in environment A. Only the activated neurons grew the light-sensitive switches, so the distribution of the switches recorded the neural correlates of the original experience of the mice in their original environment. The scientists could then turn these same neurons back on later, by shinning light on the mice's brain, thereby recreating their original experience in a totally different environment. Of course, this doesn't explain how mice remember things when they *haven't* been engineered to grow light-sensitive switches in their neurons. The experiment explains exactly nothing about the mechanism of memory storage simply because it *bypasses* it altogether. It was the scientists who recorded and stored the information, and then used this information to create a pattern of brain activity, *not the mice.* How do the mice do it when there are no scientists to record, store and re-launch the information in their brains?

The experiment also says nothing new about the nature of experience. That experience is correlated with certain patterns of brain activity is very old news. That they could create an association between two events by activating their respective patterns together in the brain is also no news, since this has been shown by classical conditioning since the time of Pavlov. The only novelty – and, make no mistake, it's amazing and important, just not in the way the article portrays it – is the scientists' ability to record and then re-activate a particular pattern of brain activity. This may have important future applications in, for instance, new treatments of brain illness and perhaps even in education. But don't expect a 'Recall' shop near you any time soon. Don't expect a solution to the 'hard problem of consciousness.' And don't expect an answer to the nature and location of episodic memory.

To me, the key insight here is how, through lack of rigor and misplaced enthusiasm, an entirely undemonstrated notion can be hyped by the mainstream media to the point of looking fully established. How many well-meaning people out there, who briefly read this article, weren't thinking: 'Wow, it's a done deal... memory and consciousness really are in the brain'? Could we even blame them? I suspect that many journalists feel safe to exaggerate if they're backed by the clout of the mainstream metaphysics; what could go wrong, right?

While reading this essay, you're thinking more critically about this specific study. But how many similar articles about other studies have you casually read over the years? How many of your implicit beliefs and convictions today – 'facts' you take for granted – have been subtly created through exposure to similarly misleading hype? Scary, isn't it?

3.5. Psychedelics and the mind-body problem

Early in 2012, a study was published on the effects of psilocybin – the active ingredient of magic mushrooms – on brain function.[88] It received enormous media attention over the subsequent months. Indeed, the study attracted my own interest because the researchers observed only *reductions* in brain activity while subjects were having mind-boggling psychedelic experiences. This is, of course, counterintuitive from a materialist perspective: how can an extreme *increase* in the breadth and intensity of experience occur without an accompanying increase in brain activity? Even worse: how can it happen with a *decrease* in brain activity?

Preliminary reports on this psychedelic study had already indicated that the researchers had observed reductions of activity,[89] but the explanation could have been that the drug selectively affected *inhibitory* brain processes, thereby allowing other processes to grow unchecked elsewhere. Let me unpack this a bit for you: under materialism, inhibitory brain processes are like bouncers guarding the entrance to the club of consciousness. Brain processes become conscious if they get into the club, but the bouncers prevent many from entering, so we never become aware of them. If the drug took out the bouncers, the idea is that many processes that would otherwise remain unconscious could then grow and flood into the club. This would explain the 'trip.'

The problem is that the researchers observed *no* brain activation *anywhere* in the brain. Quoting the study: 'We observed no increases in cerebral blood flow in any region.'[90] You see, if the club of consciousness got flooded because the bouncers were taken out, the researchers should still have seen, *somewhere in the brain*, the increases in activity corresponding to the new, now-uninhibited processes growing within the club. But they didn't. In fact, they observed that *the more the drug de-activated the brain, the more intense were the subjective experiences* reported by the subjects.[91] This is highly counterintuitive under materialism. Subjects reported experiences like 'geometric patterns,' 'extremely vivid imagination,' seeing their 'surroundings change in unusual ways,' as well as experiences with a 'dream-like quality.'[92] Without brain activations observed anywhere, and with the subjects stuck inside a brain scanner, this is difficult for a materialist to make sense of. One would expect, for instance, visions of geometric patterns to be caused by activations of visual areas of the brain. But the researchers not only did not observe these activations, they reported that 'there were ... additional ... signal decreases ... in higher-order visual areas.'[93]

If you want to have an idea of the kind of structured, coherent, evocative and disconcertingly intense subjective experiences that people have under the effect of psilocybin, I recommend the *Erowid* online experiences vault.[94] If you browse through the reports in there, you will likely convince yourself that, if consciousness were merely the result of brain metabolism, such experiences could not occur without measurable increases in this metabolism. Yet, the opposite happens.

Surprisingly, the researchers went as far as acknowledging that their results suggested that the brain was at least partly akin to a consciousness localization phenomenon (as I argue in essay 2.1). They wrote that their findings were 'consistent with Aldous Huxley's 'reducing valve' metaphor ... which propose[s] that the mind/brain works to constrain its experience of the world.' To help you know precisely what Huxley's hypothesis was, here is the appropriate quote from his book *The Doors of Perception and Heaven and Hell:*

The suggestion is that the function of the brain and nervous system and sense organs is in the main eliminative and not productive. Each person is at each moment capable of ... perceiving everything that is happening everywhere in the universe. The function of the brain and nervous system is to protect us from being overwhelmed ... by shutting out most of what we should otherwise perceive or remember at any moment, and leaving only that very small and special selection which is likely to be practically useful.[95]

Also interesting is the researchers' observation that the highest de-activations of the brain occurred in areas associated with the ego.[96] This is consistent with the age-old idea that the ego prevents us from perceiving the unity and transcendence of consciousness. As discussed in essay 2.1, I liken the brain to a whirlpool in a transpersonal stream of experiences. So when I read this part of the study, I couldn't help but visualize the de-activation of the ego as analogous to a disruption of the whirlpool, which allows consciousness to partly and temporarily de-localize beyond the spacetime locus of the body. When some specific brain functionality is taken out, consciousness de-clenches and expands.

Eminent neuroscientist Dr. Christof Koch and I once had an indirect debate on this study via interviews we both gave to the same Internet talk-show.[97] Koch claimed that my position – as discussed above – was too simplistic, given that conscious experience isn't directly proportional to global brain activity due to the role of inhibitory processes. I already discussed above – and, much more extensively, in my earlier book *Why Materialism Is Baloney*[98] – why references to inhibitory processes do not solve the problem. Whichever way one presents the issue, under materialism a fully inactive brain cannot be conscious because consciousness allegedly *is* some kind of activity somewhere in the brain. Therefore, despite the role of inhibitory processes, a significant increase in the breadth and intensity of experience *must* correlate with a corresponding increase in activity *somewhere* in the brain.

This becomes clear when you consider this: lucid dreams and psychedelic experiences are similar in that neither can be attributed to sensory inputs. Yet, in a lucid dream, when we do something as dull as clenching our dreamed-up hands, scientists can discern the corresponding brain activations from the baseline of brain activity.[99] But when we have unfathomable psychedelic excursions into 'other universes,' scientists see no brain activation whatsoever when contrasted to the baseline. If this isn't an anomaly under materialism, then materialism makes no significant predictions as far as consciousness is concerned and might as well be declared operationally irrelevant.

Whatever the ultimate *interpretation* of these results will be, it is important that the results themselves be reported *factually*. But look at this quote from a CNN news piece reporting on the study in question:

> [The researchers] scanned the brains of 30 healthy volunteers after they had been injected with psilocybin and found the more primitive regions of the brain associated with emotional thinking *became more active* and [a region] associated with high-level thinking, self-consciousness and introspection, was disjointed and less active.[100]

What can one say? *According to the study report, there were no increases in activity anywhere.* What increased was coupling in some regions, but that's not activity. The news piece essentially conveys *the opposite* of what was found.

The same team of researchers continued their efforts to understand the effects of psilocybin in the brain and published another scientific article in 2014 elaborating on their new results.[101] Once again, the media seems to have reported misleadingly on the findings. The news piece in question stated that the researchers had 'found *increased activity* in regions of the brain that are known to be activated during dreaming.'[102] If this were true, it would contradict the conclusions of the earlier 2012 study. But let's look at what the researchers were investigating this time:

> ...the effects of psilocybin on the *variance* of brain activity parameters across time has been relatively understudied and this line of enquiry may be particularly informative ... Thus, the main objective of this article is to examine how psilocybin modulates the dynamics and *temporal variability* of resting state [brain] activity.[103]

Clearly, unlike in the 2012 study, the researchers this time weren't reporting on brain activity, but on the *variability* of that activity; that is, on how much and how fast it changed over time. Naturally, a brain displaying higher levels of activity *variation* can still have, overall, much lower levels of activity than normally. A jetliner in cruise flight has very high speed, but very low speed *variability*. You will experience more speed *variability* if you are riding a motorcycle downtown – constantly stopping in traffic lights, accelerating on long stretches of straight road, slowing down before turns, avoiding other traffic, etc. – but the speed of the motorcycle will still be much lower than that of the jetliner. Do you see the point?

The researchers went on to report on their findings:

> In summary, increased *variance* in [brain activity] was observed ... This change in variance is the expression of an increased amplitude of [brain activity] *fluctuations* ... bursts of high amplitude activity have been seen in human rapid-eye movement (REM) sleep ... Given that phenomenological similarities have previously been noted between the

psychedelic ... and dream states, it is intriguing to consider whether [this] may be an important common property of these states.[104]

What was found to increase was thus the *variability* of brain activity in dream-related regions, not activity itself. As such, the new study doesn't contradict the earlier findings.

The confusion could, in principle, have arisen from simple misunderstanding. The language used in the 2014 scientific article, although strictly accurate, is indeed conducive to just this kind of misinterpretation. For instance, the article talks about the 'total spectral *power*' of brain activity in certain regions having '*increased.*'[105] This seems to suggest that brain activity increased, doesn't it? But it has nothing to do with it. The word 'power' is misleading here, for it's used in a very specific technical sense: it corresponds to the square of each frequency component of the original brain activity signal, wherein phase information is discarded. Therefore, an increase in 'total spectral power,' in and of itself, neither implies nor suggests that brain activity increased.[106]

The use of language like '*higher* total spectral *power*' and '*increased amplitude* variations' seems to suggest that, unable to make sense of their own 2012 results, the researchers were looking for some quantifiable neural parameter that *did increase* during psychedelic trances. It is as if they were pressed to find that something – anything – *increased.* After all, the materialist intuition screams that, if consciousness *expands,* something in the brain *must increase.* Since materialism today offers no coherent explanation for how consciousness allegedly arises from matter (see essay 3.1), it is conceivable, in principle, that experience could arise from *variations of neural activity level,* as opposed to activity itself. Nonetheless, this would contradict a whole host of other correlations routinely observed between experience and the sheer level of brain activity, such as the lucid-dreaming study referred to earlier.[107] Materialism cannot have it both ways.

I initially attributed the confusion to science journalism lacking rigor and in-depth grasp of the research. But then I found a popular science piece written not by a journalist, but by one of the researchers himself: Dr. Carhart-Harris. Titled 'Magic mushrooms expand your mind and *amplify your brain's dreaming areas*,' Carhart-Harris goes on to say that psilocybin *'increased the amplitude ... of activity'* in brain regions associated with dreaming.[108] This is not corroborated by the 2014 technical paper, which reports an increase only in the amplitude *of variations* of brain activity levels. Carhart-Harris then speculates that psychedelics enabled *'disinhibited activity'* in neural systems associated with emotions.[109] This again suggests that activity increases somewhere in the brain as a result of psychedelic use, both in contradiction to Carhart-Harris' own 2012 results and without substantiation in the 2014 technical article. In another popular article in which Carhart-Harris is quoted, he goes beyond mere suggestion: 'You're seeing these areas getting *louder, and more active*,' he is quoted as saying. 'It's like someone's *turned up the volume* there.'[110] What's going on here?

Puzzled, I emailed Carhart-Harris asking for clarifications.[111] He and Enzo Tagliazucchi, the main author of the second study, replied promptly and very generously. The email exchange that ensued over several days confirms my assessments above. Namely:

- Indeed, they found just an increase in the *variability* of the brain activity signal, that is, an increase in fluctuations as opposed to a constant, unchanging signal.[112] Phase information is lost in the variability analysis, so no conclusions can be extracted about the average amplitude of the signal.
- Tagliazucchi interprets the *variability* of brain activity during rest as analogous to *actual* brain activity when the

subject is engaged in performing a task. The variability may show how often spontaneously-occurring neural processes engage and disengage, thus providing a measure of 'something going on' in the brain while the subject is at rest.[113] As such, variability could be looked upon as a kind of 'meta-activity' measurement that may correlate better with the qualitative changes in subjective experience reported by the subjects.

• Actual brain activity has *not* been found to increase anywhere in the brain.

After having seen an earlier draft of this essay, the researchers requested that I do not quote their email messages to me; a request I find disappointing but which I am honoring. All I can thus say is that, following extensive and in-depth exchanges with them,[114] it is my genuine understanding and conviction that Carhart-Harris' popular science piece and some of his statements quoted in the press were outright false; they misrepresented his own studies in a way that, accidently or not, made them seemingly more consistent with materialism. Carhart-Harris himself has neither explicitly agreed with nor denied this assessment, although I believe it to be an *inescapable implication* of the email communications I've had with him and Tagliazucchi. To me, these events illustrate how easy and forgivable it is to err on the side of the reigning materialist worldview, so as to perpetuate it even in view of data that contradicts it.

You see, I see nothing wrong with exploring the idea of 'meta-activity.' In fact, I applaud it. I just feel that the terminology should be used rigorously and unambiguously to avoid misleading readers and the media alike. Brain activity – that is, metabolism – is one thing; *variations* of brain activity are another thing entirely. Speed is not the same as acceleration. A car that repeatedly stops, accelerates and then stops again is not necessarily a car that travels fast. The theoretical hypothesis that 'meta-activity' may be a more useful measurement does not make it valid to use the word 'activity' as shorthand for 'activity variability.'

The bottom-line is this: when one sees *more* consciousness consistently accompanied by *less* brain activity, one is forced to contemplate the possibility that brain function is associated with a localization of consciousness, as opposed to its production.

4. On skepticism and science

As a culture, we've come to believe that skeptical science now understands most of the mysteries of our ordinary world. There may be unanswered questions regarding parallel universes and other remote abstractions, but we assume that most of the facets of concrete life have been explained by rational scientific theories, from the weather to health, to psychology, to social dynamics. We believe unquestioningly that the Faustian power of rationality, skepticism and the application of the scientific method have answered – or are on the cusp of answering – all questions of any practical relevance to our daily lives. But is that really so? What reasons do we actually have to believe it? Could it be that the apparent runaway success of science – and, more generally, of our rational faculties – is as much illusory as it is factual? Could it be that we live in a world of illusions enabled precisely by a spectacular *failure* of skepticism?

Essay 4.1 explores – in a metaphorical manner – the insanity of our deification of rational faculties. Essay 4.2 illustrates how the belief that science has explanations for most of the events of our daily lives is nothing more than an illusion. Essay 4.3 discusses the unexamined and tendentious philosophical *beliefs* adopted by many scientists when it comes to extracting conclusions from the available data. Essay 4.4 goes deeper into this subject by exploring how most scientists have come to conflate scientific observations with philosophical *interpretations* of these observations. Essay 4.5 discusses a true taboo that pervades science as practiced today, and which so often corrupts proper scientific assessment of the empirical facts of reality. Essay 4.6 confronts the question that underlies the culture wars: does the scientific evidence in favor of evolution by natural selection imply that life is meaningless and purposeless? Finally, essay 4.7 argues that the solution to the prejudices of scientific thinking today is not a departure from skepticism but, surprisingly, its *revitalization*.

4.1. Intellectual fundamentalism

Important disclaimer: this essay adopts the format of a fictional medical description of a fictional psychiatric condition – called 'intellectual fundamentalism' – for the purposes of social and cultural criticism. This essay should not be interpreted literally. The signs, symptoms, causes, risk factors, treatments and preventive steps described below are not – insofar as I am aware – medically recognized.

Intellectual fundamentalism is a dangerous condition that affects increasing and alarming numbers of people worldwide. Though its origins can be traced to the West – some think René Descartes was the index case – modern means of communication and easy travel have allowed it to spread far and wide into the East as well. This essay is an attempt to raise awareness of this dangerous epidemic, so people can identify the early signs of the condition and take appropriate steps.

Definition

Intellectual fundamentalism is characterized by a severe psychological imbalance: exaggerated focus on one specific psychic function – namely, the rational intellect – to the detriment of all others, including intuition, poetic imagination, emotional intelligence, artistic sensitivity, empathy, perceptual awareness, etc. Curiously, the intellect isn't always the patient's dominant psychic function: often, those whose intellect is relatively limited also fall victim.

Signs and symptoms

Patients tend to implicitly or explicitly deny the efficaciousness and reliability of all psychic functions except the intellect. They insist that the intellect is the only valid avenue for approaching reality, even though they are unable to coherently justify why.

The condition blinds them to this obvious cognitive dissonance and causes them to arbitrarily consider their position self-evident. If, while in therapy, the patient is confronted with the fact that the human psyche is equipped with many other forms of cognition beyond the intellect, he will typically point to historical events in which these other faculties have been unreliable, while ignoring all other historical events in which they have been vital. Such tendency to consider evidence selectively is a hallmark of intellectual fundamentalism.

In social interactions, the condition manifests itself clearly in the patient's approach to communication. A psychologically healthy individual, when conversing, tries to look beyond the particular logical and grammatical constructs used by his interlocutor, so to understand what the interlocutor is actually trying to say. In other words, a healthy individual is interested in what his interlocutor *means,* as opposed to what his interlocutor *says.* A sufferer of intellectual fundamentalism, on the other hand, loses interest in intended meaning and focuses, instead, on the *form* of the logical and grammatical constructs used by his interlocutor. The patient will fixate obsessively on what is said, losing sight of what is meant. When a logical flaw is found in what is said, the patient will construe it as sure evidence that his interlocutor is unworthy and completely close himself up to the intended message. This fixation on form above intended meaning is not only detrimental to the patient – who misses out on much of the subtlety and nuance of what others try to convey to him, particularly those who have most to contribute for seeing the world in a different way – but also to his interlocutors: it is frustrating for family, friends and acquaintances to interact with someone who insists in finding flaws in the finger pointing at the moon, instead of looking at the moon.

Indeed, sufferers of intellectual fundamentalism derive great satisfaction from finding logical flaws, ambiguities and inaccuracies in the way others communicate. Since they see the intellect as the only valid psychic function, differentiating themselves from others on an intellectual basis provides them with powerful feelings of self-worth and adequacy, hiding whatever other unpleasant psychic issues might be present. This narrow field of awareness may seem counterproductive and silly to an external observer, but it is sincerely embraced by patients and ranks very high in their value system.

Because patients are severely dissociated from most other aspects of their own psyches, they become delusional and believe that *all* reality is amenable to intellectual modeling and apprehension, despite the complete lack of any rational reason for such belief. In other words, patients believe arbitrarily that all reality fits into the only psychic function they acknowledge as valid: the intellect. This delusion is a natural self-defense mechanism attendant upon the condition: were the patient to acknowledge otherwise, he would have to face the anxiety of great uncertainty. Moreover, he would also have to acknowledge the severe limitations of his own psychic state, with associated feelings of inferiority, inadequacy and shame. The delusion is, thus, the patient's effective way to avoid distress by losing contact with reality. For this reason, intellectual fundamentalism is considered a psychosis, as opposed to a neurosis.

Associated with this, sufferers of intellectual fundamentalism display a tendency to interpret everything *literally*. Since they are alienated from the cognitive faculties necessary to capture the deeper meaning of symbols, metaphors and other indirect ways of conveying ineffable meaning, they have no alternative but to try to make sense of reality on a purely literal basis. Indeed, many patients deny even that anything at all exists that can't be described or conveyed in literal form. They then project their inability to see beyond the literal onto all other human beings, deeming others' attempts to communicate ineffable meaning to be drivel.

Depending on the severity of the condition, the denial of

all forms of cognition other than the intellect usually grows to become a fixation. At this point, if still left untreated, the condition has the potential to further evolve into a hero syndrome, which drives the patient to try to 'save the world' by attempting to eradicate all human activities, views and general outlooks that do not conform to intellectual value systems. If and when this happens, the patient may become a threat to the community. The condition is also particularly contagious at this advanced stage.

Causes

The causes are not yet fully understood, but well-substantiated hypotheses have been put forward. Some speculate that attempts at self-affirmation during adolescence can evolve into intellectual fundamentalism in later years. A hypothesis is that children who are socially impaired and have difficulties commanding the respect of their peers find self-worth, instead, in lonely intellectual pursuits. Other times, an individual might even be reasonably well integrated into his peer group, but eventually discovers that he has an intellectual edge over others, which he then attempts to profit from. The self-worth found in both cases is, naturally, directly proportional to the individual's belief that the intellect is superior to all other cognitive faculties: one needs to narrow the playing field to the particular segment where one has a perceived advantage. This way, there is significant psychological incentive for the individual to dissociate from the rest of his cognitive faculties, eventually leading to full-blown intellectual fundamentalism.

The tendency displayed by sufferers to try to humiliate others during intellectual exchanges arises from the need to increase this engineered perception of self-worth. Compensation for bullying suffered in early years is strongly believed to be a factor in this process, as well as the general psychological predisposition colloquially referred to as 'nerdish.'

Risk factors

- Receiving high academic education in science or engineering;
- Working in academic, scientific or engineering environments;
- Being publicly recognized as an expert in a scientific or engineering discipline;
- Episodes of bullying in childhood or adolescence;
- Having a 'nerdish' predisposition in childhood or adolescence;
- Lack of appreciation or patience for art, poetry, psychology, mythology or religion;
- Lack of empathy and sensitivity.

Prevention and treatment

The cultivation of a rich variety of outlooks is essential for preventing intellectual fundamentalism. For instance, if one's professional life is highly specialized and focused on science or engineering, one can reduce one's risk by cultivating hobbies such as play-acting, reading poetry and the classics, volunteering for social work (particularly with senior citizens), cultivating a vegetable garden and other forms of interacting directly with nature, attending exotic religious rituals about which one hasn't developed early prejudices, cooking, painting, attending art exhibitions, meditating, going to silent retreats, etc. It is important that one insists in pursuits that one's first instinct is precisely to avoid.

If intellectual fundamentalism has already taken hold, talk therapy with a qualified depth-psychologist is recommended in addition to the steps above. With the guidance of the therapist, one can slowly bring up to awareness one's repressed psychic functions and cognitive faculties. In severe cases, confrontational therapy or medically supervised journeys with legal and safe psychedelics can be last resorts, though neither is guaranteed to be effective.

This essay has been written by a recovering intellectual fundamentalist who still experiences frequent relapses of the condition.

4.2. Living in a cocoon of mere hypotheses

In logic, there is a strong distinction between so-called *deductive* and *inductive* inferences. Here is an example of a *deductive* inference:

Amsterdam is the capital of the Netherlands. Therefore, to go to Amsterdam I must go to the Netherlands.

Clearly, a deductive inference is necessarily implied by its premises. As long as the premises are correct, a proper deduction is a *certainty*, not a guess or a hypothesis. Now consider the following *inductive* inference:

My house has been broken into and there are unidentified footprints in the backyard. Therefore, the footprints were left by the burglar.

Here the inference cannot be derived with certainty from the premises. There is only a reasonable probability that the footprints were made by the burglar. Indeed, they could have been made, for instance, by the gardener who came by to collect some tools. A deductive inference isn't a certainty, but a mere *hypothesis*.

Inductive inferences are entirely dependent on our ability to correctly evaluate probabilities. Only because we know that all other possibilities – including the gardener coming by – are comparatively unlikely in view of the data, can we infer that the footprints were made by the burglar. However, probabilities are notoriously tricky to evaluate without the benefit of past observations of equivalent situations. Consider this hypothetical case:

> For the past 10 years, 90% of the times the postman came by my house I had already woken up. Therefore, I infer that tomorrow I'll be awake when the postman arrives.

Here the probabilities are easy to estimate based on past observations; 10 years of it, to be precise. These previous observations constitute a so-called 'reference class.' The probability of the inductive inference can then be calculated based on the reference class: in this case, there is a 90% chance that the inference is correct. But what about cases where no proper reference class is available? For instance:

> George saw a luminous object in the sky performing maneuvers impossible for any known aircraft. Therefore, George saw an alien spaceship.

How many times have similar observations been *known* to be caused by spaceships from another planet? Here is another example:

> Vicky returned from verified clinical death claiming to have seen the doctors working on her body as if she stood outside it. Therefore, Vicky's story is a post-event confabulation based on earlier memories.

How many times have similar stories, told in equivalent situations, been *known* to be confabulations? A final example:

> The fundamental laws of nature have been the same across

space since the birth of the universe.

Where are the reference classes in all these three cases? Our estimates of probabilities here aren't based on past statistics. Instead, they are based solely on subjective values, assumptions and beliefs, which suggest to us what should be possible and impossible. In other words, *they are based on a subjective paradigm.* According to this paradigm, we've already catalogued every phenomenon that could conceivably be produced by our earthly environment, so George could *only* have seen a spaceship from another planet. Still according to this paradigm, consciousness is a product of brain activity, so Vicky could *only* have confabulated her story. And finally, if the laws of nature could change over time our celebrated cosmological theories would be baseless, so the laws could *only* have stayed the same.

In all these cases, the form of the thought is this: since all other alternatives allowed by the paradigm can be discarded, then the only alternative left must be true. In other words, we extract conclusions by *elimination of alternatives.* The problem is that, in order to correctly make inductive inferences by elimination, *we must know all the alternatives.* In other words, we must assume that there is no yet-unknown aspect of reality lying outside the paradigm. This is a supremely conceited assumption; one that history has shown again and again to be untenable.

We don't know all the parameters and dynamics of our earthly environment, so postulating a non-earthly agency to explain certain bizarre observations is rash. Nobody has a clue how the material activity of the brain can possibly generate consciousness, so discarding the possibility that consciousness can exist independent of brain activity is unjustified. Finally, we just cannot know whether the laws of physics have been the same since the Big Bang. Yes, we have models based on this assumption that seem to explain the universe, but this amounts to inverting the argument: these models were built *in order to* make the assumption work.

These apparently inconsequential examples betray a very serious problem in science and in our culture: *the mainstream worldview is based on just this kind of inductive inferences unsupported by empirically derived reference classes.* Inductive inferences motivated only by subjective paradigms lead to worldviews that are at least as much a reflection of our own biases and limitations as of nature at large. Our experience of the world is thus largely shaped by subjective values, beliefs and expectations, as opposed to empirical facts. Indeed, we tend to hold many more ideas about what reality is – and is *not* – than the empirical facts warrant. In science, this is reflected in the way *the validity of models is routinely extrapolated way beyond what observations actually corroborate.* Let's unpack this claim slowly.

Models are mathematical mock-ups that are to the world like a map is to the streets of a city. In the case of science, however, only very few positions in the map are empirically tested against the actual configuration of the myriad streets it's meant to represent. But since the map is generated by a coherent mental procedure – that is, an internally-consistent set of axioms, rules and derivations – by confirming only a few of its predictions we gain confidence of the validity of the procedure and, therefore, of the entire map.

For instance, the Standard Model of particle physics is a map of matter at the subatomic level. It correctly predicts laboratory observations of relatively simple systems of particles. In other words, when we test the map against a few, small, isolated alleys of the city, we find an excellent match. And since the map wasn't put together arbitrarily, but derived from a coherent mental procedure, we extrapolate these simple matches and *inductively infer* that the map accurately represents all the streets, highways, junctions, tunnels and overpasses of the entire city. However, as any inductive inference, this is a mere *hypothesis.* It is motivated by a *subjective,* paradigmatic assessment of probabilities. We don't *know* that it's true.

Nobody has ever simulated any remotely complex, macroscopic phenomenon, starting from the basic laws of particle physics, to check if the simulated results would match up with the realities we ordinarily experience. In other words, nobody really knows if the weather, the oceans, forests, people, bothersome neighbors, office intrigues, illnesses, marriages and divorces, teenage delinquency, politics, history, etc., can really be reduced to the modeled behavior of subatomic particles. As a matter of fact, nobody knows even if the behavior of larger microscopic systems like protein molecules or DNA can be reduced to the basic laws of particle physics. Laughlin and Pines, writing in the *Proceedings of the National Academy of Sciences of the USA,* went as far as to say that this can't ever be known. Referring to the basic laws of particle physics as the 'Theory of Everything,' they wrote:

> [The] Theory of Everything is not even remotely a theory of every thing. We know [its] equation is correct because it has been solved accurately for small numbers of particles (isolated atoms and small molecules) and found to agree in minute detail with experiment. However, it cannot be solved accurately when the number of particles exceeds about 10. No computer existing, *or that will ever exist,* can break this barrier because it is a catastrophe of dimension.[115]

We just *assume* that complex phenomena can be reduced to the basic laws of particle physics, because such an assumption is an axiom of the current paradigm. But who is to say that as-of-yet unknown and irreducible causal forces or organizing principles don't kick in at higher levels of complexity? Who is to say that nature isn't mostly governed by these higher-complexity principles or agencies, which only come into play when enough subatomic particles interact in a way too complex to simulate or test under controlled conditions?

As such, the widespread cultural notion that science has explained most of the world is scandalously unjustified. For all we know, we've explained only very, very little; practically nothing. We just don't know what kinds of fundamental causal forces and organizing principles may kick in when systems become complex enough to be seen with the naked eye outside a laboratory. Inability to acknowledge this represents a catastrophic failure of skepticism. We can only claim to have explained – and even then only partially – extremely simple microscopic systems for which most variables can be controlled. Unfortunately for the neo-priesthood of science (see essay 5.1), the world we all *actually* inhabit is visible and unfathomably complex. That we've come to believe that science understands how most of this complex world works is just a reassuring illusion; a wish.

An argument often mentioned in defense of science is the broad and impressive effectiveness of technology. The contemporary world is driven by computers embedded everywhere, wireless communications, drugs designed at the molecular level and all kinds of machinery controlling every aspect of life. One might claim that this is proof that science correctly understands the larger world, not only laboratory experiments. Yet, a little reflection shows this argument to be very weak: *technology is designed to eliminate – by construction – the influence of all but the potentially small set of causal forces that are understood by science.* Electronics and computer engineering, for instance, are entirely dependent on techniques for increasing the so-called 'signal-to-noise ratio,' which ensures that the influence of 'noise' – that is, unknown factors deemed to be random – is reduced to negligible levels. We don't need to understand those allegedly random factors in order to eliminate their influence in practice. And then, for all we know, among the discarded factors may lie undiscovered forces and organizing principles (see essays 4.3 and 4.6). *Because technology is deliberately insulated from the unknown, its effectiveness in the larger world is no evidence that science has a significant understanding of that larger world.*

As a human activity, science embodies the human tendency to extrapolate the little we know and construct vast networks of inductive inferences to replace the mystery with; cocoons of mere hypotheses taken for facts. Culture goes even further: from the moment we begin to understand language, we start getting entangled in a web of uncorroborated assumptions and suppositions conveyed under the guise of knowledge. As a result, later in life we end up taking for granted that we are our brains; that our consciousness is a product of brain activity, even though there isn't even a tentative explanation for how this could possibly be the case (see essay 3.1). We take for granted that all reality is amenable to our rationality and perception mechanisms, even though we know that earthworms can't say the same. We accept that death is the end of consciousness, even though a growing volume of data published in leading medical journals seems to cast doubt on this notion.[116] Clearly, our experience of the world has become largely a matter of education and culture – of inductively inferred hypotheses – not of hard empirical facts. If one looks critically and skeptically enough, there is precious little of the latter to go by.

Reality is far too diverse, broad, elusive, ambiguous and complex for us to pin down. Even the limited empirical data we do manage to collect can only be interpreted within the framework of a subjective paradigm.[117] It is, therefore, not really neutral. But in our desperate search for closure and reassurance we confabulate abstract entities and explanations to construct huge edifices of assumed truths. They make up the world we actually experience; a self-woven cocoon of stories, not facts.

4.3. Scientific dogmatism and chance

Years after it was first aired, I watched a 1994 BBC documentary series called *Heretics of Science*. Episode 5 was about Prof. Robert

Jahn, former Dean of the School of Engineering and Applied Science of Princeton University and the founder of the Princeton Engineering Anomalies Research Laboratory (PEARL), original home of the Global Consciousness Project. The documentary gave a fair assessment of Prof. Jahn's work and his conclusion that mind can directly influence matter to a small degree. It then went on to expose the dogmatism of the scientific orthodoxy when confronted with such paradigm-breaking results. Inspired by this documentary, I want to share some thoughts here on the symbiotic relationship between scientific dogmatism and the always-tricky interpretation of statistical data in science.

In the documentary, a Nobel-laureate physicist rather cavalierly dismissed Prof. Jahn's results – instead of offering specific criticism of his methodology, experimental design or analysis – by stating that, were the results to be correct, they would invalidate four centuries of refinement of our current scientific paradigm. I don't think this conclusion follows at all from the results but, be it as it may, the unspoken assumption is that *observations cannot be right if they don't fit our current expectations.* Is this scientific?

To be sure, evidence in favor of a small mind-over-matter effect does not invalidate the scientific edifice built over the past four centuries. It only invalidates certain subjective *extrapolations* and *interpretations* of it. Pure science is about investigating and modeling the consciously observable patterns and regularities of nature. None of the patterns and regularities we've discovered and verified empirically over the years would suddenly vanish if the effect were confirmed. They would simply be shown to be *incomplete,* which would hardly be a surprise. None of our technology would stop working. Only certain scientific *prejudices* – like the primacy of matter and the epiphenomenal character of consciousness – would have to be revised. Revolutionary indeed, but in no way a negation of four centuries of work.

We would like to think that science is immune to dogmatism;

that the neutrality of data provides us with a fail-proof basis for assessing truth, independent of psychological biases. Yet we've known since Thomas Kuhn that, in fact, such an idealized picture of how science works is not at all true.[118] The difficulty of interpreting statistical data compounds the problem, which is vividly illustrated by the reactions to Prof. Jahn's work. You see, all modern science is based on statistics. It's not enough to observe an effect only once. After all, different kinds of unforeseen circumstances could potentially produce the effect by chance. So to tie the effect to a specific cause – or exclude a certain cause – one needs to observe it a sufficient number of times. This is where statistics come in.

The experiments carried out at the Princeton lab tested whether mind can directly influence the data produced by random number generators – electronic coin flippers – thereby inducing a discernible pattern in what should otherwise be a patternless string of numbers. The problem is this: although random data is defined in information theory as lacking pattern, there is a non-zero theoretical chance to find *any pattern* in truly random data. This contradiction renders the interpretation of statistical results highly vulnerable to subjective biases and prejudices. Allow me to elaborate.

If one's statistical conclusions are in accordance with the reigning scientific paradigm, it is enough to demonstrate that the odds of a certain effect occurring against chance are very small. However, *if the conclusions contradict the reigning paradigm, critics can always dismiss the evidence on the basis that, theoretically, any pattern can be found in the data if random effects can't be completely ruled out.* This, obviously, is a double standard that injects bias in what should be objective science. For instance, the results from the Princeton lab are now claimed to have odds against chance of more than a trillion to one.[119] If this claim holds true, then, according to any unbiased scientific standard, it should be enough to conclusively prove the effect.

Yet, critics continue to dismiss the results on the basis that any pattern can theoretically be found in random data.[120] Shouldn't we then reconsider the reality of certain subatomic particles whose celebrated discoveries entailed odds against chance of *only* about a million to one?[121] You see, if we stretch such double standards a little further, we can make the reigning paradigm virtually unfalsifiable.

As an activity carried out by people, science is as vulnerable to psychological biases as any other human endeavor. The tricky and even contradictory nature of chance and randomness, as discussed above, renders scientific judgment vulnerable to bigotry and dogmatism, particularly when it comes to statistical evidence. Though scientists may fancy their art as something above human shortcomings, they themselves are still just humans. It is up to the rest of us to remain cognizant of this and maintain critical judgment of what we hear from the bastions of science.

4.4. Science and the defacement of reason

I once elaborated upon how, in my view, true science differs from the way it is presented to the public today.[122] My concern back then was to defend science from the defacement I believe it is suffering at the hands of those expected to protect and promote it. Since I wrote those words, however, I've come to realize that my archetypal view of science is more a personal ideal than an objective reality. More than some kind of Platonic Form, *science is what scientists do in practice.* As such, the reality of the situation may be the opposite of what I had wished it to be: actual science may be the culprit, not the victim. To distinguish my archetypal, idealized view of science from the reality of science today, I will follow my friend Alex Tsakiris and refer to the latter as 'science-as-you-know-it.'[123]

Archetypal science is metaphysically neutral: it is a method for unveiling and mathematically modeling the observable patterns and regularities of nature. But science-as-you-know-it implicitly adopts the materialist metaphysics, which is merely one way to interpret these observable patterns and regularities. For example: an observed regularity of nature is that objects fall when dropped, which can be modeled through a simple mathematical equation. One possible *interpretation* of this regularity and its respective mathematical model is that there are material bodies fundamentally outside conscious observation, which attract each other and also give rise to conscious observation itself. This interpretation is the metaphysics of materialism. As such, materialism isn't itself an observation; it is a metaphysical interpretation that seeks to make sense of observations. It is a philosophical inference, not a scientific conclusion. The problem is that many scientists – and even philosophers – today seem to conflate science with materialism, observation with interpretation. This is illustrated in a rather alarming manner in a book by Alex Rosenberg.[124]

Of course, not all scientists conflate science with materialism. Perhaps even only a minority does. But this minority is vocal and influential. It controls how science-as-you-know-it is presented in the media, in school curricula and in the culture at large. This is how it has turned science-as-you-know-it into a synonym of materialism. The spokespeople of this minority are prodigies of rhetoric and specialized puzzle-solvers who often ignore rigorous logic, epistemology and ontology. And the institutions of science seem to be in no hurry to correct the situation. As such, they and their members are guilty, at least by omission, of this sorry state of affairs.

As argued in essays 2.1 and 2.2, materialism is a fantasy. It's based on unnecessary postulates, circular reasoning and selective consideration of evidence and data. *Materialism is by no stretch of the imagination a scientific conclusion, but merely a metaphysical opinion that helps some people interpret scientific conclusions.* Yet, the emperors with no clothes who promote the materialist belief on

TV, in books and what not, present themselves as spokespeople of science itself. When these people promote their flawed logic in the media as an expression of *reason,* the irony is painful. As such, science-as-you-know-it, with all the funding and respect it has accumulated as enabler of technology, has become the chief promoter of a philosophical worldview that is not only false, but corrosive, demeaning to the human condition and a threat to a sane and healthy future for our children. As much as its continuing positive contributions to civilization cannot be ignored, science-as-you-know-it has also made itself part of a great threat.

The materialist belief that is now intrinsically associated with science-as-you-know-it limits the horizons of scientific research. Many interesting and promising phenomena do not get studied because, according to materialism, they are *a priori* decreed to be impossible. Interesting data, which could point the way to entirely unexpected and promising avenues of research, get discarded because, according to materialism, they cannot be valid. By adopting materialism, science-as-you-know-it has surrendered its openness. How many healing methods, amazing technologies and ways of improving our lives will not be discovered because of this? How many new horizons that could bring great meaning, excitement and unimagined possibilities to the human condition won't be opened? Instead of being a force for impartial exploration, science-as-you-know-it is turning into a strait jacket for the human spirit. By projecting all reality onto abstract matter and then denying the value of philosophical inquiry,[125] science-as-you-know-it is draining the meaning out of the human condition.

It is true that we have to be extraordinarily careful. To simply get rid of science would be a catastrophe, setting us back hundreds of years. A quick look at the fringes of the culture shows the dark tides of delusion, hysteria, nonsense and fundamentalism waiting at the sidelines. But this real risk cannot justify accepting the prospect of slow but sure spiritual annihilation that scientific materialism now presents us with. The human spirit cannot tolerate the starvation of meaning and the limited horizons that science-as-you-know-it is forcing upon us. The collective human psyche will rebel. When it does, our challenge will be to channel those erupting energies in a way that balances their destructive and constructive aspects. It is most definitely a good idea to prepare for it starting already now. Future generations will be thankful.

4.5. The taboo against meaning

Many people, scientists included, believe that the greatest taboo in science is the one against 'magic.' After all, science is a method for explaining things and phenomena in terms of measurable, concrete causes. *'Magic,'* on the other hand, *entails an appeal to undetectable or ethereal causes, only their effects being concretely observable.*

Defined this way, however, one can find many historical precedents for the acceptance of 'magic' in science. For instance, during the Renaissance, scientists attempted to explain electrostatic attraction by postulating the existence of an invisible substance, called 'effluvium,' which supposedly stretched out across bodies.[126] Needless to say, effluvium was undetectable by any direct means, only its effects being concretely observable. As the Renaissance gave way to the Enlightenment, scientists began trying to explain every phenomenon in terms of interactions between concrete material particles through direct contact. Any explanation that did not conform to this template was considered 'magical' and, therefore, invalid. That is why the ideas of an English scientist called Isaac Newton were ignored and even ridiculed at first: Newton dared to propose that objects attracted one another at a distance through an ethereal force he called 'gravity.' Yet we know how that story developed.

You see, magic is not really a taboo in science. It has never been. After all, the chain of reduction has to end somewhere. One cannot keep on explaining one thing in terms of another forever. Eventually, one must postulate primary facts of nature that are not reducible to, or explainable by, anything else. These primary facts are what they are simply because that's how nature is. At their level, science must necessarily accept 'magic.' Electromagnetic waves vibrating in a vacuum sounds pretty much like magic – After all, what is it that vibrates? – but that's just how nature apparently behaves. Imagining the fabric of spacetime twisting and bending in the presence of matter also sounds like magic, but who are we to judge it? It's just the way things apparently work. Throughout the history of science we have chosen different things to consider primary facts, many of them entirely abstract. Each time this choice changed, the previous one was made to look like silly 'magic.' But at all times have we accepted 'magical' primary facts of nature. Moreover, with the advent of quantum mechanics, string/M-theory and multiverse cosmologies in recent times, the list of undetectable, ethereal, wholly abstract phenomena that science considers legitimate has become seemingly endless.

No, magic has never been a taboo. The real taboo is *meaning*.

Once scientists thought that the Earth was at the center of the universe. Ptolemaic astronomy could explain nearly all celestial observations of its time based on just such an assumption. That gave us humans a sense of being special, significant, *meaningful*: we were at the center of existence; the heavens turned around us. But it was not to last. Once scientists realized that our planet was just a rock going around the Sun along with countless other rocks – other planets, moons, asteroids, etc. – a great sense of humiliation must have ensued. How presumptuous and stupid astronomers must have felt, all their aspirations of meaning and significance shattered beyond repair. What fools!

And it happened again; and again. For instance, for centuries many scholars believed that living creatures differed fundamentally from inanimate objects in that we were powered by a special force later called '*élan vital*,' or 'life force.' Such distinction was construed to be sure evidence of purpose for our existence. Life was significant. We were significant. But again, it was not to last. Today, the majority of scientists extrapolate the little we know about molecular biology and assume that life is merely a complicated mechanical process. As discussed in essay 2.5, I think this assumption is wrong, but the point is that it is nonetheless accepted by the majority of scientists. In their view, after centuries of foolishly believing in our significance, it turns out that we are just machines, not fundamentally different from rocks except in that metabolism operates a little faster than crystallization or erosion. Again we fell flat on our faces; or so most scientists suppose. We aren't significant. We serve no higher purpose. We're just like dust.

Psychologically, these are defining experiences. When you have aspirations of significance and nature conspires to show you, very publicly, how deluded you have been and how unimportant you actually are, the shame that ensues shouldn't be underestimated. It is easy to see how this could have built right into the culture and core values of science a deep phobia of delusions of meaning. After all, it's better to assume the very worst and be positively surprised, than to expect some kind of significance and be, again, disappointed and ridiculed. It's better to assume – as a matter of principle – that there is no meaning and then let nature prove us wrong. This way, we turn the tables on nature: we challenge her to try and humiliate us again, if she can! For this time we are ready with our shields of cynicism. Never again will we be made to look like fools... or so the unacknowledged thought might go.

The problem is that, over time, what may have begun as a cautious value system has turned into a taboo; a cynical idea that has been instinctively taught and learned by osmosis over generations, and whose validity is now thoughtlessly taken for granted.

A taboo against meaning has the potential to be as naïve and delusional as the hope for meaning. The idea behind the taboo is that there allegedly is no basis to assume that our existence has any significance in the grand scheme of things. But you see, *who are we to decree that it doesn't?* What do we know about the grand scheme anyway? As discussed in essay 4.6, even evolution by natural selection doesn't preclude the possibility of there being meaning and purpose to life. Our earlier conceptions of meaning have historically been proven hollow because they were ingenuous. Today, who would think that being physically located in some kind of cosmic center is a precondition for purpose and significance? The ingenuousness and failure of our earlier conceptions of it doesn't imply that meaning itself is illusory.

At the end of the day, the fact is: the universe exists; life exists. Assuming that it all came out of nowhere for no reason is as much a leap of faith as anything can be.

4.6. Darwinian evolution: an open door to purposefulness

Rather simply put, the key idea behind Darwinian evolution is that species evolve from other species by the accrual of genetic mutations that provide a survival advantage. This has become known as *evolution by natural selection* and the evidence for it is overwhelming: it comes not only from the fossil record, but also from comparative genetics and comparative anatomy of living species. Laboratory experiments have also confirmed the phenomenon on a small scale.[127]

The problem, however, is that Neo-Darwinists conflate the established fact of evolution by natural selection with another hypothesis that is anything but established: that the genetic mutations at the root of the entire process are themselves *random* or *blind*.[128] I believe such failure to separate belief from known fact is motivated by the Neo-Darwinist program to drive purpose and meaning out of nature.[129]

Indeed, the notion of 'random mutations' is hardly questioned today, hitching an easy ride with evolution by natural selection as if all the evidence for the latter were also evidence for the former. Many people uncritically take these two ideas to be intimately associated, but little could be further from the truth. In this essay, I will make the case that *there is no convincing evidence that the mutations at the root of evolution are random,* which opens up the possibility that evolution is a *purposeful* natural process.

Each segment of an organism's DNA is either associated with a functional characteristic – an aspect of anatomy or physiology – or consists of non-coding DNA with no known phenotypical role.[130] This non-coding DNA accumulates over time through evolution due to certain genetic amplification processes.[131] For now, let's consider only the functionally active part of the DNA. It is mutations in this part that lead to *speciation,* or the creation of new species. To say that the genetic mutations at the root of evolution are random implies this: if we simply looked at the functional changes caused by each raw genetic mutation before natural selection either fixed or deleted it, we should *not* be able to identify any phenotypical pattern or trend. There should be no preferential direction or gradient in the kinds of functional changes caused by the raw mutations over time. *Only after natural selection should this be the case.* This way, all the obvious patterns we can identify in the fossil record – as well as all over nature today – are allegedly the result of natural selection alone, the underlying mutations themselves being random.

There are formal randomness tests in information theory.[132] Given a data set, we can run one of these tests and verify whether or not the data in it has discernible patterns. For this to be feasible, however, the data set has to be either complete or very densely sampled, since patterns can be easily lost if pieces of information are missing. Let us illustrate this with a simple example. Consider the number sequence below:

$$1 - 2 - 3 - 4 - 3 - 2 - 1 - 2 - 3 - 4 - 3 - 2 - 1$$

Suppose that this is our original, *complete data set*, representing a given phenomenon. Clearly, the phenomenon isn't random, for the numbers follow a pattern: they ascend from 1 to 4, descend back to 1 and then the process repeats itself. Now imagine that, for whatever reason, we lost some of the numbers in our data set (marked with an 'X' below). We now have only an *incomplete data set:*

$$X - 2 - 3 - X - 3 - X - 1 - X - 3 - 4 - X - X - 1$$

Or, more simply:

$$2 - 3 - 3 - 1 - 3 - 4 - 1$$

Clearly, this incomplete data set shows no pattern or trend. It isn't representative of the original phenomenon. Because of the gaps in the data, we are unable to discern the underlying pattern and might wrongly conclude that the original phenomenon itself was random.

Like the incomplete data set above, the fossil record preserves only a small amount of the raw genetic mutations – or their functional, phenotypical correlates – that occurred during the course of evolution. Of all successful and unsuccessful species that have ever lived on Earth from the dawn of life, and of the countless unique organisms with non-viable mutations that never reproduced, how many have been preserved in the fossil record? And of those preserved, how much of the full range of their anatomy and physiology can be inferred from the record? In technical terms, our sampling of the complete data set is extremely sparse. Most of the data has been lost. Whatever patterns might have been present in the original phenomenon cannot be reasonably assumed to be recoverable from such sparse sampling. Therefore, when one talks of 'random mutations,' one is precariously inferring, based on a massively *incomplete data set,* that the original phenomenon was patternless. There is no sound basis for such a conclusion. To say that the genetic mutations at the root of evolution were random – that is, patternless – is a paradigmatic statement of faith, not of empirical fact. *We have never run a randomness test on a sufficiently complete set of raw genetic mutations to know the answer either way.*

Let's now turn our attention to the present, as opposed to the fossil record. How much can be inferred about the complete historical set of raw genetic mutations from the DNA of living organisms today? Not much. Natural selection ensures that most mutations in the functionally active part of the DNA are not preserved. Therefore, nature itself, by construction, continuously eliminates large chunks of the original information. The non-coding DNA is a slightly more promising avenue: since it isn't necessarily filtered out, it may indeed preserve a kind of sparse genetic history. However, there are two reasons why this isn't enough: first, the patterns we are hypothesizing here have to do with the functional characteristics – the phenome – of the organisms. In other words, the hypothesis is that the raw mutations themselves, not only natural selection, are biased towards certain anatomical or physiological trends at different points in time. Since non-coding DNA, by definition, has no role in anatomy or physiology, it is irrelevant for the hypothesis. Second, even if non-coding DNA were relevant, it would still be unreasonably optimistic to imagine that a sufficiently dense sampling of all raw mutations that have ever taken place in the history of life on Earth could have been preserved this way.

In conclusion, one cannot assert that the raw genetic mutations underlying evolution are random on a geological scale. We are in no position to test this, for we simply do not have the necessary data over sufficiently long periods of time and across a sufficiently large population of species. That such a belief gets casually conflated with evolution by natural selection itself – for which *there is* overwhelming evidence – is incredibly misleading. It conveniently enables those who espouse a mechanistic view of nature to claim evolution as evidence in their favor.

Science is about finding the patterns that underlie nature. It is a fundamental premise of scientific activity that there may be patterns in natural processes where we can currently see none. To deny this amounts to arbitrarily decreeing an end to the process of scientific discovery. Indeed, openness to – and even hope for – the possible presence of as-of-yet undetected patterns are integral to scientific inquiry. After all, new scientific conclusions arise from the patterns we *do* find, for these are the footprints of the laws of nature. *Neo-Darwinism is an aberration in that one of its key conclusions arises precisely from the alleged* absence *of pattern, even though no substantial evidence for it exists.*

To be sure, I am not outright stating that there is a pattern or a purpose behind the raw genetic mutations underlying evolution. I do not know it, since we do not have the data to conclude either way. What I am saying is that the possibility that there indeed is a purposeful pattern is scientifically as good as that there is none.

As discussed in essay 2.1, I hold the view that all reality is grounded in a transpersonal form of consciousness that I call mind-at-large. Each living creature is merely a dissociated complex, or *alter,* of mind-at-large. Since intentionality is a paradigmatic attribute of mind, it isn't then unreasonable to hypothesize that, underlying the evolution of life, there is a transpersonal form of intentionality. As such, evolution by natural selection could reflect an iterative attempt of mind-at-large to reach certain goals. This doesn't mean that mind-at-large knows exactly where to go, otherwise there would be no need for iterations. Rather, the hypothesis is that nature is a *laboratory of experimentation.* Natural selection may work as the evaluation function used in the experiments to determine their degree of success. In the process of experimentation, mind-at-large may make mistakes: mutations that are useless or detrimental are continuously tried out. But through iterative trial-and-error, it may adjust its strategies and advance towards its goals.

Some may claim that there is no conceivable mechanism for closing a feedback loop in this hypothetical learning process. In other words, they may claim that there is no way in which the mere existence of organisms arising from natural selection could influence future genetic mutations at a microscopic level. But this criticism ignores what we have learned from quantum physics over the past century. We know that genetic mutations are, at bottom, probabilistic quantum events. We also know that, at the quantum level, even arbitrarily distant physical events in the canvas of spacetime cannot be said to be fundamentally separate.[133] This opens the door to the possibility that the results of natural selection can tilt the probabilities of future genetic mutations through quantum effects. In other words, the performance of an organism in the theater of nature could hypothetically correlate with the raw genetic mutations that happen next, thereby inducing a non-random pattern.

Finally, some may argue that my hypothesis is unnecessarily convoluted and inflationary, since there is no need for there to be feedback loops that create patterns in the mutations themselves. The proven mechanism of natural selection is allegedly enough to explain the emergence of all biological complexity we can see. But this, of course, begs the question: *we simply don't know whether natural selection really is sufficient as far as its explanatory power.* We haven't run a controlled evolution experiment on the scale of the Earth, over almost four billion years, wherein all genetic mutations were generated strictly randomly, to see if similar variety and richness of life would have emerged under those controlled conditions. So we just don't know. If anything, the astonishing richness and variety of life we see around us today seems to suggest precisely that some form of built-in intentionality is at play at the root of the evolutionary process. Of course, this whole hypothesis seems highly implausible under the subjective value system of a materialist, mechanistic worldview. Perhaps precisely for this reason, Neo-Darwinists feel the need to pass the alleged randomness of mutations for fact, when it is merely a hypothesis. Be it as it may, the alternative scenario I am putting forward here is entirely plausible under the framework discussed in essay 2.1. Indeed, given all the evidence, it is entirely plausible to imagine that the evolution of life serves a universal purpose. This in no way whatsoever contradicts the established fact of evolution by natural selection.

4.7. To understand the anomalous we need *more* skepticism, not less

In September of 2014, arch-skeptic Michael Shermer, publisher of *Skeptic* magazine and field marshal of militant skepticism worldwide, wrote a surprising piece for the *Scientific American* magazine.[134] In it, Shermer relates a synchronicity that had recently happened to him and his wife Jennifer in the occasion of their wedding ceremony. A vintage, long-defunct radio set that originally belonged to Jennifer's late grandfather had suddenly began to play music again right at the start of the ceremony, suggesting to Jennifer that her grandfather was somehow present. Such meaningful coincidence reportedly impacted both Michael and his wife on a deep emotional level. Shermer confessed in his piece that the synchronicity – which he termed an 'anomalous event' – had shaken his skepticism to the core. Personally, I think this is unfortunate; it may reflect a generalized misinterpretation of what skepticism actually means. Indeed, I think the problem with the militant skeptic movement is that *it isn't skeptical enough*. Like an army attempting a forward-escape when pushed into a corner, I think the solution to Shermer's dilemma is not to abandon skepticism, but to embrace it more fully, in an internally consistent manner.

Skepticism is a general and healthy attitude of doubt. In terms of ontology and cosmology, a skeptical attitude translates into a preference for parsimony: if we can explain empirical reality with less theoretical entities, why postulate extra, unnecessary ones? Theoretical entities should be doubted unless they are necessary to make sense of things. The parody of the 'Flying Spaghetti Monster'[135] evocatively illustrates why parsimony is preferable from a skeptical perspective. While we can't disprove the existence of the monster, we don't *need* to postulate it in order to make sense of the world. Another example: if you find footprints in your backyard one early morning, you could infer (a) that a burglar tried to break into your house during the night, or (b) that aliens from another dimension landed their spaceship in your neighbor's property, somehow stole his shoes, and then went for a stroll in your backyard before departing back to space. Although you cannot disprove explanation (b), the reason you will certainly prefer (a) is parsimony: it only requires entities that you already know to exist – namely, burglars. Explanation (b), on the other hand, requires postulating a number of new theoretical entities: aliens, spaceships and extra dimensions. Clearly, skeptical parsimony is a good and important guiding principle in our efforts to understand reality.

But parsimony regarding theoretical entities is not the same as parsimony regarding nature's degrees of freedom. Less theoretical entities may actually imply that nature has *more* degrees of freedom to operate. Let me unpack this with an example: during the 17th century, so-called 'effluvium' theories dominated research on static electricity.[136] For centuries it had already been observed that a piece of amber would attract chaff when rubbed with a cloth or fur. Researches postulated that the rubbing dislodged a material substance – called 'effluvium' – which then stretched out in space mechanically connecting the amber to the chaff and, like an elastic band, pulled the chaff to the amber. The problem with this theory is that it could not account for electrostatic *repulsion*. So committed to their effluvium theories researchers were at the time, they couldn't even *see* repulsion: they would describe chaff mechanically 'rebounding' or 'falling from' the amber, but not being *repulsed* by it.[137]

Precisely by postulating an extra, unnecessary theoretical entity that acted mechanically between bodies – that is, effluvium – researchers artificially constrained the degrees of freedom of nature: they could not accept electrostatic repulsion, only attraction. A failure of skepticism at the level of theory led directly to misplaced skepticism at the level of empirical phenomena. So much so that researchers would even refuse to *see* instances of electrostatic repulsion when it was right in front of their eyes. Electrostatic repulsion was turned into what Shermer would call an 'anomaly.'

Shermer, as many of those engaged in militant skepticism, seems to conflate parsimony regarding theoretical entities with parsimony regarding the degrees of freedom of nature. Proper skeptical parsimony is not about declaring things to be impossible. It has nothing to do with pruning the degrees of freedom of reality. After all, reality remains what it is regardless of our theoretical abstractions. Proper skeptical parsimony is about making sense of reality with as few postulated theoretical entities as possible. The very concept of 'anomaly' is a reflection of this misunderstanding of parsimony: an anomaly, if true, is simply a phenomenon that doesn't conform to our theoretical *expectations*. It doesn't have a different ontological status than any other phenomenon in nature, for the same reason that electrostatic repulsion doesn't have a different ontological status than electrostatic attraction. Both are equally normal and natural.

Today, the metaphysics of materialism postulates an extraordinarily complex theoretical entity: a whole universe fundamentally outside the only carrier of reality anyone can ever know for sure, which is consciousness itself. Materialists do this for essentially the same reason that researchers earlier postulated effluvium: it seems to be a reasonable inference that explains most aspects of nature (provided that you refuse to see the anomalies, of course). The problem is that it makes an implicit and fallacious assumption: that reality cannot be made sense of without the postulated world outside consciousness. If it can, then, based on the application of proper skeptical parsimony, it is as unnecessary to postulate a world outside consciousness as it is to postulate the Flying Spaghetti Monster. Indeed, I discuss in essays 2.1 and 2.2 how we can explain *all* of reality on the basis of excitations of consciousness alone.

The very moment we succeed in explaining reality with less theoretical entities, we realize that what materialism considers anomalous is, in fact, entirely natural. When we dropped effluvium, electrostatic repulsion also became natural. What Shermer considered a shattering anomaly can, under this more parsimonious and skeptical metaphysics, be seen as ordinary. And that reality is allowed to have more degrees of freedom under this view does not, in any sense whatsoever, contradict the proper application of skeptical parsimony. Much to the contrary.

In conclusion, in order to make sense of anomalies what we need is *more* skepticism of the proper kind: skepticism about postulated theoretical entities like the Spaghetti Monster and a whole universe outside consciousness. More skepticism of the proper kind will allow us to see that nature has more degrees of freedom to operate than we could accept to be the case before. As we've seen, this won't even be the first time in history that we make, and then correct, this kind of mistake. Michael Shermer has no reason to abandon skepticism. If anything, he now has an extra reason to embrace his skepticism more fully and in an internally consistent manner.

5. On culture and society

Human beings naturally long for wonder, transcendence, mental landscapes beyond the boundaries of ordinary life. Something in the human spirit shouts loudly that there is more to ourselves than the spacetime confines of the body. This obfuscated part of our psyche demands lucid recognition of what it knows to be the true breadth and depth of our existence. Throughout much of our history as a species, we've given it its due recognition in the form of myths, mostly of a religious nature. Indeed, religious myths encode a form of symbolic truth that can't be described or made sense of directly, in literal terms. Yet, it resonates intensely with the deepest obfuscated layer of our psyche, giving it its due voice in our lives.

Since the Enlightenment, however, our culture has come to reject all truths but the ones amenable to literal articulation. In doing so, it has withdrawn the tacit acknowledgement of the obfuscated psyche, creating an inner state of conflict. Our everyday sense of reality and self-identity, as outlined by our culture, is now in direct contradiction with what the deepest layer of the psyche *knows* to be true. This conflict creates an unstable situation. The gap left by the arbitrary denial of all symbolic truths demands to be filled in some way. It is this irresistible gravitational pull towards some form of transcendence, artificial and precarious as it may be, that lies at the root of the dangerous cultural and social ailments of our time. These ailments, and the specific dynamics that motivate and underlie them, are examined in this chapter.

Essay 5.1 argues that the spokespeople of contemporary science are attempting to replace priests as intermediaries between people and transcendence. The move is meant to invest them with inauthentic power previously reserved for ecclesiastic authorities. Essay 5.2 argues that our educational system has become almost entirely utilitarian, turning people into controllable tools, as opposed to equipping them to fully express themselves in the world. Essay 5.3 laments the ever-diminishing role of philosophy in laying down reasonable, coherent maps to transcendence, a responsibility many academic philosophers have tragically forfeited. Essay 5.4 discusses the dangerous cultural aberrations that arise out of our odd denial of the validity of myths. Essay 5.5 attempts to rekindle our sensitivity to the notion of enchantment, the loss of which – one of the greatest tragedies of the Enlightenment – has made our world small and claustrophobic. Essay 5.6 relates our current cultural dilemmas to some of our subtle psychological predispositions, attempting to raise awareness of their unexamined but far-reaching and detrimental effects. Essay 5.7 argues that a sane future for our culture and society can only be nurtured through a balanced integration of direct experience, philosophical inquiry and psychological awareness. Finally, essay 5.8 suggests that, because of the desperately unstable state of our culture and society today, significant change at all levels can be expected in the not-so-distant future. It also discusses the shape such changes may take.

5.1. The idolatry of a new priesthood

In the summer of 2014, a contentious public exchange broke out between Deepak Chopra, a well-known physician and author, and Brian Cox, a physicist and TV personality who is famous for his science documentaries on UK television. The exchange was rather tendentiously covered in an article published in the *New Statesman*.[138] Below, I want to discuss what it seems to reveal about the appalling state of our culture.

The exchange began when Chopra publicly stated that no scientific cause could be ascribed to the primary event that created the universe. He did it in support of his contention that all reality is in a form of transpersonal consciousness that he calls 'cosmic consciousness,' a legitimate term already used by psychiatrist Dr. Richard Bucke at the turn of the 20th century.[139] Cox then proceeded to publicly deride Chopra's statements.

The particular details of the exchange are unimportant for the purposes of this essay. What *is* important is this: Chopra may not have articulated his position with the rigor that Cox might have preferred, but he said nothing whose essence couldn't be substantiated with hard science. For instance, we know from the Borde-Guth-Vilenkin theorem[140] that there has to have been a primary creation event that gave birth to the universe – or multiverse – and, for being primary, such an event could not have had a scientific cause.[141] Moreover, there is plenty of experimental data suggesting strongly that reality, after all, can't be outside consciousness.[142] Whether the spirit of Chopra's claims proves to be ultimately right or wrong, there was simply no scientific reason for scorning them.

I suspect that this contentious exchange was merely a small symptom of a much broader and concerning cultural trend. Because our operational knowledge of nature in many fields is growing exponentially, the specialists who hold much of this knowledge feel that only *they* are qualified to interpret reality for the rest of us. This subtly frames them as a kind of neo-priesthood, as Amir Aczel forcefully put it.[143] No longer are we, mere mortals, able to develop a direct relationship with truth, but should instead subject ourselves to the benevolent intermediation of specialized elites. This is disturbingly similar to how priests were supposed to act as intermediaries in our relationship with divinity.

Instead of vicars and ministers, we now have highly-trained and often disturbingly narrow-minded specialists, not uncommonly disconnected from their own humanity. Despite efforts to come across as no-nonsense skeptics, what they preach is often as belief-based as what the older priesthoods did. For instance, instead of heaven and hell, we now hear about uncountable – and unprovable – parallel universes with alternative versions of you and me. Again like the older priesthoods, their discourse seems designed to bewilder and draw stupefied admiration and respect. We, average people, are supposed to admit that we need the neo-priesthood in order to maintain a crucial link with what is really going on, for we, poor dears, can't interpret the world on our own. How dare Chopra bypass the priesthood and attempt to develop a direct relationship with truth?

Because our culture mistakenly takes technological success for evidence of a deep understanding of the underlying nature of reality (see essay 4.2), we are all guilty, at least by omission, of allowing the neo-priesthood of science to appoint themselves arbiters of truth. This is as insane as appointing a five-year-old kid, who happens to break records playing computer games, chief architect at a major computer company. Does the kid's game-playing prowess necessarily imply deep understanding of the underlying computer engineering? The fact that one has figured out, through expensive trial and error, how to play the game of technology does not imply any deep understanding of what's actually going on. Our failure as a culture to truly grasp this has allowed the appointment of five-year-olds to the role of civilization's guides.

Our growing cynicism has long ago driven out true wisdom. We have given up on the idea of elders: those who, irrespective of formal education, are firmly in touch with the full spectrum of their humanity and its intimate connection to the universe at large. We have given up on our poets, artists, healers and philosophers as guides. But the archetypal human need to receive guidance and reassurance from an external source remains intact. We naturally need to place our projections of wisdom and superior knowledge onto something or someone else. The gap left had to be filled. And in our technology-obsessed culture, we tragically filled the gap with the spokespeople of science. Having done so, we now find ourselves in the position of expecting wisdom and guidance from intellectual specialists who can solve abstract mathematical puzzles but are often largely disconnected from life. No teenager would make this mistake among their own circle of friends, as a visit to any schoolyard will show you. Yet we, as a culture, do it all the time.

Why do we behave like this? What are we getting from these foolish projections of wisdom? An interesting analysis by James Sheils may help shed some light on the question. Sheils argues that 'Cox's science documentaries stupefy the public into remembering disconnected and obscure ideas they do not understand.'[144] Yet, the public is fascinated by these documentaries because the obscure mysteries they hint at instigate a misplaced sense of 'amazement and awe.'

Shiels may be on to something here. Our progressive abandonment of our relationship with the mysteries of transcendence since the Enlightenment has left a gaping hole in the human psyche. Our culture is desperate to get intellectual permission to believe in something else instead, to peek into some new and obscure mystery, so long as it inspires the same amazement and awe previously reserved for transcendence. The neo-priesthood of science sensed an opportunity and rushed to fill the gap.

It is we, as a culture, who project onto the spokespeople of science maturity, authority and wisdom they've often never had. And, as any psychologist will tell you, those who receive such projections begin to believe them themselves, in a process sometimes called 'inflation.' They then take their preferred methods, values and particular way of thinking to be the only valid ones, snubbing all others. As a consequence, true intuition, imagination and direct experiential knowledge are disregarded today in favor of purely conceptual exercises in abstraction. Our projections have given narrow human beings the power to impose their idiosyncratic values and dominant psychic functions onto the rest of us. This has been costing our culture more than we dare imagine.

But if we have been enablers of this situation, we can also reverse it by withdrawing our projections. Let's take the members of the neo-priesthood for what they truly are: confused human beings like you and me, potentially beset by hubris, narrow-mindedness, prejudices, agendas, circular reasoning, projections, hidden insecurities, neuroses, lack of self-reflection and the entire gamut of human limitations. In doing so, we may lose some of the anchors that ground our lives: we may feel lost in the jungle, without guides. But those anchors were illusory to begin with. We need wisdom, not narrow intellectual prowess. We need guides, not puzzle-solvers. We need people who are self-reflectively aware of, and in touch with, their humanity, in all its beauty and horror.

5.2. Education and the meaning of life

Education is universally recognized as a key prerequisite for a healthy, vibrant, viable society. Hardly anyone would dispute that. Yet, there doesn't seem to be a broad consensus on what one should be educated *for*. Although there certainly are many more facets to this question, I will limit myself here to contrasting two of them, which I consider most relevant to our present time: *utilitarian education* versus *philosophical education.*

A utilitarian education aims to equip one for the performance of practical tasks that have a direct and relatively short-term function in a society. Electricians fix power distribution networks; engineers build dams, computers and all kinds of handy apparatuses; physicians fix our bodies; diplomats avoid wars by resolving conflicts. The value and importance of these practical tasks to our society is unquestionable: through them, we can live longer, physically more healthily and perform our own tasks more effectively. But they ignore bigger questions: *Why do we live in the first place?* How can we express our full potential in the world? What should we know and understand in order to live meaningful, fulfilling lives?

This is where a philosophical education comes in; an education that equips us to look critically and thoughtfully at the world around and inside us; an education that helps us understand nature, history and the dynamics of the human mind; an education that helps us take the lead in driving our lives to meaningful goals, as opposed to falling by reflex into the role of mindless consumers who only in their deathbeds come around to asking, 'What has all this been about anyway?' A philosophical education equips us to make something truly meaningful out of our lives.

We live in an age that – especially after the 1960s – turned so drastically towards pragmatism that we've nearly forgotten to ask why we live in the first place. Utilitarian advancements are important in that they extend and optimize our lives on a practical level, but leaving it at that is akin to restoring and turbo-charging your car so you can leave it in the garage. We're so focused on living longer, optimizing the performance of necessary tasks, communicating faster and more frequently with one another, accumulating wealth and, most visibly, consuming and entertaining our way to depression that we've almost entirely forgotten to ask what this is all about. Why do we live? What is love all about? What is art all about? What have philosophers and poets alike been trying to say for the past few thousand years? *What is going on?*

It's legitimate to optimize our lives on a practical level, but obviously not at the cost of failing to explore what life is about in the first place. Failing to provide a philosophical education that foments the growth and expression of thoughtful and sensitive human beings, attuned to their own place in nature, cannot possibly be a healthy way forward. Yet, the educational system in most modern societies today is almost entirely focused on utilitarian aspects. Why is this so? It doesn't take much imagination to understand: a purely utilitarian education tends to turn people into controllable tools; cogs in the machine. Unequipped to even conceive coherently of the higher questions of existence, we're left with no option but to blindly leverage our utilitarian skills day in and day out, contributing to economic output and wealth generation. From the point of view of entrenched power structures – which stand to gain most from this wealth generation – the benefits may seem to outweigh the risks: not only does the current educational approach favor production, it may be seen to increase social stability, reduce unrest and, perhaps most importantly, ensure the preservation of the power structures. The more unquestioningly one performs one's tasks in the system, the less commotion and disturbances are to be expected.

Of course this isn't natural. Human beings aren't tools. We're here to *express* ourselves – What else? – not to be cogs in a mechanism. A civilization of stupefied drones going blindly about their practical tasks is constantly flirting with collapse. But the power structures may believe that this can be managed through the right combination of alcohol, tobacco, television, pornography, commoditized shopping culture and, in more severe cases, cognitive behavioral therapy[145] and dependency-creating psychiatric drugs.[146] *The mainstream metaphysics of materialism enables this by rendering culturally legitimate the outrageous notion that unhappy people are simply malfunctioning biological robots.*

The way to wake up from this all-too-real nightmare is a form of education that we, worryingly, seem to have lost familiarity with. Only a *philosophical* education can provide a truly *human* alternative for our future. Some may argue that, without a strong focus on optimizing the practical aspects of life, we would be so busy with securing food and shelter that we wouldn't have time or opportunity to consider philosophical questions. Yet, a superficial look at the world's pre-literate cultures *proves* this to be simply false: aboriginal societies have always made significant room for philosophy – which, in their case, we call *mythology* – despite their ever-present and rather formidable survival challenges.[147] We look upon them as primitive and unenlightened whilst, in fact, it's *we* who have become sick. Unfortunately, our sickness seems to play right into the hands of entrenched power structures and, in this way, self-perpetuate.

5.3. Has academic philosophy lost its relevance?

Philosophy is the discipline of human thought that allows us to interpret our experience of ourselves and of the world at large, thereby giving meaning to our existence. While science constructs models of nature that predict the behavior of matter and energy, philosophy asks how those models relate to our condition as conscious entities. Without philosophy, science is merely an enabler of technology; it tells us nothing about the underlying nature of reality. Science provides practical tools that mostly work, but it is philosophy – even when unthinkingly and precariously done by scientists – that relates these tools to the framework of our being. This way, the importance of philosophy for giving meaning to our lives cannot be overestimated. Yet, for several decades now, I believe philosophy has lost its way and become nearly irrelevant to most educated people.

If you ask an average educated person to make a short list of key philosophers in chronological order, he or she will likely start with Socrates or Plato, mention a few Renaissance or Enlightenment names such as Spinoza or Descartes and probably end with Nietzsche or Heidegger. Nietzsche's contribution to human thought and his cultural influence are undeniable. He guided the transition of our culture away from uncritical theism, tackling the immense implications it had as far as our need for finding meaning in life. Political movements, such as the Nazi regime in Germany, have misappropriated and distorted his ideas for political gain. Though I personally disagree with many of Nietzsche's key tenets and believe his thought to largely reflect his own troubled nature, it is undeniable that the man had tremendous influence in society. Right or wrong, wise or pathological, he was a true, relevant philosopher, brave enough to face the depths of the human condition in all its glory and horror. But Nietzsche died at the turn of the 20th century. How many philosophers of the past few decades do you know to have had similar impact on our culture? Heidegger published his masterpiece *Sein und Zeit* in 1927. What happened to philosophy since then?

What happened is that philosophy became increasingly more academic and departmentalized. In itself, there was nothing wrong with it. But a side effect was that, in trying to emulate science and mathematics to gain more respect within academia, academic philosophy ended up formalizing itself into irrelevance. It begun to resemble a highly abstract form of mathematical logic or linguistics, far removed from our immediate experience of reality. It forfeited its links to what is of significance to the average educated person. The great questions of existence, like the nature of reality and the meaning of human life, so cogently tackled by the likes of Nietzsche, Goethe – who I consider a philosopher before a poet – Plato and even Jung – who I consider a philosopher before a psychologist – were left out. They couldn't be framed in sufficiently formal terms.

Today, the role academic philosophers should play in helping us all make sense of our lives, of our minds, of our culture and science, of our historical nexus and of our condition as living entities in general, has been left to others: priests and preachers, inspirational speakers, self-help literature, questionable gurus, reductionist psychiatrists and even scientists. This is a tragedy. It has caused our civilization to lose its bearings. Where are the Platos, Nietzsches, Goethes and Jungs of our times? Who is guiding us to construct sensible worldviews and relate to reality in a mature manner? Not academic philosophers but the evening news anchor; because academic philosophers are, by and large, locked away in obscure conferences discussing abstract issues of little relevance to the educated person on the street.

With a few honorable exceptions,[148] academic philosophy has largely shunned its own humanity, losing its link to our culture in the process. It has succumbed to the foolish notion that the original approach of classical philosophy, which harmoniously integrated the subjective and objective aspects of the total human being, was inferior – instead of complementary – to those of science and mathematics. It began to believe that to 'prove' an idea is more important than for the idea to *resonate* with the innermost selves of people and, thereby, make a true difference.

Like a teenager unsure of their identity and self-worth when standing next to bigger bullies, academic philosophy has become blind to its own value, seeking instead to turn into something it didn't need to be. In doing so, it forfeited its own role and relevance in our culture. You see, the only carrier of reality anyone can ever know for sure is experience. And experience, while projecting objectivity onto the world at large, is fundamentally affective. By denying the affective nature of reality, academic philosophy has alienated itself from a large and significant part of what it means to be a human being alive in the world. *In seeking to become more objective and real, it ended up distancing itself from reality.*

As our civilization begins to face the inherent contradictions of the way it relates to life and the world, we need philosophy more than ever. The absence of true, wholesome philosophy is both a symptom and a *cause* of the current world crisis. Academic philosophers must wake up, find their own identity and cultural role again and make a palpable contribution to society at large. We cannot go through this crisis without qualified guidance. A new path must be found; one that brings academic philosophy closer to the people and the culture. The matter is urgent.

5.4. Myths in contemporary culture

Myths have been part and parcel of human life since primordial times. They have given expression to our obfuscated psyche – which depth-psychology calls the 'unconscious' – and their telling around the fire has been critical for the psychic health of our ancestors. Indeed, our ancestors did not make a sharp and hard distinction between myths and facts. To this day, members of aboriginal cultures do not understand why we, civilized peoples, make such a distinction, since both myths and facts are realities of the mind.[149]

At some point, Western society defined a rigorous boundary between these two worlds: it emptied the world of myth from its significance, reserving all ontological value for the world of consensus facts. This has been going on for several hundred years, with the effect of progressively impoverishing our mental lives, as Jung sought to highlight.[150] Now, in the early 21st century, a new dynamics seems to be at play: the obfuscated but powerful collective segment of the human psyche is trying to restore the connection between myth and fact; this time, however, with a new and dangerous twist.

Continuous repression of, and alienation from, our own obfuscated psyche – the realm of myths – has left an open and festering wound. We've become unable to derive psychic energy from anything but the stories that we believe to be objective facts. The cultural indoctrination that deems myths to be inconsequential has left us, as adults, unable to discern meaning and significance in our own imagination the way a child can. The craving that results from such alienation from ourselves has been accumulating in our society for centuries now. We try to numb it by increasing the 'loudness' of what we know to be 'mere' fantasies: ever brasher music, ever more action-packed movies, 3D, virtual reality, high-tech role-playing games, etc. But, deep inside, we continue to live in psychic poverty, for we 'know' that those are 'just fantasies.'

In unacknowledged desperation, we turn to newscasts, reality television and other sources of 'real' stories, which we grant ourselves permission to believe in. But there, ultimately, we only find disappointment: 'real' reality is too constrained and static to even approach the evocative power of myth. Poor we continue to be, despite our desperate attempts to find meaning and significance somewhere 'out there.'

Realizing that the source of this poverty is the hard divide between myth and fact, the obfuscated psyche seems to have now found a dangerous and frantic way out: while it cannot close the divide, *it can attempt to convey myth under the guise of mind-independent fact, so we again give ourselves permission to derive significance from it.* In other words, there seems to be an astonishing readiness, on the part of many of us over the past few decades, to believe as literal fact that which is clearly mythical. Only through such belief do we allow the stories to again reach us, bringing their richness into our psychic lives without the inevitable dismissal reserved for anything deemed unreal. Our willingness to believe in the *literal* reality of fantastic stories has reached incredible levels in some corners of society. As the collective psyche must always maintain its global equilibrium, this very tendency towards unreasonable beliefs feeds into the development of an equally hysterical and biased pseudo-skeptical movement, which is now better organized and funded than ever before in history. Action and counter-action: balance is maintained at a global level. Whoever tries to remain individually balanced now finds themselves isolated and friendless in the crossfire between these extreme poles.

A quick look at a list of popular books and videos over the past couple of decades reveals a recurring attempt to pass myth for literal fact: well-meaning extraterrestrials trying, as you read this, to free humanity from the tyranny of secret societies and other caricatural conspiracies; invisible inter-planetary wars taking place every day as we blindly go to work in the morning; energy waves from the galactic center re-architecting our DNA to grant us access to higher dimensions; channeled messages from Pleiadeans who are about to re-enter human history to rescue the chosen ones among us; special souls incarnating in human form with a specific mission to prepare the rest of humanity for some kind of ontological shift; ancient alien visits that explain everything not yet understood – and even much of what *is* understood – and for which every archeological finding is evidence; etc. Mind you, these stories are conveyed as literal fact, not metaphors. Their authors are telling you that this is what is *actually* happening. Some go as far as presenting them as *scientific* fact, pointing to an unlikely array of dubious, obscure, pseudo-scientific work on the one hand, and sometimes-outrageous misrepresentations of legitimate scientific work on the other hand.

As discussed above, such ideas likely arise from overactive imaginations seized by the obfuscated collective psyche, hungry as it is for meaning, richness and significance. As such, and in all fairness, their authors are simply meeting a demand. They are tools of a transpersonal process, not culprits of a crime. There would be no motivation for any of this if there weren't a collective need for rich and meaningful myths conveyed *under the label of 'fact.'* If they were to be conveyed in any other form, their power would dissolve. We want to be deceived; we need to be deceived. That's the only way the obfuscated psyche has found to restore significance to what has otherwise become a vacuous and purposeless existence, devoid of much of its original evocative power. After all, as Michael Prescott so forcefully put it, the materialist worldview of our culture entails that

None of the key developments in your life was somehow meant for you. No one is looking out for you. No events in your past happened for a reason, and they aren't building up to any future purpose. The story of your life has no continuity and no destination – heck, it's not even a story – and there is nothing to strive for. You were not put here for a reason, you don't matter, and you're deluded if you think you have a 'mission' in life. Face facts! You have no calling! The universe couldn't care less about you! Just give up!!!¹⁵¹

Such a situation is psychically unsustainable. Indeed, it's a wonder that we've accepted it for so long.

It may look to you as though I were just psychologizing the contemporary phenomenon of fantastic realism and dismissing the corresponding stories as mere delusions. But to conclude so assumes that I don't see anything significant in the psychic dynamics behind all this. I do.

As discussed in essay 2.1, I hold the position that consensus reality is a projection of mind. The continuity and seeming autonomy of the world arise from collective structures in the obfuscated parts of our psyche. The world, as such, is merely the visible tip of the collective mind's iceberg. What I am thus suggesting is that the collective mind is restless: it can no longer accept our cynical view of reality. It craves new significance, new richness, new meaning. And if consensus reality is the tip of the psychic iceberg, these obfuscated mythical needs, if continually unfulfilled, are bound to end up manifesting themselves, in some form, in reality. In other words, if we insist in denying ourselves permission to derive fulfillment from anything deemed unreal, our obfuscated mythical aspirations may eventually infiltrate consensus facts. After all, a bland reality loses the evocative power that is its *raison d'être*, defeating its own purpose. What the exact nature of this process will be, however, is anybody's guess.

5.5. Enchantment: the lost treasure
When young, we were all familiar with the enchanted places of

fairytales. Even as adults, we still hear others describe special places in the world as enchanted, which we take to be some kind of allegory. But what is enchantment? What do people mean when they say that a place or a thing is enchanted? As I child, I intuitively knew the answers to these questions. Only later in life, however, could I begin to articulate those ideas to myself in words.

Once, while playing blitz chess with an old, very traditional chess set, I suddenly had the sense that the pieces had come alive. It coincided with my intuitively *sensing* – not calculating – a forced checkmate combination several moves ahead, which assured me of victory. As I began to play the moves out on the board, the pieces became a living, breathing army, resolutely marching towards their opponents with a harmony, iridescence and purposefulness that nearly made them glow. They were moving themselves, my hand merely a tool under their control. It was a brief, elusive experience, but the token fell: *that, my friend, was enchantment.*

One night, in the spring of 2012, the Moon, Venus and Jupiter were all very close to one another in the lower Northwestern sky. While I contemplated this cosmic alignment against the faint silhouette of my house, they seemed to come alive. It occurred to me at once that they had been right up there, without fail, throughout my life. It was as if they were watching over me from my earliest childhood up until that very moment, through every important event of my existence: my first day at school, my first kiss, the death of my father, university graduation, my first job, wedding, etc. The celestial bodies were a kind of forgotten cosmic family of mine. On that night, they became *enchanted.*

Yet, enchantment is more than that. It also entails a brief ability to imagine the world through the eyes of another. When seen through the eyes of an insect, a mere bush becomes enchanted: it transforms itself into an uncanny, mysterious forest. When seen through the eyes of a rabbit, mere shrubs in a shallow depression take on the glow of a cozy, warm village: something akin to a hobbit shire in Middle-Earth, with huts, trees, fields and all. When one is in a peculiar, indefinable state of mind – when one has the 'eyes of enchantment,' so to say – passages through rock formations become gateways to fairyland: a feeling as elusive and hard to catch at work as it is heartwarming.

One may say, rather cynically, that it is all in the eyes of the beholder; that there is no such a thing as objective enchantment, but only one's own thoughts and emotions projected onto consensus reality. Such a view is as correct as it misses the point. After all, *all* experiences entail interplay between subject and object. No object – no reality – is ever experienced in or by itself, but always as an amalgamation between observer and observed. It is thus true that enchantment exists only in one's mind, *in exactly the same way that all experienced reality exists in mind;* and, as discussed in essay 2.1, in mind *alone.* As such, enchantment is as real as anything can be.

Enchantment is the lost treasure of our culture. In our shame-driven strive to avoid foolishness (see essay 4.5), we got rid of the baby along with the bathwater. In glorifying the object, we totally lost sight of the subject as the matrix of all reality. Because the whimsical and moody subject is not amenable to the objective methods of science, we basically removed it from our picture of reality. And since the object is merely pixels if not imbued with the meaning bestowed on it by the subject, the world we live in became hollow and bland. What a loss! *What is the world for if not to evoke and reflect back to us, as mirror, the obfuscated aspects of ourselves?* In denying the world the significance of our psychic life, we deny ourselves our own significance.

5.6. A cultural narrative of projections

In analytical psychology, projection is the act of attributing to other people qualities of ourselves that we do not acknowledge. For instance, a spouse who has repressed thoughts about having an affair may project these thoughts onto their partner, suspecting them of infidelity. On a more positive note, we may project our own inner wisdom onto figures of authority such as doctors, therapists or teachers. In doing so, we see in another an aspect of ourselves. Indeed, we live in personal worlds populated with projections: we don't really see people for who they are, but for the aspects of ourselves that we project onto them. This way, the world inadvertently enacts our own psychic dynamics. We have even developed cultural institutions, such as religious organizations, to catalyze projection: priests, preachers and gurus reflect our own inner wisdom back to us; altar boys and children's choirs reflect our innocence; the church or temple the protective maternal matrix within us all, etc.

Projection is thus the amazing mental mechanism by which we create 'the other' out of ourselves, like Eve from Adam's rib. It enables the magical rise of a second person from the first person, the 'you' from the 'I.' Through it, the 'outside' world becomes a mirror for the most hidden and unacknowledged aspects of our psyches, so we can, in essence, interact with ourselves by proxy. We get a chance to dance, unwittingly, with that which is repressed within us. It is easy to see how conducive this can be to personal growth, *provided that, at the end, in one of those Oh-My-God moments, one recognizes one's own projections.* No amount of books or conceptual understanding can rival the direct insight into one's own nature that is experienced in that precious moment: *'I am that! That is me!'* It is disarming, merciless, visceral. It cracks one's mind open and broadens one's intuition of self and reality like nothing else could.

For those who suddenly become cognizant of the projections they've been placing, the power of the phenomenon is disconcerting. They ask themselves: 'What other elements of the world 'out there' may actually be projections of my own right now? Is there anything about reality that I can be absolutely sure to *not* be my own material?' Indeed, it is difficult to delineate a sure boundary for our ability to project. How far does it go? Does it stop at people or does it perhaps permeate the inanimate aspects of nature as well?

The question isn't absurd. The mainstream cultural narrative today is that the world is made of matter, which allegedly exists outside consciousness. We, conscious beings, supposedly arise as elusive, ephemeral material arrangements. Yet, if you step back for a moment and contemplate this situation thoughtfully, it's easy to see that matter is a *concept* whose existence arises and resides *in our consciousness.* All the qualities we attribute to matter – solidity, concreteness, permanence, etc. – are *experiences* before we ever engender the thought that such experiences are caused by something outside consciousness. Whatever matter may be beyond experience isn't, has never been and will never be part of anybody's life. Therefore, we *project* our own experiences onto the *concept* of inanimate matter.

Moreover, consciousness is the *sine qua non* of our identity. Before myriad conceptual constructs arise in our minds regarding who or what we are, we are *conscious*. Being conscious is the very essence of what it means to be whatever it is we are. But what does our culture say about this? It says that consciousness arises out of particular arrangements of matter. The projection here is so in-your-face that it may be hard to see: *we are projecting ourselves onto matter!* We are projecting the essence of what it means to be us onto concepts created and existing within consciousness. Lost and afraid in a crowd of our own alienated facets turned other, we create a cultural narrative of pure projection to try to impose some order onto the chaos.

As suggested above, projections are useful for self-discovery and understanding. They mirror back to us aspects of ourselves that would otherwise remain hidden, repressed, obfuscated. Unable to be acknowledged directly, those repressed aspects get a chance to confront us under the guise of 'the other.' Subterfuge this may be, but it's useful and even essential if you

141

contemplate the alternative. However, the accruing value of the charade is only cashed in when the spell breaks and we finally become cognizant of our projections. If we never do, the entire affair remains useless: we never attain the final, earthshattering insight that confers meaning to all the years, centuries, eons of delusion. At some point, we must withdraw our projections and realize that our understanding of the world is actually an insight into ourselves.

Today, we think of ourselves as whimsical, insignificant and ephemeral creatures. In the cosmic scheme of things, we are like mayflies – or so the cultural narrative goes. We also think of matter/energy as eternal, unfolding according to magnificent, reliable patterns and regularities, and constituting the ground of all existence. What will we learn, in jaw-dropping astonishment, when we finally withdraw our projections from matter?

5.7. Direct experience, philosophy and depth-psychology: why we need them *all*

In a thoughtful review of my earlier book *Why Materialism Is Baloney*, Tom Bunzel made a statement that caught my attention: 'The 'problem' with this marvelous book is that those among us who most need to confront its wisdom won't have the openness to do so. And those with the openness to do so may not really require these explanations.'[152] Bunzel's suggestion is that those who can apprehend truth in a direct, experiential fashion do not require intellectual articulations of that truth. In other words, those who experience truth do not need an explanation for it. I see his point but also believe he misses something else. Allow me to elaborate.

There are two types of knowing: *intellectual* and *experiential*. The first is an indirect form of knowing achieved through the intermediation of conceptual models. The second is a form of direct, intuitive knowing achieved through experiencing the truth of what is known. Only experiential knowing has transformative impact. In spirituality circles, people refer to this form of knowing as 'knowing with the body' or 'kinesthetic knowing.' In more academic circles, it is known as 'knowledge by acquaintance.' Philosophy, on the other hand, is about intellectual knowing. It's based on conceptual models that *point to* truths, not on a direct experience of these truths. Philosophy can help you convince yourself intellectually that, for instance, there is only one mind and the subject isn't separate from the object. Yet, every time you look at a tree you may still see a tree out there, separate from you. Every time you look at another person you may still see a person out there, separate from you. As works of philosophy, my books are about intellectual – not experiential – knowing. So why do they count?

They count because we live in a largely rationalist society where the intellect has gained overwhelming power over our other psychic functions (see essay 4.1). When we make choices in our lives, even trivial ones, people around ask us, '*Why* did you do it?' When we hold an opinion about something, people around ask us, '*Why* do you think so?' These questions demand intellectual justifications for our choices and opinions. They implicitly assume that no choice or opinion is valid without an intellectual underpinning. Society's pressure in this regard is so ubiquitous that we often require such justifications from *ourselves*. Even if our intuition or experience screams that a certain choice or point-of-view is the correct one, we do not find peace until we can attach a reasonable intellectual story to it. Many of us do not give ourselves permission to embrace a point of view that resonates with our hearts unless and until that point of view can be couched in a logico-conceptual articulation.

The intuition and inner experiences of many people today are rescuing them from the madness of materialism. Neo-Advaita, Buddhism, non-duality, mysticism in its many variations, religion lived in its symbolic form, meditation, psychedelics and many other paths to the direct experience of truth are helping to wake people up from the trance of a cultural narrative of projections (see essay 5.6). Yet, many of these people live bipolar lives: a chasm forms between their direct spiritual experience and what their intellects can accommodate and justify. On the one hand, they experience a reality of pure consciousness and no separation. On the other hand, they 'know' that a well-placed knock to the head ends consciousness quite effectively. How come? How can reality behave as though materialism were true, while our spiritual experiences inform us otherwise? (The answer to this question can be found in essay 2.2) We become split.

I believe that a person in such a split condition does not give herself the freedom to truly embrace a direct experience of truth. Deep inside we hold ourselves back, because the intellect stays conflicted and in doubt. Unless and until we can find a place in the intellect for the truth that is directly experienced, we do not let ourselves go. Unless and until we can make intellectual sense of the fact that, for instance, the brain does seem to generate consciousness, we do not allow ourselves to truly embrace, unreservedly, a non-materialist worldview. Moreover, without a logical narrative to underpin it, no direct experiential insight can truly influence the culture at a broader level, since it cannot be communicated. Philosophy gives language to experience and allows it to be passed on – rather precariously as the case may be – to those still unable to attain the experience themselves.

This is the role I believe philosophy can – and must – play in relation to direct experience. It can aid experiential knowing by couching it in reasonable, logical, empirically substantiated intellectual models. In and by itself, philosophy won't ever be as transformative as the direct experience of truth. But it can help one open up to such an experience without the reservations that could otherwise block one's progress. The brain, after all, is the bouncer of the heart. Philosophy gives people intellectual permission to truly embrace what their intuitions and experiences are already telling them to be true. It also allows those experiences to penetrate society far and wide, through the use of language, thereby positively impacting the culture.

But that's not all. Bunzel's comment points indirectly to the crucial complementarity not only between philosophy and direct experience, but also depth-psychology. The direct experience of transcendent truths can – and often is – misappropriated and misinterpreted by the ego, that small but dominating segment of our psyche. For instance, it is common to find people in non-duality circles who, after having had the experience that their personal identities are illusions of consciousness, conclude that life is meaningless. 'The world is an illusion and I don't exist anyway; so why care about anything?' This – as discussed in Chapter 8 of my book *Why Materialism Is Baloney*, as well as Chapter 8 of my book *Rationalist Spirituality* – is a conclusion that simply does not follow. Moreover, without the insights of depth-psychology, it can become very tricky to separate personal confabulation and fantasy from the authentic experience of transcendent truths. Hence, direct transcendent experience is liable to egoic hijacking and misinterpretation unless the individual has attained sufficient self-awareness and psychic integration. For this, the crucial role of depth-psychology cannot be overestimated. Without the oversight, guidance and mirror provided by therapy, many individuals engaged in the path of direct experience are vulnerable to major pitfalls. Depth-psychology, in turn, relies on direct experience if the individual is to gain transformative insight into the deeper layers of their psyche. Without this experience, the most obfuscated and transpersonal parts of the psyche remain merely conceptual and abstract. The individual cannot truly achieve the ultimate psychological goal of a fully integrated psyche – which Jung called *individuation* – without it.

A similar codependence exists between philosophy and depth-psychology, completing the synergistic triad. Without a suitable metaphysics to ground it, depth-psychology is unable to address the *real,* the road to psychic wholeness becoming thereby impassable. How to treat depression without addressing the *actual* meaning of life? How to treat death anxiety without addressing what death *actually* is? If depth-psychology avoids these crucial metaphysical questions, its efforts turn into mere academic exercises. Reciprocally, without depth-psychology philosophy becomes liable to psychic biases and vulnerable to pathologies. After all, an unbalanced psyche cannot produce balanced philosophy. Nietzsche's philosophy, for instance, while compelling and marvelously insightful, is rather clearly the biased output of a tortured psyche.

In conclusion, the path to individual and cultural sanity requires philosophy, depth-psychology *and* the direct experience of transcendence. It goes without saying that the *supportive, background* role of science remains indispensible: it *informs* and *grounds* philosophy, psychology and direct experience in the discernible patterns and regularities of empirical reality. But it is the latter triad that is most crucial for our culture to take the next step forward in the road towards truth.

5.8. Unfathomable change is on the horizon

In 2012, the Internet was ablaze with speculations about consciousness shift, the Mayan calendar, the end of the world and what not. Ultimately, nothing out of the ordinary seems to have happened that year. But the hoopla illustrated one thing beyond any doubt: the visceral human need for – and expectation of – major *change* in the current state of the world. Change, in this context, means much more than the ordinary oscillations of the historical timeline: it means fundamental transitions of a nature and magnitude not witnessed for generations; a revolution in our very way of relating to reality.

The most obvious harbingers of change come from straightforward extrapolations of current social, economical and environmental trends: the monumental increases in consumption, waste and resource extraction; climatic and ecological impact; population growth; increasing signs of vulnerability in our economic system; etc. It is unthinkable that our current way of life and associated values can be maintained for another 50 years. But other signs of change are of a more intuitive nature, difficult to pin down, yet obvious to the sensitive, observant person. They have to do with a subtle but palpable shift in the way people seem to look upon the world. It is these that interest me most in this essay.

At any given historical juncture, the way we humans relate to reality is based on a coherent set of subjective values, beliefs and assumptions about what can be real and what cannot. In science, this is called a 'scientific paradigm.'[153] Here, we can use the word 'paradigm' more generically. One can speak, for instance, of the various religious paradigms that have emerged throughout history. A pagan paradigm, for instance, entails that nature is a conscious entity. It is to be respected as a living organism, not a depot to be plundered. A Christian paradigm, on the other hand, entails that nature is the Creation of a Higher Being, to Whom we owe respect and allegiance, and on Whose judgment we ultimately depend for salvation. This defines the Christian way of relating to the world. Moving on to philosophy, the materialist paradigm gives us license to eliminate guilt and look upon nature as a mere resource. Since it equates our consciousness and personal identity with limited and temporary arrangements of matter – that is, the body-brain system – materialism entails that our time is limited.

Truly fundamental change happens when the most pervasive paradigm of a civilization or historical nexus is suddenly transformed. This is much more powerful than a change in external circumstances, like economic crises or minor climate fluctuations. Indeed, a change of paradigm transforms the entire way we see and relate to reality. Therefore, in an important sense it changes everything. Today, with globalization, for the first time in history there is a large degree of paradigm uniformity across geographical boundaries. Human civilization is currently driven, even in the continuing presence of religion, by a tight alignment between the materialist paradigm and our economic system. A sudden collapse of that ruling paradigm would be as dramatic as to qualify for the expected 2012 event.

As the essays in Chapter 2 of this book make clear, I believe there are plenty of reasons to be skeptical of materialism. It survives partly because of inertia, but mainly because of its symbiotic relationship with our economic system. By linking consciousness and personal identity to limited and temporary arrangements of matter, materialism inculcates the following subjective values in our culture: life is short and you've only got one to live; the only source of meaning lies in matter – after all, nothing else exists – so the game is to accumulate as many material things as possible; we should consume as fast as possible, even at the expense of others or the planet, for we have nothing to lose since we're going to die soon anyway. It's easy to see how these values encourage runaway consumerism – err, 'economic growth' – and reinforce current power structures. Indeed, in a significant way, our economy depends on this value system. It isn't at all surprising, thus, to find our airwaves swamped with messages aimed at reinforcing materialism. Even governments stimulate it.

If you give this some thought, it will become clear to you where the true power of the materialist paradigm really lies. Its main strength is not necessarily how well it explains the available data; after all, there are more than enough anomalies in science today to question materialism.[154] Neither are the philosophical foundations of materialism strong, as Chapter 2 of this book illustrates. *The true strength of materialism is its symbiotic relationship with the economic system and power structures upon which we have all come to depend.* This creates a self-reinforcing loop from which it's very hard to escape. The combination of materialist metaphysics and the economy forms a point of stable equilibrium from which society can only dislodge itself by temporarily making things *worse*. In technical terms, to escape it one needs to kick the system out of a local minimum. How to pull this trick off is the most urgent question to face our civilization, for all trends indicate that the current state of affairs is unsustainable.

Now, if the underlying paradigm of our civilization does shift, this would be the most profound and extraordinary change in generations. What on Earth could cause this? What reasons do we have to believe that we won't keep on playing the same mad game of optimizing for short-term material goals until catastrophe and oblivion strike? Well, I suspect that there are forces building up in the obfuscated collective psyche that may just pull off this trick.

Never before have we been so wealthy and dominant as a species, but have our lives ever been as meaningless as today? Materialism crushed most of the myths that lent significance to the lives of our ancestors. We've become orphans of meaning. We go on chasing one material goal after the other, as if there were a little bag of magic goodies at the end that would retroactively bestow meaning on the entire enterprise. This is akin to chasing ghosts. What do we live for? Life has turned into a mad scramble for the accumulation of things and the status they confer, for the sole sake of leaving it all behind at death.

Shockingly, *it is illusions that maintain our mental balance.* We need ghosts to chase, because once we see through the game and realize what is really going on, we question the sense of it all and may succumb to apathy and depression. Therefore, instead of trusting and surrendering to our intuition, we raise the stakes. Not only do we chase ghosts, the ghosts began to chase us. Competition – so we tell ourselves – does not allow us to relax. We have to one-up the others, work even harder and more aggressively, or risk losing the precious illusions we've managed to accumulate at great cost to our families and ourselves. The more we accumulate, the more we have to lose, so the net result of achieving 'success' is the opposite of what we would have hoped: we become even more paranoid and stressed out. Life quickly turns into an appalling nightmare; a self-created horror show where we play both victim and perpetrator. And since we don't know of any other option, all we can do is engender some new ghosts to chase. This goes on and on until the cycle repeats itself enough times that the illusion can no longer be sustained. We are then left mentally broken and defeated. Many a celebrity or wealthy person has come to this sad juncture, where addictive drugs or suicide become real options.

You see, the illusion only works for as long as it lies in the future, just out of reach. Like the proverbial carrot hanging in front of the horse, the entire allure of wealth and status lies largely in *not* having them. By *not* having them, mental space remains open for our psyches to fill with fantasies onto which we project numinous meaning. It is the achievement of success – the catching of the ghosts – that gives away the game. As desirable material goods become commoditized and more available, it actually becomes *harder* to keep up the illusion. *It is the very economic success of materialism that carries with it the seed of its own destruction.* When purchasing a television set was a magical, nearly untenable consumer dream rich in projected meaning, its appeal was huge. Now, other things have to be invented that can serve as receptacles for our projections, from smart phones to cars, to porn-style commercial sex, to major promotions at work. As with any addiction, it gets increasingly harder to achieve the same high. Eventually, we will no longer be able to keep up as far as engendering sufficiently numinous material aspirations.

Might we be close to this point in the wealthy West? For a paradigm shift to take place, there is no need for the majority of the world's population to join in. Most people are so focused on survival that this entire discussion – this very book – is utterly irrelevant to them. When the economically successful and intellectually influential elite – a small minority of the people – are no longer able to derive fulfillment under the auspices of materialism, the paradigm will already change. I dare to see signs that exactly this is beginning to happen.

Most of us are pretty good at keeping appearances. We hide from even our most intimate friends – and often from ourselves – what is truly going on in our psyches. We fear being perceived as different, odd. Social animals that we are, we have an innate need to fit in and belong. Therefore, even if massive numbers of human beings were intuitively beginning to see the ghosts for what they are, it would still be hard to tell it from just watching the news or chatting with colleagues at work. Yet, from personal experience, I dare say that people are indeed beginning to see through the game. I see this process happening everywhere, though its manifestations are very subtle. Something is stirring in the collective human psyche. Critical mass is building up and we may not be too far from what Malcolm Gladwell called the 'tipping point.'[155]

Again, the only reason we insist on the old, failed game – inventing new ghosts to chase after catching previous ghosts and discovering that they were illusions – is that we don't know any better. We were never told what else to do; not by our parents, not by our schoolteachers, not by anyone. Hence, we desperately try to avoid depression and other forms of mental stress by the only means we know: replacing old projections with new ones. Nonetheless, the only sustainable solution lies in seeing through the projections. Material things only have numinous power insofar as we lend them this power. *We are the source of what we desperately seek and it has been so all along.* But given the current cultural climate, we are woefully equipped to pursue a path of self-exploration. Long ago have we dispensed with elders, with archaic traditions and myths, and many of the metaphors that could now illuminate our way. So we will have to face the inevitable breakdown of the illusion of meaning-in-things, whether it happens shortly or in many years, without much in the way of guidance.

Materialism will be replaced as a paradigm, I believe, within my lifetime. It has run its course and can no longer nurture the human psyche. We cannot survive in a vacuum of meaning. Thus, it is our own innate need for meaning that will kick the *status quo* out of the local minimum. It is our need for a new way to relate to life that will, at first, make things worse so we can find a new path forward. Our challenge will be to collectively find a way to bump the system strongly enough to dislodge it from its current equilibrium point, but gently enough not to destroy the economy. Are we capable of doing it smoothly? Honestly, I am skeptical. For the same reason that I don't believe human beings are capable of organizing themselves into huge secret conspiracies, I also find it difficult to imagine that we can organize ourselves for an orderly paradigm transition. It will be a bumpy road, but a road we need to travel regardless. We just don't have any alternative.

6. On the strange and mysterious

In the previous chapter, we discussed the interplay between contemporary cultural dynamics and the intrinsic human recognition of, and need for, transcendence. It is only natural, thus, that we now look at empirical phenomena that seem to validate our intuitions about transcendence. The essays here, due to the very subjects they address, tend to be more speculative and less rigorous than those in other chapters.

Essay 6.1 discusses the possible validity of the phenomenon of Near-Death Experiences (NDEs) from empirical and logical perspectives, exploring its implications as far as the existence of an afterlife is concerned. Essay 6.2 delves more specifically into the subject, offering a critical deconstruction of Sam Harris' attack on a particular, well-known NDE report. Essay 6.3 then switches gears and addresses the phenomenon of Unidentified Flying Objects (UFOs), offering a perhaps unique perspective on what it may represent. Staying close to the theme, essay 6.4 discusses something curiously left untouched by the mainstream media and the spokespeople of science: the implications that the discovery of (microbial) life in other bodies of our solar system would logically have in contradicting key axioms of the materialist paradigm.

6.1. Near-Death Experiences and the afterlife

Throughout the ages, people have reported amazing experiences of non-ordinary states of consciousness. Although the underlying themes of these stories seem very consistent – as argued, for instance, by Dr. Richard Bucke[156] and Aldous Huxley[157] – the metaphors used tend to be enormously varied, culture-bound and even contradictory across reports.[158] The stories of people who underwent Near-Death Experiences (NDEs) – that is, the experience of being conscious while one's body is highly compromised or clinically dead[159] – are no exception to this: while there is unquestionable consistency in the underlying themes, the metaphors and details vary wildly. For instance, some report to have met the Buddha, while others were in the arms of the Christ. Such discrepancies motivate skeptics to claim that NDE reports are mere hallucinations or confabulations. After all, if these people had witnessed a true afterlife realm, one would expect their reports to be consistent across the board and not bound to one's particular beliefs and culture. But is this expectation really logical and reasonable?

Before answering this question, let me first emphasize that *there are surprising similarities of themes underlying NDE reports.* Having read and listened to many recent testimonials, I've come up with the following list of what seems to consistently happen during a typical NDE:

- Association between a source of light and feelings of unconditional love, acceptance, bliss and peace.
- The feeling of returning 'home,' whence one's primordial self originates.
- Interactions with what are perceived as entities of some sort, variously described as angels, dead relatives or undefined presences.
- The sensation of knowing – or rather, *remembering* – the true nature of reality and of one's identity, even though one cannot articulate that knowledge later in words. This often includes the notion that life is a kind of dream.
- A life review and other experiences that transcend linear time or space constraints, as if everything happened 'here and now.'
- Transcendence of all dichotomies such as good/evil, positive/negative, past/future, I/you, subject/object, etc.
- The feeling that there is an important purpose to life.

NDE researcher Raymond Moody compiled a similar list decades ago from older case reports, which confirms the surprising consistency of themes.[160] Such consistency is indicative of a core reality underlying the otherwise contradictory reports. Yet, we do have to explain the circus of incongruous metaphors often used to 'dress' these underlying themes in an effort to describe them. Indeed, some people experience the presence of an abstract, impersonal white light, while others report an encounter with a bright bearded man, both of which are described as God. Some people report being welcomed by dead relatives, while others describe winged angels at the doors of heaven. The religious symbolism behind different reports tends to be tied to the particular beliefs and culture of the individual in question. If the events witnessed during an NDE are real, how can we explain this variety of incongruous descriptions?

The first line of explanation is simply to notice that there is likely a difference between what people report and what the experience in itself looks like. Even in our ordinary realm of reality, when different people witness exactly the same events they often describe the events in widely different ways.

But there is another, more powerful explanation for the discrepancies: because most of us have only ever experienced our own ordinary realm of reality – at least insofar as we can remember – we instinctively *assume* that all conceivable realms must share the core characteristics of our own. After all, we know nothing else. This way, *since our ordinary realm seems to be completely independent of our beliefs and expectations, we instinctively extrapolate the same independence to a hypothetical afterlife realm as well.* Let me illustrate this with an example: our ordinary realm is such that, even if a person truly believes that she can fly, she will surely fall if she jumps off a bridge. Our ordinary realm doesn't seem to care about what we believe or expect; it appears to be entirely separate from our inner subjectivity. So we instinctively imagine that all valid realms must be equally autonomous and separate from subjectivity. Notice, however, that this is no more than an *assumption*. If the afterlife is *another* realm – presumably operating under different rules and constraints – there is simply no *a priori* requirement for it to be as independent of our beliefs and expectations as our ordinary realm is. As such, that a Christian meets Jesus and a Buddhist meets the Buddha in the afterlife doesn't refute its potential reality.

Here is my hypothesis: the afterlife realm comprises a *core layer* consisting of the recurring underlying themes listed earlier. This core layer reflects the *intrinsic, essential, invariant properties* of the afterlife and is independent of the cultural background of the witness. But surrounding the core layer there is a *symbolic layer,* which is malleable and acquiescent to one's particular beliefs and expectations. This symbolic layer is a kind of bridge: it *presents* the core themes according to whatever imagery is most evocative to each personality. Different witnesses 'dress' a core theme with the symbolic 'clothes' that render it most recognizable and evocative to them. For a Christian, little could be more evocative of the core theme of unconditional love than Jesus; so it is through the Christ image that the core theme is symbolically presented to a Christian. For a sincere atheist, perhaps a dead relative is the most evocative alternative, which then determines the atheist's particular experience of the same core theme. And so on.

The expectation that NDE reports should be consistent at the level of descriptive symbols and metaphors – even when they are reported as literal – reflects merely a prejudice. That a hypothetical, *different* realm of reality is more responsive to one's beliefs and expectations than our ordinary realm is no reason to deny the validity of the former.

6.2. Why Sam Harris is wrong about Eben Alexander's visit to 'heaven'

In the week of 8 to 15 October 2012, Newsweek magazine's cover article was Dr. Eben Alexander's report and analysis of his own Near-Death Experience (NDE).[161] Alexander is a neurosurgeon and former professor at Harvard School of Medicine. In the fall of 2008, he underwent an unfathomable NDE while suffering from acute bacterial meningitis, which allegedly shut down his neocortex. Alexander's story is rich and nuanced, with many Christian overtones. One might wonder how seriously we can take a report so colored by cultural idiosyncrasies but, as argued in essay 6.1, I do not see this as reason to refute the validity of an NDE. As a matter of fact, my hunch is that Alexander's experience was authentic. Well-known atheism activist Sam Harris, however, disagrees. It is his criticism of Alexander's case that I want to comment on here.

I believe there to be a couple of faulty assumptions in Harris' argument. The most glaring one is reflected in this segment of his post:

> His experience sounds so much like a DMT trip that we are not only in the right ballpark, we are talking about the stitching on the same ball.[162]

The implicit suggestion is that, because of similarities between a psychedelic experience – DMT is a psychedelic compound that occurs naturally in the human body – and Alexander's NDE, the latter was likely generated by brain chemistry and, therefore, mere hallucination. Underlying this suggestion is the completely unsubstantiated assumption that no valid transcendent experience can be initiated by physical means, like alterations of brain chemistry.

You see, it is a fact that there are correlations between brain states and subjective experiences. This is not in dispute by any serious commentator on NDEs. The question is: what is the nature of these correlations? This is what is in dispute. So Harris' assumption that a physical trigger cannot lead to a perfectly valid NDE seems to completely miss the point in contention. After all, most NDEs are initiated by physical events anyway: trauma, cardiac arrest, infections, etc. Yes, Alexander's NDE bears similarities with psychedelic trances – at least as far as descriptions go – but the latter can also be, and probably are, entirely valid transcendent experiences not generated by the brain, but simply *triggered* by a physical means. See the discussion about it in essay 3.5. Therefore, Harris' comparison does not at all refute the validity of Alexander's NDE.

As I argued in Chapter 2 of my earlier book *Why Materialism Is Baloney,* there is a broad and striking pattern correlating transcendent, non-local experiences with reduction or even cessation of brain activity: G-force induced loss of consciousness, psychedelics, hyper-ventilation practices, strangulation, ordeals, certain forms of meditation, brain damage, cardiac arrest, etc., all lead to similar transcendent experiences. This strongly suggests that the brain is associated with a localization of consciousness, restricting it in spacetime, but without generating it. See essays 2.1 and 2.2 of this book for an extensive elaboration of this hypothesis. Reduction or cessation of the right aspects of brain function should, as such, lead to a de-clenching or de-localization of consciousness, which thus expands and gains access to aspects of reality otherwise unavailable to ordinary awareness. Ram Dass (Richard Alpert) once described the process of death as 'removing a tight shoe,' which illustrates the point rather evocatively. This, in my view, is precisely what happened to Alexander. The potential similarities of his experience with a psychedelic trance rather *corroborate* the reality of Alexander's NDE, since the mechanisms involved should indeed be analogous. After all, both Alexander's meningitis and psychedelics reduce brain activity.

Much of Harris criticism rests on an old materialist argument against NDEs: it cannot be shown that all of Alexander's brain functions were off, so it is conceivable that there was enough brain function left to confabulate an unfathomable dream. This is as promissory as it is unfalsifiable, for there might indeed always be a neuron firing somewhere. But this isn't a relevant point, is it? The point is whether the kind of brain function that ordinarily correlates with complex dreams can be plausibly expected to have been present in Alexander's case. If chaotic, impaired, residual cortical function could explain the confabulation of a complex and coherent 'trip to heaven,' then such residual cortical function should suffice for our nightly dreams too, shouldn't it? But we know it doesn't. Harris' argument is analogous to claiming that a car should drive better and faster when everything in it is broken, except for the spark plugs.

Studies of the neural correlates of consciousness have shown that significant, coherent neocortical activity accompanies the kind of conscious experiences described by Alexander.[163] To claim that such rich, vivid experiences could happen with a highly impaired neocortex raises a deeper question: What do we then need a healthy neocortex for? Even when we dream of something as trivial as the clenching of a hand, we see clear correlations with neocortical activity.[164] So how come we can supposedly confabulate entire alternative realities, rich in landscapes, entities and emotional significance, with a highly impaired neocortex?

Harris has to decide whether he thinks human consciousness requires a brain or not. If he thinks it does, he must be self-consistent and acknowledge the obvious fact that a few neurons firing somewhere deep inside the brain, even if they were there, could not possibly explain peak experiences like NDEs. And if he doesn't think the brain is needed, then he has to bite the bullet and acknowledge the obvious implications. *Harris and his materialism cannot have it both ways.*

The more regrettable aspect of Harris' criticism is an overt attempt to discredit Alexander's capacity to judge whether his

NDE could be explained by traditional neuroscience. This is embedded in a quote from his UCLA thesis advisor that Harris adds to his post:

> Neurosurgeons, however, are rarely well-trained in brain function. Dr. Alexander cuts brains; he does not appear to study them.[165]

Pause for a moment and consider this. The claim here seems to be that Alexander, a then-practicing neurosurgeon and former professor at Harvard Medical School, does not have enough understanding of what part of the brain does what, or what level of injury is sufficient to impair those brain regions. How plausible is this? What motivates this kind of attack?

I will grant to Harris that the Newsweek article is written in a rather sensationalist tone and with rather loose language. Personally, I also do not like that. But it is an article meant for lay people, not scientists or philosophers. Alexander is trying to reach people, which I do think is laudable. In the process of doing so, he inevitably has to sacrifice the more rigorous and cautious tone that is usual in science. I will go even further: scientism activists (see Chapter 4 of this book) casually take the liberty to throw all scientific caution to the wind when peddling the notion that consciousness is generated by the brain, even though nobody has the faintest idea how this can possibly be the case (see essay 3.1). Their activism flies in the face of reason, passing speculation and hypotheses for fact. It aims directly at convincing lay people of a particular agenda, rather like politicians do during electoral campaigns. In this context, I find it understandable that Alexander, in the Newsweek article, seemed to be attempting to do an analogous thing from the opposite perspective.

Harris continued his criticism in a subsequent blog post. Referring to Near-Death Experiences (NDEs), he said:

Unfortunately, these experiences vary across cultures, and no single feature is common to them all. One would think that if a nonphysical domain were truly being explored, some universal characteristics would stand out.[166]

Here Harris is projecting onto all conceivable realms of reality a particular aspect of one known realm: namely, the apparent objectivity of phenomena in ordinary consensus reality. But it is fallacious to infer, without further reasoning, this same characteristic for *all* conceivable realms. I discuss this extensively in essay 6.1, which I encourage you to read and which I make an integral part of this commentary. Moreover, as I also discussed in essay 6.1, there are indeed many commonalities across NDEs, regardless of the cultural background of the experiencer.

Harris' thinking seems to be like this: 'Since the reports of NDEs are such that I can eliminate all theoretical possibilities *I can think of,* then NDEs can only be delusions and confabulations, despite all evidence to the contrary.' Well, this thinking doesn't say much about NDEs; it speaks only to Harris' ability to devise theoretical alternatives.

He goes on:

The very fact that Alexander remembers his NDE suggests that the cortical and subcortical structures necessary for memory formation were active at the time. How else could he recall the experience?[167]

Harris seems to be casually taking for granted that memories are encoded as physical traces in the brain, just like computer files are stored in a flash card. Yet, decades of research have failed to find these physical traces. Modest recent progress in that direction is seemingly contradictory. The fact that brain damage can impair recall only establishes that *access* to information is obstructed; it doesn't establish where the information is. Upon his recovery, it's not in dispute that Alexander's brain function was largely restored. Therefore, it isn't surprising that he could again *access* the information corresponding to his earlier NDE and tell his story. I discuss all this in detail in essay 3.3, which I also make an integral part of this commentary. Memory is a mystery. We just don't know enough about it to use it to either dismiss or substantiate accounts of NDEs.

Now let's see what I consider the most peculiar part of Harris' criticism. Pay attention to this:

> If the brain merely serves to limit human experience and understanding, one would expect most forms of brain damage to unmask extraordinary scientific, artistic, and spiritual insights ... A few hammer blows or a well-placed bullet should render a person of even the shallowest intellect a spiritual genius. Is this the world we are living in?[168]

Well, yes, it is. Harris seems to ignore the literature on the so-called *acquired savant* phenomenon. It shows many cases of people who developed genius-level skills in arts, math and many other areas of intellectual activity as a direct consequence of bullet wounds to the head, stroke, concussion and even the progression of dementia. Nearly every conceivable source of brain injury can potentially trigger a savant.[169]

Harris asks why spiritual insight isn't triggered as a result of brain damage. Well, it is. Let's leave aside the wealth of anecdotal evidence and focus on controlled studies: a 2010 study published in the neuroscience journal *Neuron* shows precisely a correlation between surgery-induced brain damage and spiritual insight.[170] Moreover, most, if not all, techniques for the attainment of spiritual insight seem to operate by causing a reduction of brain activity – think of ordeals, hyper-ventilation, sensory deprivation, psychedelics, meditation and even prayer – which is entirely consistent with the hypothesis that the brain is the image of a localization of experience.[171]

Harris' quote above describes the facts precisely as we know them, even though he uses it rhetorically, as if it were all obviously untrue. The only part of the quote that I think is false is Harris' statement that *'most forms* of brain damage' should lead to new insights. We don't know whether this should be the case for 'most forms,' for we do not yet understand all the correlations between brain function and localization of experience. All we can say is that, *for at least some forms* of brain damage, new insights should be triggered. And this is an empirical fact that Harris, as a neuroscientist, should have been aware of.

Harris goes on to refute the so-called 'transmission hypothesis,' according to which consciousness is a kind of radio signal received by the brain. He argues that, if the hypothesis were correct, it would imply that we are the signal, not the radio. So the fact that the radio captures only a small part of the signal should not lead to a narrowing of what we experience. This stretches the 'radio' metaphor beyond its intended scope but, be it as it may, I ultimately concur with Harris' argument here. Yet, the notion that the brain is the image of a localization of experience is not the same as the transmission hypothesis. In fact, the transmission hypothesis is dualist: it posits that brain and consciousness are two fundamentally different media. My view, on the other hand, is monistic: I assert that *there is only consciousness.* The brain is merely an outside image of a process by means of which consciousness localizes itself, like a whirlpool in water. Notice how this answers Harris' question: instead of being an external signal, consciousness folds in on itself in the form of a vortex, limiting its own breadth. The image of this vortex is our body-brain system. The brain is simply what our thoughts and emotions look like from the outside. We are consciousness, and yet consciousness self-limits. To say that electrochemical processes in the brain are the cause of consciousness is as illogical as to say that a whirlpool is the cause of water. For an extensive elaboration on this view, see essays 2.1 and 2.2.

In conclusion, whether Eben Alexander's 'trip to heaven' was a valid experience or not, Sam Harris' arguments against it simply don't hold up to reason, empirical honesty and clear thinking.

6.3. UFOs: even more mysterious than you'd think

Reports of Unidentified Flying Objects (UFOs) have fascinated me since early childhood. I've spent many a night lying on the deck of my childhood home, staring at the sky and waiting – no, *hoping* – for something 'strange' to happen. As Jung wrote, UFOs are symbols of powerful processes in our obfuscated psyche, which explains people's fascination with them.[172]

Later in life, what was a childhood fascination became a more serious, scholarly interest. I've read much of the literature on UFOs just to become highly disillusioned with what people make of the phenomenon and the evidence. Today, I am very critical – even cynical – of much of what takes place within 'UFOlogy.' I hold the opinion that the field is riddled with fantasies, delusions and outright deception aimed at commercial gain or personal fame. So much so that, if not for the work of one man – a voice of reason and integrity in a morass of hysteria – I would have dismissed the whole affair once and for all. This man is French UFO investigator Jacques Vallée.

What I find refreshing in Vallée's work is his readiness to follow the evidence wherever it leads. Most 'UFOlogists' today seem committed to the notion that UFOs are material spacecraft from another star system. This is the so-called 'Extraterrestrial Hypothesis' (ETH) and its motivations are clear: in a field already characterized by weirdness, the last thing investigators want is to compound the weirdness by proposing a hypothesis that doesn't fit neatly into our mainstream materialist worldview. *But the evidence doesn't support the ETH at all.* In Vallée's own words:

The accumulated data base exhibits several patterns tending to indicate that UFOs are real, represent a previously unrecognized phenomenon, and that the facts do not support the common concept of 'space visitors.' Five specific arguments ... contradict the ETH: (1) unexplained close encounters are far more numerous than required for any physical survey of the earth; (2) the humanoid body structure of the alleged 'aliens' is not likely to have originated on another planet and is not biologically adapted to space travel; (3) the reported behavior in thousands of abduction reports contradicts the hypothesis of genetic or scientific experimentation on humans by an advanced race; (4) the extension of the phenomenon throughout recorded human history demonstrates that UFOs are not a contemporary phenomenon; and (5) the apparent ability of UFOs to manipulate space and time suggests radically different and richer alternatives.[173]

So if the ETH doesn't hold up in view of the evidence, how else can we make sense of UFOs? I have elaborated extensively upon it in my earlier book *Meaning in Absurdity*. In this essay, I'd like to offer a different spin on my hypothesis.

Before I can do that, however, I need to share with you my view of the fundamental nature of reality: I believe all reality – including our bodies – is in consciousness, not consciousness in our bodies. As such, consensus reality is an imagined story emerging from obfuscated, collective parts of our psyches, like a shared dream. Our individual psyches are thus dissociated 'alters' of a single consciousness – which I call 'mind-at-large' – underlying all known and unknown reality. Consensus reality is a particular 'dream' of mind-at-large. I am well aware that this view sounds peculiar at first sight, but essays 2.1 and 2.2 of this book substantiate it in depth. Here, all I ask is that you temporarily suspend your disbelief and entertain this view for the sake of argument.

If mind-at-large can dream up an entire world and also has the potential to split itself into dissociated alters, then nothing precludes the possibility that multiple dreams may be unfolding concurrently in mind-at-large. Allow me to unpack this: as mentioned above, each person is a dissociated alter of mind-at-large, partaking in a collective dream that we call consensus reality. Our individual psyches unite at a deep, obfuscated level, and the dream of consensus reality is anchored in that unified level. This is why we are able to share the dream. *But perhaps there are multiple, hierarchical, nested and parallel levels of dissociation and alter formation.* Perhaps our individual psyches unite not at the ground level of mind-at-large, but at an intermediary level that is itself dissociated from other intermediary levels. *We human beings may be alters of a meta-alter, and there may be multiple, parallel meta-alters in mind-at-large.* As a matter of fact, there may be meta-meta-alters, and meta-meta-meta-alters, etc.

So the hypothesis is that, as our consensus reality is the dream of a meta-alter in mind-at-large, other meta-alters are having other dreams in parallel to ours. Each of those dissociated dreams is a world in its own merit. Multiple, perhaps countless dreams are unfolding in the hierarchy of dissociation of mind-at-large, somewhat analogously to the parallel universes that physicists like to talk about. Each of these dreams has its own storyline: its own internal logic, physics, history *and living inhabitants.*

And here is where UFOs and 'aliens' come into the picture. Have you ever had a dream in which an event in the waking world penetrated the dream without waking you up immediately? For instance, I once went to sleep with the window of my hotel room open while on holidays abroad. In the middle of the night, while I lay asleep, there was a storm and some drops of rain began landing on my bare feet. The wind was also moving the curtains about, which caused some noise in the room. I was dreaming whilst this was happening. At some point in my dream, I found myself walking on a beach with my feet in the surf. The feeling of wetness on my real-life feet morphed seamlessly into the feeling of dragging my feet in the seawater. The sound of the wind and moving curtains inside my hotel room morphed seamlessly into the sound of waves breaking on the beach. I realized all this because I woke up in the middle of it and, for a few brief seconds, could simultaneously feel the surf and the raindrops landing on my feet; I could simultaneously hear the wind in the room and the waves on the beach. During those brief moments, I *knew* that these experiences, while different, were in a way also the same. *The 'dream' of waking life had penetrated my nightly dream.*

This is the key: dissociated dreams can perhaps – under exceptional, delicate circumstances – penetrate each other. Separate storylines can momentarily overlap and cross-influence one another. When this happens, the protruding element from a source storyline – say, the raindrops in my hotel room – gets 'dressed up' in an image that is amenable to integration into the destination storyline – that is, the surf in my dream. Indeed, there were no raindrops in my dream; just surf. There was no perceptible wind in my dream; just waves. The protruding element isn't perceived as it appears in its source storyline, but in an alternative form characteristic of the storyline it penetrates. In a sense, the protruding element gets 'hijacked,' co-opted by the narrative it penetrates so to become an integral part of it. Yet, the underlying, intrinsic attributes of the protruding element remain the same and are accommodated by the form it acquires in the destination storyline: the wetness of the raindrops was preserved in the form of surf; the oscillating, flowing sound of the wind and curtains was preserved in the form of waves. Although the form these protruding elements acquired inside my dream was very different than their original form, their intrinsic, fundamental attributes were preserved.

By now, I'm sure you've already guessed where I am going with this: what if UFOs and aliens are protruding elements of parallel 'dreams' unfolding in mind-at-large, which penetrate our consensus reality and acquire a form amenable to integration within it? It isn't then surprising that this acquired form should resemble advanced versions of concepts we are familiar with and can place within our storyline: spaceships, humanoid life forms, medical procedures, computer technology, etc. These acquired forms often look internally inconsistent, cartoonish or even absurd simply because they aren't the original forms of the protruding elements. Instead, they reflect a rather precarious accommodation, in our own storyline, of the *intrinsic attributes* of something that fundamentally transcends our logic and physics. Here, I suggest, lies the reason for the 'high strangeness' of UFO and so-called 'alien abduction' phenomena.

If even a very small percentage of reported UFO and 'alien abduction' cases are valid and accurate, we have no alternative but to envision rather unusual, speculative hypotheses for making sense of it. The high-strangeness character of the phenomenon demands no less and this is what I attempted to offer here. Alternatively, we can simply deem all the evidence to be invalid and sleep more easily at night.

6.4. Extraterrestrial life: implications for the materialist paradigm

There has been growing expectation among scientists that extraterrestrial microbial life will be discovered in our solar system within the next few decades, perhaps in one of the moons of Jupiter or Saturn. I've asked people close to me whether they thought this would be a paradigm-breaking event, and the response has been mostly in the 'no' camp. Such a reaction is understandable: scientists have been acknowledging for years that life may be common and widespread in the universe, so why would its discovery in a neighboring celestial body break any paradigms? Nonetheless, I think we may be overlooking something important here, which may have vast implications for how we look upon ourselves and reality at large.

Our culture's mainstream view is that life is a mechanistic process explainable entirely by the known laws of physics. In other words, life is merely an epiphenomenon of dead matter. There is supposedly nothing to life but the same movements of subatomic particles behind erosion, crystallization, combustion, the weather, etc. As such, life is allegedly not fundamentally different from erosion or crystallization, except perhaps in that metabolism operates faster. Biological organisms are mere 'robots,' entirely analogous to a computer. Life is believed to have arisen by mere chance, through the random collisions of atoms and molecules in a primordial chemical soup on primitive Earth. So the question is: if biology were discovered in a celestial body next door, would this raise new and difficult questions for such a mechanistic view of life? I think it would.

Nobody knows today how life could emerge from dead matter. There are dozens of theories and even more loose avenues of speculation, but no one has ever managed to re-create life from dead matter – a process called 'abiogenesis' – in a laboratory. Therefore, there is just no proof that life could ever have arisen from non-life through purely mechanistic means. Yet, mechanistic abiogenesis is indispensible for materialism. Without it, materialism would fall apart, for it would fail to explain that which conceived materialism in the first place: human life.

The problem is that, not only do the different structures necessary for metabolism need to arise concurrently in an organism, very complicated mechanisms for the *replication* of these structures – that is, reproduction – need to arise along with them. Otherwise, life would pop into existence just to disappear again. Francis Crick, the Nobel Prize laureate and co-discoverer of DNA, once thought it impossible for the self-replication mechanisms essential to life to arise spontaneously, mechanistically, from a chemical soup on primitive Earth. He thought the complexity required was just too great.[174] Although Crick later felt that he had been a little too pessimistic in his original assessment, the key point still stands: mechanistic abiogenesis, if at all possible, is extraordinarily unlikely.

Now, how does this tie in with the possible discovery of extraterrestrial microbial life? Well, if we were to find independently-arisen life in our immediate cosmic neighborhood – right here, next door – the obvious implication would be that abiogenesis is a very common occurrence in the cosmos. After all, what are the chances that a rare event would happen, independently, twice within the same star system? But if it's common, then life can't be the kind of accidental, mechanistic phenomenon that it is purported to be by materialist science. Mechanistic abiogenesis, after all, can at best be extraordinarily rare; if at all possible. The discovery of a second instance of abiogenesis in our solar system would, therefore, force us to consider the possibility that life is the expression of yet-unrecognized but intrinsic organizing principles in nature. It would force us to consider the possibility that nature is, in a way, *meant* to produce life. This, by any measure, would indeed be a paradigm-breaking conclusion.

7. On free will

Perhaps no other topics of debate encapsulate the current culture wars as powerfully as the triad encompassing: (a) evolution by natural selection, (b) the afterlife and (c) free will. Evolution was already addressed in Chapter 4 and the afterlife in Chapter 6. This leaves free will to be examined here. Indeed, whilst the mainstream materialist worldview precludes the possibility of any true free will, does a different metaphysics – such as that discussed in Chapter 2 – allow for it?

Essay 7.1 offers a generic definition of free will that does justice to our innate intuition of it. Essay 7.2 then discusses the validity of true free will under idealism.

7.1. What is free will?

We all have an intuitive understanding of free will but, upon trying to state it in words, we often misrepresent the essence of our intuition and end up in contradiction. On the one hand, free will is clearly linked to our capacity to choose without our choices being *determined*. On the other hand, if our choices are entirely *non-determined*, they become simply random, like the flip of a coin. Randomness isn't consistent with our intuition of free will either, for true choices should reflect our goals and purposes; that is, they should be *biased* by intent. One could then say that a free choice is determined solely by our intent. But how does an intent come about? Is the intent itself determined by something outside us? Or is it merely random? This conflict between determinism and randomness muddies the waters when it comes to understanding the very meaning of the words 'free will.'

Having pondered about all this for a long time, here is what I believe to be an accurate and helpful definition that avoids the conflict altogether:

Free will is the capacity of an agent to make a choice unhindered by any factor outside that which the agent identifies itself with.

Let's exemplify this definition by taking the agent to be a person. Personal free will is then the capacity of a person to make a choice unhindered by any limitation, requirement or power that the person does not identify herself with. Notice the emphasis on what a person *identifies herself with,* as opposed to what a particular metaphysics entails the person to be. Materialism, for instance, entails that a person is merely her physical body. This way, the person's choices are allegedly the outcome of physical processes in her brain, which are part of what the person supposedly is. Yet, most of us would intuitively and promptly reject the notion that the outcome of brain processes is an expression of true free will. Why? Because, for whatever reason, *we do not identify ourselves with processes in our brains.* We say that we *have* a brain, as opposed to saying that we *are* a brain.

Most people identify themselves with the particular thoughts and emotions they are lucidly aware of, as subjectively experienced. Therefore, true free will is the case if, and only if, all determining factors behind the making of a choice are part of the person's thoughts and emotions: the opinions, beliefs, preferences, tastes, likes and dislikes, goals, sense of purpose, etc., she is lucidly aware of. The fact that a particular metaphysics, such as materialism, states that there is nothing to thoughts and emotions but brain activity, is merely a conceptual abstraction; it bears no relevance to how a person actually experiences her own identity and freedom. Even if you are a sincere materialist, you still won't *experience* yourself as electrochemical reactions inside your skull. This way, the view of free will I am offering here is independent of particular metaphysical positions, such as materialism.

Notice that other arguments for free will – like Lucas' Gödelian argument and Tallis' intentionality argument – are immersed in particular metaphysical contexts. Lucas, for instance, argues that certain human actions cannot be determined by the function of an objective, computer-like brain. His attempt is thus to prove free will – which he implicitly defines as human action *not* determined by objective brain function – through refuting the metaphysics of mechanistic materialism.[175] Clearly, this reflects a metaphysically-bound conception of free will. Similarly, Tallis implicitly acknowledges the existence of a material world fundamentally outside consciousness, which is governed by deterministic chains of cause and effect. He then proceeds to argue that humans operate from within an emergent, mental 'space of possibility' – a concept I find rather ambiguous – which somehow escapes the material chains of cause and effect. His defense of free will seems to be intrinsically linked to this ambiguous form of metaphysical dualism.[176]

My attempt here, on the other hand, is to take a step back from all these abstract conceptualizations and offer a perspective on free will that is centered in our direct experience of it, while remaining independent of any metaphysical system (see essay 7.2 for a discussion on how I tie my understanding of free will to idealism). Indeed, my contention is that the existence of free will does not need to be 'proven,' for it doesn't rest on intellectual conceptualizations and abstractions. Free will, if we define it in a way that does justice to our intuition, is an undeniable experiential reality. Everything else is merely conceptual and, as such, less real. True to this spirit, I reject attempts to label my position on free will according to any of the classical philosophical 'boxes,' such as compatibilism, libertarianism, determinism, etc.

As a matter of fact, the perspective I am offering here circumvents the insoluble problem of libertarianism, the notion that a truly free choice must be completely non-determined. The problem with it is that, from a logical and semantic perspective, a choice is either determined by some process – even if the process is yet-unknown, mysterious, unfathomable, ineffable, transcendent, spiritual, ethereal, etc. – or merely random. It seems impossible to find semantic or logical space for libertarian free will if we insist on distinguishing it from both randomness and determinism. According to my definition above, however, *true free will can be the expression of a fully deterministic process, as long as the determining factors of that process are internal to that which the choosing agent identifies itself with.* In other words, my choice is truly free if it is entirely determined by what I perceive as *me*.

To say that a free choice is determined by processes we identify ourselves with does not, in any way, contradict the essence of our intuition of free will. The appearance that it does is merely a linguistic illusion. Let me try to illustrate this with an example. I may say: 'I made choice A but I could have made choice B.' This statement is a clear assertion of my free will; in fact, it captures the very core of what free will entails, doesn't it? Yet, the statement implies that the choice was indeed determined: it was determined by me! In other words, it was the perceived essence of what it means to be *me* that determined the choice. Therefore, I can rephrase the statement in the following way, without changing its meaning or implications: 'I chose A because it is my perceived essential nature to do so, although there were no external factors preventing me from choosing B.' Formulated this way, the statement is clearly consistent with the definition above.

When one says that one's choice cannot be determined by anything in order to be truly free, what one actually means is that one's choice cannot be determined by anything *external to that which one identifies oneself with*. After all, unless the choice is random, it must be determined by something, even if that something is no more than the perceived essential nature of the agent that makes the choice. True free will holds in this latter case.

I hope this brief articulation helps sort out some of the linguistic and logical confusion that so often clouds discussions about free will. In its essence, free will is a very simple matter.

7.2. Where is free will to be found?

In essay 7.1, I discussed a generic, metaphysics-neutral definition of free will that honors our direct experience of making free choices. In this essay, I want to try to link that generic notion with my views regarding the underlying nature of reality. After all, many people find it important to know whether their perceived freedom to choose can be corroborated by a sound intellectual model of the world.

The generic definition in essay 7.1 states that free will is the capacity of an agent to make a choice unhindered by any factor outside that which the agent identifies itself with. In simpler words, *my choice is only free if it is determined solely by what I perceive as me.* Now, most people identify themselves with their thoughts and feelings. They feel they *are* their subjective inner life. This is entirely natural, since all we ultimately have is our subjectivity. Therefore, *metaphysical free will is only valid under models of reality that allow for choices to be made unhindered by factors outside our own subjectivity.* If a metaphysical view posits that choice is merely the outcome of the operation of mechanical laws in a strongly-objective brain, then there can be no metaphysical free will under such a view.

As discussed at length in essay 2.1, I am a proponent of idealism. According to this view, the world is exactly what it seems to be: a *qualitative* phenomenon unfolding in consciousness. Indeed, a world outside consciousness is an unprovable and unnecessary abstraction. We can explain all reality without it, as discussed in essay 2.2. The implication is that all nature is then fundamentally subjective. The difference between the 'outside' world perceived through our five senses and the 'inside' world of thoughts and feelings is merely one of misidentification, not of essence. We misidentify ourselves with a particular subset of our stream of experiences – namely, thoughts and feelings – while deeming the rest of the stream – sensory perceptions – to come from a world outside ourselves. Both parts of the stream, however, are still entirely subjective in nature. Think of it in terms of your nightly dreams: you misidentify yourself with a character within your dream, believing the rest of the dreamscape to be external to you. Once you wake up, however, you immediately realize that your mind was creating the whole dream. In this sense, *you were the whole dream*, not only a character within it. Moreover, idealism posits that our neurons and their electrochemical activity are merely what our thoughts and feelings *look like* from a second-person perspective; they are the *image*, not the *cause*, of our thoughts and feelings. This is so in the same way that lightning is what atmospheric electric discharge looks like, not the cause of atmospheric electric discharge.

Idealism is thus, in principle, conducive to the idea of metaphysical free will insofar as it denies anything outside subjectivity. However, as I emphasized in my earlier book *Why Materialism Is Baloney,* it remains an empirical fact that our experiences of consensus reality obey strict patterns and regularities that we've come to call the laws of nature. That it all happens in consciousness, as opposed to a strongly-objective world outside consciousness, doesn't change this undeniable fact. This way, if our choices – purely subjective as they may be – are still the deterministic outcome of mental chains of cause-and-effect, the spirit of metaphysical free will seems to be defeated.

Indeed, according to idealism, choice is the outcome of mentally deterministic processes, in the sense that these processes follow patterns and regularities that Jung called 'archetypes.'[177] The archetypes are not reducible to the known physical laws; rather, the known physical laws are particular, partial manifestations of the archetypes.[178] Moreover, since feelings and emotions are also manifestations of archetypes and valid determining factors in the making of choices, the mental determinism I am suggesting here encompasses – but goes far beyond – physical determinism. Be it as it may, *it is still a form of determinism.* How can mental determinism be compatible with metaphysical free will?

To answer this we have to look more deeply into the meaning of free will. As discussed in essay 7.1, if we mean by it that a free choice is entirely arbitrary, we end up with randomness. Clearly, randomness is not the spirit of free will: we know that we make our choices based on our prior experiences, preferences and goals. Therefore, a true choice must be *determined.* But it is only a *free* choice if all determining factors are *internal* to the agent that makes the choice. Under idealism, our individual psyches are dissociated complexes – *alters* – of a transpersonal mind-at-large. The entirety of existence unfolds as a stream of experiences in this transpersonal consciousness. Since there is nothing outside mind-at-large, all determining factors of all possible choices can only be internal to it. All archetypes are within it. Hence, *mind-at-large as a whole certainly has metaphysical free will.*

At this point, you may be wondering if I am not unduly conflating the notions of desire and necessity; 'want to' with 'have to.' After all, if the experiences of mind-at-large are the inescapable manifestation of its own intrinsic nature – that is, its archetypes – it seems more appropriate to say that mind-at-large *has to* undergo these experiences, rather than to say that it *wants to* do so. Notice, however, that the semantic difference between desire and necessity rests on the corresponding imperatives being *external* in the latter case. I only say that I *have to* work because the imperatives of society – which are external to me as a person – require me to do so. If the imperatives that compel me to work were, instead, *internal* to me – say, an inner imperative to feel useful and productive – I would say that I *want to* work. Indeed, *what is a desire but the direct experience of an inner imperative?* Now, since mind-at-large is the whole of existence, there is nothing external to it. All imperatives are internal. And since mind-at-large is consciousness itself, all imperatives are experienced. Hence, at its level, the difference between 'have to' and 'want to' disappears. What mind-at-large has to do *is* what it wants to do; what it wants to do *is* what it has to do. The necessity is the desire; the desire is the necessity. We can say that mind-at-large desires irresistibly to do precisely what it does, because it is its nature to desire so. That it is free to carry out what it desires is the very expression of its unbound metaphysical free will.

Let's recapitulate briefly: idealism entails that reality is the unfolding of experiences in a transpersonal form of consciousness that I call mind-at-large. Since this entails that all choices are purely subjective, idealism is conducive to our intuitions of free will. Yet, it is inevitable that the unfolding of experiences must obey determining factors: whatever mental processes take place in mind-at-large, they must necessarily be the manifestation of the intrinsic nature of mind-at-large. What else could they be? The behavior and choices of mind-at-large can *only* be a deterministic consequence of what it essentially *is*. In this sense, existence is mentally deterministic. But since all determining factors involved in the unfolding of experiences are necessarily internal to mind-at-large – there being nothing external to it – there is metaphysical free will at its level. The necessities of mind-at-large *are* its desires.

The crucial question that remains open is this: Is there also metaphysical free will at our *personal* level? Do we, dissociated alters of mind-at-large, also have free choice? To answer it, let's go back to our definition: we only have free will if our choices are determined solely by factors internal to what we perceive ourselves to be. Therefore, to the extent that we identify only with a particular *idea* of self – that is, with a particular dissociated thought – our personal free will be rather limited. As dissociated complexes of mind-at-large, we are immersed in a much broader and powerful archetypal matrix that influences much of our inner lives and actions. Can we freely control the flow of our emotions? Can we choose which thoughts *not* to have? In the language of analytical psychology, the ego has limited free will. Like a tiny boat in stormy seas, it can choose where to point its ruder but can't control the currents, waves or the wind. It may be free to identify and select the most affordable mortgage package, the most comprehensive health insurance plan or the fastest route to work in the morning, but it is otherwise at the mercy of broader, obfuscated psychic forces. These forces are responsible for everything from instinctual reflexes and drives to the person one falls in love with, to one's choice of profession, to creative inspiration, to neurotic feelings and behaviors, to visions and hallucinations.

However, all is not lost. By its very definition, metaphysical free will is a function of that which we identify ourselves with. If we identify with our ego – a particular, dissociated set of ideas – we turn the universe at large, and even our own intrusive thoughts and unwanted feelings, into oppressive tyrants. They become external factors that constrain and coerce us. If, on the other hand, we identify not with particular dissociated ideas but with consciousness itself – with that whose excitations give rise to *all* thoughts and feelings – we attain unfathomable metaphysical free will. This arises not from the power of the ego to control the world, but from the realization that we *are* the world. How could we feel oppressed by that which we are? Our free will is limited within our nightly dreams only because we identify with a particular character in the dream. But when we become lucid without waking up, and realize that the entire dreamscape is *us*, we attain unlimited free will; even if nothing else changes as far as the further development of the dream's storyline. Do you see the point?

To finally answer the question posed in the title of this essay, metaphysical free will is to be found *everywhere* under idealism. At the level of mind-at-large, it is unbound. We, on the other hand, as dissociated complexes of mind-at-large, are immersed in, and at the mercy of, powerful transpersonal forces. As such, to the extent that we identify with our own dissociated thoughts and feelings, our metaphysical free will is limited. But insofar as we identify with consciousness itself, the matrix of all thoughts and feelings, we partake in the unlimited metaphysical free will of mind-at-large.

8. On practical applications

We've turned into a pragmatic bunch. Our cultural value system entails that nothing is really worth anything if it doesn't have practical applications. A new insight or understanding is allegedly pointless if there's nothing we can really *do* with it. This very notion is a symptom of our confusion. Nonetheless, it would be naïve to ignore it as I attempt to communicate alternative insights and understandings. This chapter, thus, represents not my surrender to a confused value system, but my attempt to work from *within* it in order to convey a different way to relate to life.

Essay 8.1 confronts the confusion head-on: it deconstructs the cultural notion that all value is derived from applications. Essay 8.2 elaborates, in a fair level of detail, upon the practical differences that a transition from materialism to a more mature worldview would make in our lives and society as a whole. Essay 8.3 then zooms into one specific area where these differences would be particularly significant: healthcare. Essay 8.4 tackles a question that is often asked in connection with the philosophy of idealism defended in this book: if all reality is in consciousness, can our thoughts and wishes directly influence the world? The correct answer is subtler than a mere 'yes' or 'no.' Essay 8.5 closes the chapter with an unexpected twist on the question that started it.

8.1. Pragmatism and the meaning of life

When talking to people about my ideas and writings, be them friends, interviewers or event managers prior to a talk, I often hear the following question at the end of the conversation: 'OK, but now, how can people *apply* all this in practice?' In the early days, the question struck me as entirely legitimate, so I used to feel a little embarrassed for not having addressed it upfront. But as I stepped back to ponder the motivations behind it, a whole new avenue of insight regarding our culture opened up before me. To anticipate the conclusion of this essay, and without for a moment meaning to criticize anyone who has ever asked me this, I think the question reflects a generalized state of psychic imbalance in our culture; so generalized that it comes across not only as perfectly appropriate, but even smart.

Ultimately, the reality humans experience is a phenomenon unfolding in consciousness. Even if there were indeed an outside world independent of consciousness, our only access to it would be through our inner experiences. Without consciousness, the whole universe might as well not exist. Therefore, any practical application of our insights to an 'outside world' only has meaning, ultimately, insofar as it translates back into something we experience within. For instance, if an engineer has a brilliant idea and applies it in practice to get better results for his clients, the results will have human reality only insofar as they are *experienced* by the engineer and his clients. At the end of the day, it all comes back to an internal phenomenon in consciousness. The 'outside world' is just an abstract, conceptual intermediary between idea and *experienced* result. Only the internal reality of consciousness can confer any meaning to human life.

Now, philosophy is an expedition into the land of conscious insight. And conscious insight is already an internal reality; a gestalt of *experience* unfolding in the human psyche. As such, philosophy requires no applications – though it may have many, as essays 8.2 to 8.4 illustrate – for it isn't necessarily a means to an end. It already addresses the end-goal directly. It enriches life not in a roundabout way, but by nurturing the very matrix of life itself: the psyche. Asking about the applications of philosophy is akin to asking how to get the bus home when you are already at home.

Why did you get an education? To be able to work, I guess. Why do you work? To make money, of course. Why do you want to make money? To buy things. Why do you want to buy things? To be able to live and have rich experiences... what else? Yes, exactly! *At the end of the day, it's all about experience.* And experience is what unfolds in consciousness. All practical applications are mere means to arriving at certain experiences. And since conscious insight is a primary experience that frames, shapes and colors most – if not all – other experiences, why wonder about its applications as far as people's actions in the world 'outside'? We are already dealing with the core issue, already sitting on the couch at home. Why ask about the bus?

Even after reading the above, you may still feel that something is off with my argument; that everything should have some kind of concrete, practical application in order to have any value or meaning. There is a kind of uneasiness associated with embarking on an intellectual journey when the journey's guide tells you, upfront, that he doesn't care whether the journey will have any practical application. You aren't alone in this feeling. It is shared by our entire Western culture; a culture that has now invaded the whole world, the East included.

The problem is that we project all meaning onto the 'outside.' We stopped living the inner life of human beings and began living the 'outer life' of things and mechanisms. In the words of Jung, 'Swamped by the knowledge of external objects, the subject of all knowledge has been temporarily eclipsed to the point of seeming nonexistence.'[179] All meaning must lie – we've come to assume – somewhere without and never within. I even dare to venture an explanation for how this came to pass: because of Western materialism, we believe that we are finite beings who will, unavoidably, eventually cease to exist. Only the 'outside world' will endure and have continuity. Although this is nothing but a fairytale – as argued in essays 2.1 and 2.2 – it causes us to project all the meaning of life onto the 'outside world,' for only things that endure can have any significance. The world within is seen as ephemeral and, therefore, meaningless. Such is the unsustainable imbalance of our way to relate to life. We emptied ourselves of all meaning and placed it all outside. Yet, even that 'outside world' is, ultimately, an abstraction of mind; an abstraction of the world within.

When people talk to me about my ideas and their own philosophical speculations, I sense that, deep inside, they know that life is a journey in consciousness and nowhere else. They know that what we are talking about is already it; it's already all that matters. But towards the end of the conversation, when the enchantment of the discussion wanes and concedes ground to the analytical ego, they remember about the all-important practical applications. It is as though a failure to address them left the joke without a punch line; something akin to winning the bet but forgetting to cash in the chips. They compulsively need to tick that box. After all, if the ego doesn't get anything to *do* with the new insights, it has no role. Why have we lost our ability to just *be* with new insights?

Life is a laboratory for exploration along only two paths: feeling and understanding. All else exists only as connotative devices: 'tricks' to *evoke* feeling and understanding. All meaning resides in the emotions and insights unfolding within. While I, as a human being, also walk the path of feeling like the rest of us, my writing focuses on the path of understanding. Are there practical applications for my philosophy? Absolutely, as the remainder of this chapter discusses. But they are means to an end that previous chapters have already tackled directly.

The world can only advance from its currently dire state when we, human beings, make peace with and nurture our feelings, while advancing our understanding of self and reality. Can you conceive of a practical application with more significance than this?

8.2. What difference does it make if reality is in consciousness?

As discussed at length in essays 2.1 and 2.2, my metaphysical position is that all reality is in consciousness. There is no universe outside, or independent of, subjective experience. However, I also do not deny that reality exists independently of individual, *personal* psyches. When you look out and see the world, that world unfolds without caring about your individual, personal opinions, wishes or fantasies. Indeed, I maintain that empirical reality is the image of experiences in a transpersonal consciousness (see essay 2.6), which I call 'mind-at-large' in honor of Aldous Huxley. As such, empirical reality would still exist as a dream of mind-at-large even if there were no biology in the universe.

The misunderstanding that may arise from the above is to conclude that, since in both cases the world exists independently of personal psyches, there is no difference between this transpersonal mind-at-large and a material world fundamentally outside consciousness. Nothing could be further from the truth!

There are two lines of argument to clarify this. The first one is philosophical and rigorous: when we say that our personal psyches are merely segments of a broader mind-at-large, all we are doing is *extrapolating* a known and empirically undeniable ontological category – namely, consciousness itself – beyond its face-value spacetime limits. But when we say that there is a whole universe outside consciousness, we are inferring a whole *new* ontological category; one that is unprovable. These two things aren't equivalent by any stretch of the imagination. Here is a rather dramatic analogy to help you gain some intuition about this: in order to model the early universe, physicists *extrapolate* across space and time the validity of the laws of physics known on Earth today. Doing so is obviously different, and much more reasonable, than inferring an unprovable Flying Spaghetti Monster to be the causal agency behind all things![180]

The second line of argument rests on the different *implications* and *practical applications* of these two alternatives:

- If all reality is in consciousness, then your consciousness is not generated by your body. Therefore, there is no reason to believe that your consciousness will end when your body dies. Your body is simply the outside image of a particular *configuration* of consciousness that you experience when you are alive. When you die, that configuration – or state – of consciousness will change, perhaps dramatically. Changes in your state of consciousness, however, happen all the time: when you wake up suddenly from an intense nightly dream, your consciousness changes its state rather dramatically as well. Now, would we live life differently – perhaps in a less anxious, more present and grounded manner – if we knew that death isn't the end of consciousness? If the fear of death were no longer viable as an instrument of social control or economic gain, what would be the practical consequences for our culture, economy and society at large? And if you knew that your consciousness isn't going to end when you die, wouldn't you be interested in investing a bigger part of your life in preparing yourself for the transition – so it isn't traumatic – and perhaps for what might come next?
- If all reality is in consciousness, then your physical body is also in consciousness, not the other way around. As such, your body is the *outside image* of psychic processes unfolding in what analytical psychology has come to call your 'personal unconscious.' I consider the word 'unconscious' a misnomer, as I discuss in essay 2.1, preferring to call it 'personal obfuscated psyche' instead. Be it as it may, the implication is clear: your physical health isn't merely 'connected' to your psychic state; it *is* your obfuscated psychic state. I discuss this in greater

detail in essay 8.3, but the gist is that it opens up an entirely new avenue for treating physical illness through forms of suggestion, clinical psychology and many other treatments currently considered alternative or even fringe. Indeed, the implication is that medicine could advance beyond currently acknowledged boundaries by adopting a holistic mind-body approach, whose impact on our health and wellbeing are hard to overestimate.

- If our personal psyches are merely dissociated complexes – alters – of mind-at-large, then, at bottom, our psyches are fundamentally one and the same consciousness. This validates the *possibility* of so-called psi phenomena, like clairvoyance and telepathy. If the *a priori* bias against parapsychology were to disappear, so that critical resources and people could be committed to it in scales much greater than ever before, what could science discover in this field? What practical applications could emerge from more widespread and better-funded parapsychological research? In what variety of very practical and pragmatic ways could that impact our personal lives and those of our loved ones?

- If subjective experience is primary in nature – not merely a secondary phenomenon of the mechanical behavior of matter – then our feelings and emotions carry much more weight and relevance than otherwise. They are much more significant to our sense of who or what we are, what reality is, as well as to the meaning and purpose of our lives. If love is actually primary – material chemicals suffusing your brain being just an *outside image* of love, not its cause – wouldn't it make a difference regarding how you look upon your relationships? If your subjective sense of calling or purpose is primary – not merely a chemical trick to keep you motivated to survive and reproduce – wouldn't it make a difference regarding the decisions and risks you take in your life to try to make your dreams come true? Wouldn't we, as a culture, have to take another look at current psychiatric best-practices if we acknowledged our feelings to be primary, not merely the outcome of chemical imbalances to be corrected with drugs?

Notice that none of the implications and practical applications listed above would hold under a materialist metaphysics; that is, under the notion that reality exists fundamentally outside and independent of consciousness. It makes an enormous practical difference whether reality is mental.

8.3. The case for integrative mind-body medicine

Integrative medicine encompasses a variety of approaches to healthcare focusing on mind-body interaction. Unlike mainstream materialist medicine, which treats a patient's body as a biological mechanism, integrative medicine seeks to heal the whole being, including – and often starting from – one's psychic, emotional functions. It is a more holistic approach to healing that, because of the metaphysical bias carried by our culture's mainstream materialist worldview, has largely been neglected over the past several decades. In this essay, I want to elaborate on how a sane and parsimonious understanding of reality provides credibility and strong rational foundations to the integrative approach. The time has come for our culture to overcome the narrow and artificial materialist boundaries that for so long have impaired healthcare. We have suffered long enough.

Let me begin by summarizing the worldview discussed at length in essays 2.1 and 2.2. I maintain that all reality is in consciousness, though not in your *personal* consciousness alone. This way, it is your body-brain system that is in consciousness, not consciousness in your body-brain system. Think of reality as a collective dream: in a dream, it is your dream character that is in your consciousness, not your consciousness in your dream character. This becomes obvious when you wake up, but isn't at all obvious while you are dreaming. Furthermore, I maintain that the body-brain system is an *outside image* of a process of localization in the stream of consciousness, like a whirlpool is the image of a process of localization in a stream of water. It is this localization that leads to the illusion of personal identity and separateness. For exactly the same reason that a whirlpool doesn't generate water, your brain doesn't generate consciousness. Yet, because an outside image of a process correlates tightly with the inner dynamics of the process – like the way the colors of flames correlate tightly with the microscopic details of the process of combustion – brain activity correlates with subjective experience. Motivated by this correlation, materialists naively mistake an *image* of the process for the *cause* of the process.

Whereas particular types of brain activity are the outside image of egoic processes in consciousness, *the rest of the physical body is an outside image of our personal obfuscated psyche; that is, an image of our repressed, forgotten or otherwise unacknowledged psychic activity.* I maintain that the ego corresponds to self-reflective processes in consciousness – that is, processes that you are aware that you are conscious of – while the obfuscated psyche corresponds to non-self-reflective processes also in consciousness. As such, there is no true unconscious, but simply processes in consciousness that become obfuscated by the 'glare' of self-reflective awareness, in the same way that the stars become obfuscated by the glare of the Sun at noon. Now, as the body is an outside image of our *personal* obfuscated psyche, the universe at large is an outside image of a *collective* obfuscated mind, which I call mind-at-large (see essay 2.6). The collective aspect of this deeper part of the psyche is the reason we all seem to share the same world. In summary:

- An outside image of (self-reflective) egoic processes in consciousness is particular types of brain activity.

- An outside image of the (non-self-reflective) personal obfuscated psyche is the metabolism in the rest of the physical body.
- An outside image of the collective obfuscated psyche (mind-at-large) is the physical activity in the rest of the universe.

The key point in this whole story, as far as integrative medicine is concerned, is this: beyond certain specific types of brain activity that correlate with self-reflective egoic awareness, *the rest of the physical body is an image of our personal obfuscated psyche.* The body isn't merely a lump of matter fundamentally independent from, and outside, our psyche. Instead, it is what buried emotions, feelings, beliefs and cognitive processes that escape the field of our self-reflective awareness look like from the outside. Now, just as blue flames are the image of hotter combustion and red flames the image of colder combustion, so a healthy body is an image of healthy psychic activity and an ill body is an image of unhealthy psychic activity in the personal obfuscated psyche. This way, if we need to speak in terms of causation, it is fair to say that unhealthy psychic activity in the personal obfuscated psyche *causes* all illnesses. This shows the importance of integrative medicine: *we can treat all illnesses by influencing obfuscated psychic activity.*

A note of caution is required at this point. Many alternative healing techniques are promoted today that focus on the ego: affirmations, positive thinking, visualization, etc. But for as long as the corresponding psychic activity remains in the ego – that is, remains in self-reflective awareness – it won't affect the rest of the body. Because the body is an outside image of *non-egoic* psychic activity, whatever remains in the ego cannot influence the body. How many people get seriously ill despite assiduously practicing positive thinking and visualizations? How many people continue to suffer from the conditions they try to overcome with their daily health affirmations? Clearly, it isn't enough to refurnish the ego: the new furniture has to sink into the cellar of our personal psyches if it is to have bodily effect. It has to be assimilated by the obfuscated core of one's being.

This isn't necessarily bad news, for it works the other way around as well: hypochondriacs, for instance, need not worry about 'attracting' the very illnesses they are constantly anxious about. Their anxiety resides in their self-reflective egoic awareness, this being precisely the reason why they suffer. Remaining self-reflectively aware of unhealthy psychic activity causes psychological distress, for sure, but it also prevents that activity from becoming somatized as physical illness. Depth psychology has, for decades, insisted in the need to bring unhealthy psychic activity into the light of self-reflective awareness, where it does less damage and can be more easily treated through talk therapy.

Nobody needs to feel guilty about 'attracting' illness due to a negative mood disposition, since such disposition isn't obfuscated or 'unconscious.' If it were, you wouldn't be aware of it and wouldn't feel guilty to begin with. Do you see what I mean? Generally speaking, you cannot know at an egoic level whether your psychic dispositions are going to compromise your health, for the dispositions that can do so are, by their very nature, obfuscated. Case in point: a meta-study reported that

Extremely low anger scores have been noted in numerous studies of patients with cancer. Such low scores suggest suppression, repression, or restraint of anger. There is evidence to show that suppressed anger can be a precursor to the development of cancer, and also a factor in its progression after diagnosis.[181]

This is entirely consistent with the explanatory framework I am putting forward here: anger only becomes somatized if it escapes egoic awareness and drops into the personal obfuscated psyche. But the irony is clear in the quote: it is precisely *low* anger scores that indicate *high* internalized levels of, well, anger! How is a patient to tell a healthy lack of anger from internalized, obfuscated anger? Should people who do not feel angry start worrying about anger-caused cancer? That would be preposterous. Only trained therapists can differentiate between a healthy lack of negative emotions and deeply buried emotions; and even then only tentatively. Either way, worry is illogical.

Another thing to take into account is this: as the image of our personal obfuscated psyche, the body is connected not only to the ego on one side, but also to the collective obfuscated psyche – what analytical psychology calls the 'collective unconscious' – on the other side. Since the physical world we perceive around us is an outside image of the activity in this collective mind, it is no surprise that environmental stressors like viruses, bacteria, exposure to the elements, nutrition, physical trauma, pollutants, drugs, etc., all influence our bodily health. The problem is that this is the only avenue of influence that materialist medicine acknowledges. Therefore, it misses half of the problem and half of the avenues of healing: the connection with our self-reflective, egoic thoughts and feelings.

The view that all reality unfolds in consciousness points to the following twin-avenues for effective integrative medicine: first, the patient must be helped to bring all unhealthy psychic activity into the light of self-reflective awareness, so it doesn't become somatized. The patient's ego must acknowledge and welcome the patient's buried, repressed material. Once this happens, the patient can be treated through the oldest, simplest and most effective healing method ever devised by humankind: heart-to-heart interaction between patient and healer. Second, healers can influence the psychic conditions in the personal obfuscated psyche – the seat of all illness – through the egoic channel. But for this to be effective, healers must help patients *internalize* the treatment, so it drops past the ego and into the deeper layers of the psyche. Here is where the art and skill of the healer comes into play, for this 'dropping in' must be accomplished through bypassing egoic barriers and defense mechanisms. A form of benign manipulation is required, which may conflict with present-day notions of ethics.

A case in point is the so-called placebo effect. Current practice in approving new drugs and treatments is that they must be demonstrated to be more effective than the proverbial 'sugar pills.' A serious problem for the pharmaceutical industry is the growing effectiveness of placebos in combating illness, which makes new drugs increasingly more difficult to approve.[182] The elephant in the room, obviously, is that placebos work, and more so in recent years. Clearly, through the power of suggestion and a form of benign egoic manipulation, a real effect is produced in the patient's personal obfuscated psyche; an effect whose image is renewed bodily health. To close one's eyes to the greatly beneficial implications of this fact is unwise. Even the ethical questions often raised – 'Can we deliberately deceive the patient?' – are based on prejudices: *there is no deception if the method works.* It is hardly relevant, for instance, whether reiki or homeopathy work for the theoretical reasons claimed by their practitioners or for entirely different reasons, *as long as they do work.* As a matter of fact, the theoretical reasons offered by the practitioners may be integral to the treatment, insofar as they provide the patient's ego with models and images that help lower the ego's defenses. Without those, the treatment may never fully penetrate the patient's egoic barriers and drop into the personal obfuscated psyche, the only place where physical healing can occur. Moreover, even mainstream science depends largely on convenient fictions such as, for instance, force-carrying subatomic particles.[183] We claim these convenient fictions to be legitimate because we can build working technology based on them: empirically, things work *as if* the fictions were true and that's good enough. Why not apply the same sensible pragmatism to the healing arts? Maybe acupuncture works *as if* energy meridians were true and, until we know better, that's good enough too.

We have every logical reason – not to mention myriad empirical ones – to give ourselves rational permission to embrace and trust integrative medicine. It explores effective avenues of treatment that have been left largely untouched by mainstream materialist medicine. Today's healthcare systems treat us as biological robots because the materialist metaphysics defines us as such. Consequently, doctors often behave as mechanics, instead of healers. But for millennia prior to modern medicine, it was the sheer strength of the healer's personal presence, as well as the psychic effects of his or her often-intricate techniques, that helped people to heal. Back then, we lacked the avenue of the collective obfuscated psyche in the form of effective drugs and surgery. Now, the situation has been reversed: we focus solely on drugs and surgery, ignoring the egoic channel. The time has come to explore both of these avenues concurrently. Human health and wellbeing demand no less.

8.4. Can our thoughts directly affect reality at large?

A recurring theme in popular culture, at least since the birth of the New Thought movement in the 19th century, has been what I call the 'intentional mind-over-matter hypothesis': the notion that our thoughts can deliberately and directly influence the world. According to the hypothesis, we should be able to purposefully mold the world – at least to a small extent – to our own wishes by the use of mental practices such as positive thinking, visualization, affirmations, etc. Documentary films and books like *The Secret* have given a renewed, modern spin to this idea, spreading it far and wide.

As discussed in essay 2.1, my own view is that reality unfolds entirely in consciousness – the medium of all thoughts – as opposed to a strongly-objective world outside consciousness. This view is called *idealism*. One may then legitimately wonder if idealism doesn't lend support to the intentional mind-over-matter hypothesis. After all, if both thoughts and empirical reality are in consciousness, it doesn't seem to be at all implausible that they could influence each other. But is the possibility of an intentional mind-over-matter effect a necessary implication of idealism? The answer isn't as straightforward as it may seem.

Before we can address the question fairly, some brief background is required. According to idealism, the world is in a *transpersonal* form of consciousness that transcends your *personal* psyche alone. Thus, it is your body-brain system – as a part of the world – that is in consciousness, not consciousness in your body-brain system. The body is an *outside image* of a process of localization of experiences in transpersonal consciousness, like a whirlpool is the image of a process of localization of water in a stream. For exactly the same reason that a whirlpool doesn't generate water, your brain doesn't generate consciousness. Yet, because an outside image of a process correlates with the inner dynamics of the process, brain activity correlates with localized subjective experience. Active neurons are what our personal experiences *look like* from the outside, not their cause.

As such, it is true that positive thinking, affirmations and visualizations can affect the reality *of our personal psyches and bodies:* they can change our emotions, general outlook on life and even our physical health, as discussed in essay 8.3. After all, these thoughts, affirmations and visualizations are experiences created by, and unfolding within, the whirlpool that we identify with as personal entities. Disturbances arising within the whirlpool can, of course, directly influence the whirlpool's inner dynamics. They can also *in*directly influence the broader stream through contact with the rim of the whirlpool: with the use of our arms and legs, we can physically act upon our thoughts to change the world at large. We do this every day when we wipe the floor, move furniture around or build a house with our own hands.

The question, of course, is whether our localized mental activity can influence the world *without* the physical mediation of our body. Can a disturbance created within the whirlpool remotely affect the flow of water on the other side of the stream, without any form of contact with the rim of the whirlpool? Framed this way, the answer doesn't seem all that obvious anymore, does it? Indeed, idealism doesn't necessarily imply that we can 'attract' a promotion or the ideal lover by merely visualizing it. It doesn't necessarily imply that thoughts or imagination within the whirlpool can remotely affect anything outside of the whirlpool. The consensus world clearly unfolds according to stable patterns and regularities that we've come to call the 'laws of nature.' Idealism doesn't deny this; it simply brings these patterns and regularities into the scope of consciousness: they become certain 'laws of consciousness,' so to speak.

Yet, idealism also doesn't *refute* intentional mind-over-matter effects. It is true that disturbances arising within a whirlpool can influence the stream outside by going through the rim of the whirlpool – that is, through body-mediated physical intervention in the world. But there may also be ways for disturbances to propagate 'under water.' Indeed, what we call the physical world is the ripples propagating on the surface of mind-at-large. They are all we can ordinarily perceive. The glare of the surface obfuscates the currents and disturbances that may be flowing underneath, so we can't discern them in a self-reflective manner. It is thus conceivable that thoughts and imagination originating in our personal psyche, *if they somehow sink into the deepest, most obfuscated, collective levels of consciousness,* could indeed affect consensus reality without physical mediation.

According to idealism, the physical world is an outside image of transpersonal mental processes. See essay 2.6 for details. But the *image* of a process doesn't necessarily reflect all there is to know about the process. Flames don't tell all there is to know about combustion. Lightning doesn't tell all there is to know about atmospheric electric discharge. Our physical appearance doesn't tell all there is to know about our state of health. Therefore, what we ordinarily perceive as physical cause and effect reflects merely the *visible* regularities of the unfolding of those transpersonal mental processes. There may be a lot more going on beyond our view. Moreover, our understanding of even these visible regularities is very incomplete, as argued in essay 4.2. *We do not know that the physical world is causally closed, or self-contained.* As such, the empirical reality we ordinarily perceive may be just the surface of an ocean of untold depth. Unfathomable complexity may lie immersed, obfuscated from view by the glare of the surface.

In one of his many wonderful talks, Alan Watts related a very evocative analogy for what we call physical causality: he asked his audience to imagine themselves sitting in front of a wooden fence, with just a thin slit allowing them to see what lies on the other side of the fence. If a dog were to walk along the other side, one would first see the dog's head through the slit and, a little while later, the dog's tail. Every time the dog would walk along the fence, one would first see the head and then the tail. Watts then argued that we would, very naturally, conclude that *the dog's head causes the dog's tail.* The logic behind this conclusion seems indeed impeccable.

You see, if all we have is a *partial* view of what is actually going on – a small slit in the fence – our understanding of the chains of cause-and-effect in nature may be very limited and inaccurate. The dog's head obviously doesn't *cause* the tail, even though every empirical observation through the slit would consistently reinforce this erroneous conclusion. The head and the tail are just regularities of a broader pattern unfolding beyond ordinary perception; namely, a walking dog. If consensus reality is merely a partial image of obfuscated, collective mental processes, our position as its observers may be entirely analogous to that of the person sitting in front of the wooden fence. The true, complete causal processes behind our observations – that is, the actual dog walking by – may lie in obfuscated depths below the surface. It is thus conceivable that, by somehow allowing our self-created thoughts and imagination to sink into the lower depths of the psyche, we could plug them into the *actual* causal chains of nature, whose effects could spread far beyond us. By allowing them to sink in we could conceivably release them into wide-ranging underwater currents.

In conclusion, idealism does not necessarily imply that one can directly influence consensus reality through positive thinking, affirmations or visualizations. In fact, it implies precisely that, for as long as our self-created thoughts and imagination remain in our personal psyche, they *cannot* influence the world at large. At best, they could influence our mental and emotional outlook, as well as physical health. But idealism does leave a door open for intentional mind-over-matter effects when our self-created thoughts and imagination are allowed to sink into the lower, transpersonal levels of the psyche. How this form of release can be intentionally accomplished is unclear. After all, for as long as our personal intentions remain *personal,* they are still circumscribed by our personal psyches and cannot affect the world. But it is conceivable that techniques or skills for achieving the effect may have been developed through the course of history. It is also conceivable that the effects could grow if the techniques or skills were to be applied by a large number of people working in synch, as some studies on meditation suggest.[184]

8.5. It starts and ends with us: what can we do individually?

In early 2013, I was discussing with a reader what could be done to prevent the growth of meaninglessness and isolation in the heart of our culture from crossing the point of no return. Although my conversation with her included more practical issues, such as the alarming environmental deterioration and dangerous geopolitical trends we all bear witness to, here I want to focus more on the psychological and 'spiritual' – a word I use with caution, since its meaning is so loose – health and wellbeing of humanity. On this specific point, my young reader felt strongly that vocal and decisive initiatives should be undertaken by those with insight into the situation; that something should be *done* in the form of practical actions. It wasn't lost on me what she was trying to suggest she expected of me.

I confess to feeling some hesitation about this 'doing' approach, though. By and large, I believe that real and lasting change arises naturally from within the individual. My attitude could probably be construed as too passive – too little, too late – which I suspect was my reader's take on it. A big part of me even acknowledges this. Shouldn't I then suggest that we do something more proactive? Shouldn't we take more responsibility, as inhabitants of this planet and members of humanity, for changing our presently suicidal course?

I pondered much about it and finally found a way to reconcile my conflicting attitudes: instead of suggesting what we should try to *do*, I will instead suggest what we could *stop* doing so to improve our circumstances. Indeed, I believe that much of the damage arises from our own misguided actions. We blindly go about life doing all kinds of things that ultimately harm us. As such, perhaps the best way to stop the downward spiral into madness is not to do yet more things, but to *stop* doing a few things. In fact, it is a symptom of the imbalances of Western culture – which now pervades the whole world – that all useful thinking must translate into actions. Ours is a culture of do, do, do. However, when someone is pounding his own head with a hammer, the right solution is not to look for a helmet, but to stop the hammering.

So here are my five suggestions – Only five! – of things we could all, individually, stop doing to help improve our collective sanity and wellbeing. None of the entries in the list below requires effort, since they are not proactive but passive. Yet, if most of us would stop doing these five simple things, I am convinced that our psychological and spiritual health would improve substantially, both individually and collectively. As a direct result of that, we might even find our culture and civilization on a path back to meaning.

1. *Let us stop compulsively stupefying ourselves.* We all feel, in the unacknowledged depths of our psyche, that our ordinary life is becoming increasingly empty and meaningless. Our obfuscated psyche tries to correct our course through an array of signals: unexplained unease, depression, anxieties, intuitive epiphanies and odd drives. We then diligently proceed to ignore and repress all these signals through distractions: idiotic television shows, fanatic rooting for sports teams, alcohol, retail 'therapy,' hollow social networking, compulsive money-making and status-chasing, compulsive casual dating and whatnot. This is understandable in that nobody likes to remain exposed to the anguish, frustration and anxiety emerging from the obfuscated psyche while it attempts to force a change. But if those feelings are not allowed self-reflective mental space to be acknowledged, processed and integrated, not only will they harm us even more from within – think of psychoses and even physical illness, as discussed in essay 8.3 – we will not give ourselves any chance to find the meaning of our lives again. Self-reflective psychological distress, whatever else it may be, hints at a corrective direction for our lives.

2. *Let us stop believing so readily.* Here I don't mean just belief in the hysterical claims shouted from the fringes of the

culture, but also belief in the materialist nonsense that is spoon-fed to us by academia, the educational system in general and the mainstream media. In fact, I often find it hard to decide which of these two beliefs is more detrimental and dangerous. While the hysterical fringes are often pathological, the materialist worldview is demeaning to the human spirit and runs counter to the full expression of psychic life. What alternative do we have then? The words of the poet John Keats offer an avenue:

> At once it struck me what quality went to form a Man of Achievement, especially in Literature, and which Shakespeare possessed so enormously – I mean Negative Capability, that is, *when a man is capable of being in uncertainties, mysteries, doubts,* without any irritable reaching after fact and reason.[185]

Indeed, if one is rigorous and honest, one must recognize that there is precious little that can really be concluded from consensus fact and reason. In our grasping attempts to ease our insecurities and anxieties, we often *conjure up* facts and *overstretch* reason. Materialism is an expression of this compulsive overreaching. You see, your belief is valuable currency, for the way you spend it sets the tone for your life. As any cautious buyer will tell you, there is no need to part with currency in a hurry. It's okay to live in the mystery while you consider how best to invest your belief. It's just important to keep in mind that being cautious with your belief does not mean becoming *cynical.* Cynicism, in fact, is a disguised but extreme form of belief: the often-baseless commitment to the *impossibility* of something. It spends as much currency as gullibility. Living in the mystery, on the other hand, entails an attitude of openness without commitment.

3. *Let us stop acting so much.* Let's face it: we all act. We act at work, we act at home, we act at the gym, we act at the pub, etc. We act so consistently that we mistake the acting for living an ordinary life. We try to control the image of ourselves that we make available to others, motivated by a need to fit in, to appear strong, to look attractive, etc. In psychological terms, we all wear the mask of the *persona*. We know, in our heart of hearts, how much suffering, insecurity and anxiety we actually live with. But since everybody else is acting like we do, hiding their inner truths like we do, each one of us ends up concluding that we are alone in our suffering; that we are the weakest, most inadequate and fear-ridden person on the planet. The acting causes us all unnecessary *extra* suffering. Show me a person who claims to have no significant anxieties or insecurities and I will show you a liar. The human condition isn't reassuring and we're all in the same boat. But because we try to put up this image of strength, we add insult to injury by convincing each other that we are alone in our misery. This only increases our isolation and loneliness. We forget that the only real strength is the courage to present ourselves to the world as we really are, so we can live in authentic community and help each other out.

4. *Let us stop eating so much meat.* No, I am not suggesting that we should all become vegetarians, just that we could perhaps *reduce* our meat consumption. And I say this not for the usual reasons, such as better health, less environmental impact, etc. These reasons are all true and good, but my motivation here is different: once you turn animals into *products,* you make it unavoidable that they are treated – no, *processed* – as such. Savage economic and human realities then kick in and ensure that these animals live dreadful lives and die in unthinkable agony,

as recent documentaries have shown.[186] Many more higher animals are killed for food every day than the total number of human beings killed in the whole of World War II, and often under more horrendous circumstances. This unimaginable and excruciating orgy of pain, agony and death is being carried out on our account every day, because we provide the demand for it. And if all psyches, human and otherwise, are one at their deepest, most obfuscated levels – a point I argue in essay 2.1 – try to imagine how much outrage, stress, anxiety, dread, anguish and sheer pain is being pumped every day into our collective, obfuscated mind. Do you really think that you, as an individual, are insulated from this? Can you even conceive of the magnitude of what we are doing to ourselves?

5. *Let us stop buying so much unnecessary stuff.* Do we really need to upgrade our wardrobe every year? Do we really need a bigger TV or a newer car? Or that new phone? In the throes of culturally-induced fetishism, we look for meaning and divinity in mere stuff. We think – utterly irrationally – that our lives will finally make sense and be fulfilling after we buy the things we fetishize. Yet, inevitably, stuff always disappoints us at the end. How long did your 'high' last after your latest dream purchase? Weeks? Days? Maybe only a few hours? Withdrawing our projections from mere things, and modifying our spending habits accordingly, will force a potentially painful but certainly necessary adjustment of the economic system. It will reduce the influence and power base of those who gain most from the current *status quo*, weakening the control loops that perpetuate it. As a bonus, by buying less we will also be less motivated to continue to increase our income beyond reasonable levels, freeing up time and energy in our lives for more meaningful pursuits (for

instance, those discussed in essay 5.7). Make no mistake: a quiet and entirely peaceful change in our spending habits is not only impossible to repress, it will also have a much bigger impact than any street revolution. Consumerism – so frantically reinforced by governments, the mainstream media, and validated by the academically-sanctioned delusion of materialism – is what keeps us in the role of cogs in a sick system that benefits only the pathological amongst us. By peacefully refusing to play the role of entranced consumers, we will irremediably undermine the very foundations of this system and enable positive, necessary change.

That's it. Five simple things we could *stop* doing today in order to change the world of tomorrow. How about that?

9. Takeaway message

As you may have noticed, an underlying worldview runs across the various essays in this book as a unifying theme. It is based on two simple but crucial notions: first, that what we call the 'human psyche' or 'personal awareness' is not a self-contained phenomenon inside our head, but a dissociated psychic complex – or *alter* – of a broader transpersonal consciousness. All reality unfolds as subjective experiences in this transpersonal 'mind-at-large.' Second, the formation of alters gives rise to two different perspectives from which mental processes in mind-at-large can be witnessed: the first- and second-person perspectives.

The first-person perspective occurs when an alter experiences a mental process powered and modulated from *within* the alter itself. For instance, the flow of my thoughts, which I experience from a first-person perspective, arises and is shaped entirely within me. The second-person perspective happens when the experience of an alter is powered and modulated by another mental process unfolding *outside* the alter, *but still within mind-at-large.* For instance, my sense perceptions are powered and modulated by processes unfolding outside me. More specifically, if I look at measurements of another person's brain activity taken when the person is thinking about something, I gain a second-person perspective of the person's thoughts. Notice that both first- and second-person perspectives are *experiences:* I experience seeing brain activity measurements. It's just that certain experiences in an alter are induced by *other* experiences *outside* the alter, so they end up corresponding to each other information-wise. The brain activity measurements I see correspond, information-wise, to the other person's experience of her thoughts. Even the inanimate objects I perceive around me correspond to mental processes experienced by mind-at-large. *Ultimately, thus, there's only experience.*

Naturally, the second-person perspective of an experience is very different than the first-person one. Looking at the brain activity of a frightened person feels totally different than being frightened oneself. This dramatic difference isn't at all surprising: the second-person perspective is a *secondary* excitation of consciousness, inside an alter, *induced* by another, *primary* excitation of consciousness outside the alter. The primary and secondary excitations, although corresponding to each other in certain ways, need not be even remotely similar qualitatively. As an analogy, imagine that your particular alter in mind-at-large is like a kettle on a stove. The primary excitation of burning gas outside the kettle induces the secondary excitation of boiling water inside the kettle. There are clear correspondences between the two: for instance, the water will boil faster if the flow of burning gas is stronger. *But boiling water looks nothing like burning gas.* Analogously, the second-person perspective of an experience looks nothing like the first-person perspective. Those who endorse materialism because our sense perceptions feel so different from our inner flow of thoughts and emotions simply fail to see this simple point.

It is the formation of alters that delineates boundaries between different psychic 'spaces' within mind-at-large, giving rise to second-person perspectives. After all, without a boundary there would be no 'outside,' but only a first-person perspective of every mental process unfolding in mind-at-large. It is dissociation that creates the experiential 'outside.' But this 'outside' is not outside consciousness itself; it is simply outside the alter. *Our culture has come to mistake the witnessing of mental processes outside our personal alter for the witnessing of material phenomena outside consciousness.*

This mistake is as inflationary as it is tragic. Postulating a whole universe outside consciousness requires an unprovable ontological category – namely, not-consciousness – that is also entirely unnecessary to make sense of observations. Dissociation, in turn, as a process *of* and *in* consciousness, requires only the primary datum of reality, which is consciousness itself. All empirical reality can be understood in terms of the first- and second-person perspectives of experience that arise from dissociation. As discussed in depth in this book, all evidence used to support the *inference* of a world outside consciousness can be made sense of on the basis of these two perspectives, including: the fact that we feel a clear distinction between our inner lives – our thoughts and emotions – and the 'outside world' we perceive through our sense organs; the fact that our subjective experiences can be affected by intervention in our brain (drugs, trauma, surgery, etc.); the fact that our personal awareness is firmly connected to the moving platform of our physical body; etc.

This understanding is the key to a revolution in our way to relate to reality whose time has come. In fact, it is overdue. Everything that currently motivates us to believe in a world outside consciousness can and will be understood as the effects of mental processes outside our particular alter, which we witness from a second-person perspective. If you truly grok this, you will see through our culture's delusion; you will wake up from the trance that the world around you conspires to keep you in.

Materialism represents an astonishing failure of the human intellect to see what's right under its nose. It hides nature's marvelous simplicity behind a veil of contrivance. Its continuing survival in face of the mounting odds of reason, evidence and direct experience requires constant and deliberate maintenance. Indeed, materialism serves powerful economic and political interests. 'If our confusion suits the reigning political and economic regime just fine, it is because it stands as proof that the operation to supplant the dream-space of soul and psyche with a fully controllable interface is going according to plan,' writes Jean-Francois Martel.[187] What forces stand to gain from the continuance of materialism? How do these forces manifest themselves in society?

Questions like these evoke the idea of conspiracies. Yet, our ordinary view of conspiracies tends to be rather caricatural: secret, powerful organizations working behind the curtain, whose goals and actions are deliberately orchestrated by *hierarchies of control* with an *elusive leadership* at the top. Secret meetings are allegedly held, secret orders issued and disseminated through myriad covert channels. Everybody in a position of any significance in society is allegedly involved; *everybody except us.* How plausible is all this? You see, this caricatural view of conspiracies helps to protect and preserve what is *really* going on. If our only choice is to either believe in the caricature or absolve all players of all guilt, it is easy to see how the world is kept entranced.

It has become practically impossible to reclaim the more moderate denotations of the word 'conspiracy.' So let me try a different word: *stigmergy.*[188] Stigmergy happens when agents co-ordinate their actions indirectly, through the local effects of their behavior in the environment. These local effects influence subsequent actions by other agents, whose effects, in turn, influence the behavior of yet other agents, and so on. This way, local actions by different agents reinforce and build upon each other, leading to the spontaneous rise of globally co-ordinated, systematic activity. Ant and termite colonies, for instance, operate according to stigmergy: there's no hierarchy of control, no elusive leadership, no broadcasting of secret orders. Yet, the resulting behavior is systematic – following a clear global agenda – *as if* it were centrally co-ordinated by some kind of secret cabal.[189]

There is vicious, insidious stigmergy in our society today. The agenda of this stigmergy is the maintenance of materialism. It manifests itself as a broad network of subtle local actions, biases and values, each serving powerful interests. These local dynamics build up into a system of global reinforcement; a *virtual cabal,* so to speak. The stigmergy has turned most of us into entranced drones, serving a mad state of affairs that is slowly but inexorably killing our humanity.

We must get past the delusions of our intellectual adolescence. We must escape the invisible cognitive cage where we're kept by those who stand to gain from the *status quo.* We must see through the insidious, soul-crushing stigmergy of materialism. We must summon the courage to acknowledge that some of the most celebrated intellectuals and scientists among us have been no more than arrogant children when it comes to their understanding of the nature of reality and of their own humanity. They do not deserve the wide-ranging reverence we, as a culture, seem to feel we owe them. Unexamined prejudice and foolishness are rampant even among the self-proclaimed guardians of reason. A failure to acknowledge and integrate all this at the broadest cultural level will, at best, delay our maturity and, at worst, destroy our species.

Afterword by Rupert Spira

At the time of writing this *Afterword,* I have not yet met Bernardo. At least, that would be a true statement in the context of our prevailing materialistic worldview. What do we mean when we say that we have met someone? We mean essentially that two bodies have encountered each other and possibly shaken hands or conversed.

However, in the context of the worldview expressed in this book, to meet someone, indeed the very idea of relationship itself, takes on a different and broader meaning. From the idealist point of view that informs the essays in this book, and indeed from the perspective of the perennial philosophy that underlies all the great religious and spiritual traditions, the body is an appearance in the mind and the mind is a modulation of Consciousness. As such, the body and the physical world that it appears to perceive are the smallest elements of experience. They are a limited view of the much more expansive world of mind, the larger world of mind being itself a modulation of infinite Consciousness.

Thus, to meet someone 'in the flesh' is to meet only a fraction of the 'whole person.' As physical bodies we are reasonably well defined, each with a distinct boundary, but these boundaries define only the smallest element of who we are. At the level of thoughts and feelings there are still subtle boundaries, but the distinctions here are less clearly defined and, therefore, the sense of separation less obvious. As we travel 'backwards' or 'inwards' towards the essential nature of our minds – that is, as the mind travels 'backwards' or 'inwards' towards its *own* essential nature – the forms we encounter become less distinct, and the grounds for the apparent separation between people or entities are less discernible.

At some point the mind traces itself back to its original,

irreducible essence, where there is no form – that is, no coloring of itself – and, therefore, no objects or entities present to be distinct or separate from one another. It is at this level where all humanity, indeed all apparent objects and selves, are one. From this point of view, all apparent objects and selves are expressions, modulations or vibrations of their original shared essence – unconditioned or infinite Mind, pure Consciousness itself.

What we, as human beings, experience as friendship is the echo of this original oneness of being, reverberating through shared layers of mind, which sometimes, but not always, takes the shape of a meeting at the physical level. As such, true friendship does not require a meeting in the flesh, just as a meeting in the flesh does not always reveal true friendship.

To meet someone in the flesh is to encounter the visible face of a much larger field of energies. To reduce this larger field of energies to a physical object – a person – is to diminish it, and by doing so to diminish our self. Such a relationship between two separate and distinct objects cannot be a harmonious one, for it denies the shared reality that is their source and essence.

It is in this context that I can say of Bernardo that I know him without knowing him.

What has been said above about the meeting of two people is equally true of encountering an inanimate object. I first recognized this when, as a ceramic artist, I would visit museums around the world and explore their collections of early pottery. Long before I was able to rationalize experience as I am doing now, I would frequently feel an uncanny familiarity with a particular bowl or jar, a sort of visceral intimacy that expressed itself in simplistic terms such as, 'I knew the person who made that bowl,' 'I made that jar myself,' or 'These are my friends.' In the terms in which Bernardo expresses his ideas in *Brief Peeks Beyond,* I was simply recognizing the broader field of mind that

I shared with the bowl or jar, of which my body and their forms were, as it were, cross-sections or snapshots.

Indeed, it was something about the visual image of the bowl or jar itself – my only experience of which was, as Bernardo repeatedly points out, a perception in the mind – which had the power to draw my mind away from the objective aspects of experience, through subtle layers within its own field, at least some way 'back' to its formless source and essence.

Seen in this way, such an object becomes, as it were, transparent, delivering to one's intimate experience the broader field of mind of which it is a temporary, local expression. This apparent merging of the field of the perceiver with the field of the perceived is the experience known as 'beauty.' In fact, it is not a merging of two fields, but rather the dissolution of apparent distinctions within the essentially indivisible field of their shared continuum. As such, beauty is to perception what friendship is to relationship.

Such is the function and power of art, the power that some objects have to draw attention from the finite to the infinite. A meeting of friends serves the same purpose, only we call it 'love' rather than 'beauty.' And likewise, some words, such as the collection of essays in *Brief Peeks Beyond,* have the same power to evoke in the reader not just the concept of infinite Consciousness or 'Mind Itself,' of which the apparently physical world is but a temporary precipitation, but the *experience* of it, a taste of its own essential reality.

I have been touched by the profundity of these essays and know that they will imprint their healing intelligence in the broader medium of mind, from which humanity draws its knowledge and experience, for many years to come.

Rupert Spira
Oxford, UK
December 2014

Notes

1   Lessing (1999), p. xxii.

2   Unger and Cui (1997), p. 174.

3   You can also join the forum by going to http://www. bernardokastrup.com and clicking on the 'Forum' link.

4   See, for instance: Koch (2004).

5   The 'Church of the Flying Spaghetti Monster' is a parody of religion and Creationism. Its deity, the 'Flying Spaghetti Monster' proper, has allegedly created the universe and all life forms in it. The parody aims to illustrate the absurdity of invoking complex and unprovable entities when simpler explanations suffice. For more details, see: Vergano (2006).

6   For an introduction to the depth-psychological notion of the 'collective unconscious,' see: Jung (1991). For the accumulating empirical evidence supporting its existence, see the *Journal of Transpersonal Psychology*.

7   Huxley (2011), p. 8.

8   Tegmark (2014), pp. 255-259.

9   Paller and Suzuki (2014), pp. 387-388.

10   Petrucelli (2010), pp. 79-114.

11   *Journal of Transpersonal Psychology.*

12   Coyne wrote: 'Throughout the article Kastrup implies that there is no reality independent of consciousness ... That, of course, is untenable, as there is plenty of evidence about what was going on in the Universe before consciousness evolved.' (Coyne 2014b).

13   Seth Lloyd writes: 'Although the basic laws of physics are comparatively simple in form, they give rise, because they are computationally universal, to systems of enormous complexity.' (Lloyd 2006, p. 176). Perhaps the most evocative demonstrations of how simple rules can generate unfathomable complexity come from computational

systems called cellular automata (Ilachinski 2001).

14 Lehar writes: 'Beyond the farthest things you can perceive in all directions, i.e. above the dome of the sky, and below the solid earth under your feet, or beyond the walls and ceiling of the room you see around you, is located the inner surface of your true physical skull, beyond which is an unimaginably immense external world of which the world you see around you is merely a miniature internal replica.' Lehar (1999), p. 124.

15 Libet (1985).

16 Paller and Suzuki (2014), pp. 387-388.

17 See, for instance: Blackmore (1993) and Mobbs and Watt (2011).

18 Popper (2005).

19 This is a wake-initiated lucid dream. See: LaBerge and Rheingold (1991), Chapter 4.

20 *Buddha at the Gas Pump* episode #240, published on 14 July 2014 and available online at: http://batgap.com/bernardo-kastrup/ (Accessed 17 December 2014).

21 Paller and Suzuki (2014), pp. 387-388.

22 Online article titled *Dissociation FAQ's* available at: http://www.isst-d.org/?contentID=76 (Accessed 17 December 2014). The italics are mine.

23 Coyne (2014a).

24 See, for instance: Fogelin (2001).

25 See, for instance: Zee (2010), pp. 17-25.

26 Krioukov et al. (2012).

27 Available online at: http://www.nytimes.com/imagepages/2006/08/14/science/20060815_SCILL_GRAPHIC.html (Accessed 18 December 2014).

28 For instance: Corbin (2010).

29 Cheetham (2012).

30 Goethe and Bernays (1839), p. 207.

31 Beauregard (1963).

32 Bohm (1980).
33 Personal communication on 1 November 2014. Matser is a renowned humanist, philanthropist and author.
34 Smolin (2013), p. 270. The italics are mine.
35 Ibid.
36 Plato and Zeyl (2000).
37 Petrucelli (2010), pp. 79-114.
38 Jung (1969).
39 Jung (2002).
40 See, for instance: Kim et al. (2000), Gröblacher et al. (2007), Lapkiewicz et al. (2011) and Ma et al. (2013).
41 Ibid.
42 See, for instance: Griffiths (2004), chapters 1 and 2.
43 Paller and Suzuki (2014), pp. 387-388.
44 See, for instance: Faye (2014).
45 See, for instance: Vaidman (2014).
46 See, for instance: Bacciagaluppi (2012).
47 See, respectively: Chalmers (2003) and Levine (1999).
48 Miller (2005).
49 See, for instance: Dennett (1991).
50 See, for instance: Graziano (2013).
51 See, for instance: Ramsey (2013).
52 Strawson (2006), p. 5.
53 See, for instance: Graziano (2014).
54 The original argument appeared in Searle (1980) and focused on the nature of intelligence and understanding. My interpretation of the argument in terms of consciousness is elaborated upon in Kastrup (2011), Chapter 7.
55 For instance: Graziano (2014).
56 See Novella's comment of 13 May 2014 at 1:32 pm, in Novella (2014).
57 See, for instance: Tanenbaum (1992), Section 2.4.
58 See, for instance: Zee (2010), pp. 17-25.
59 See, for instance: Greene (2003), Chapter 12.

60 Dennett (1991).

61 Dennett (2003).

62 See, for instance: Humphrey (2014). For more background on Humphrey's ideas regarding consciousness, see: Humphrey (2011).

63 Strawson (2005).

64 Blackmore (2002), p. 26.

65 See, for instance: Churchland (1989).

66 Center for Consciousness Studies University of Arizona, Anesthesiology (2012).

67 See, for instance: Zandonella (2012).

68 Wheeler (2008).

69 Gelbard-Sagiv et al. (2008), p. 100.

70 Hendricks (2009).

71 Craddock, Tuszynski and Hameroff (2012).

72 Cheu et al. (2012).

73 Hendricks (2009).

74 Center for Consciousness Studies University of Arizona, Anesthesiology (2012).

75 Paller and Suzuki (2014), pp. 387-388.

76 Jung (1972), pp. 139-158.

77 Koch (2004).

78 Shomrat and Levin (2013).

79 Pearsall, Schwartz and Russek (2005).

80 Rothschild (2000).

81 Cedars-Sinai (2013).

82 Lashley (1950).

83 Pribram, Nuwer and Baron (1974).

84 This has extraordinarily interesting implications regarding the nature of time, which echo some of Julian Barbour's ideas (Barbour 1999). Such considerations, however, are beyond the scope of the present essay and will be treated more rigorously in future works.

85 Castro (2013).

86   Ibid.

87   Ramirez et al. (2013).

88   Carhart-Harris et al. (2012).

89   Mosley (2011).

90   Carhart-Harris et al. (2012), p. 2141.

91   Carhart-Harris et al. (2012), p. 2139.

92   Ibid.

93   Ibid.

94   Available online at: http://www.erowid.org/experiences/
     subs/exp_Mushrooms.shtml (Accessed 21 December 2014).

95   Huxley (2011), p. 8.

96   Carhart-Harris et al. (2012), pp. 2141-2142.

97   See, respectively: Tsakiris and Koch (2012) and Tsakiris and
     Kastrup (2012).

98   Kastrup (2014), p. 33.

99   Dresler et al. (2011).

100 Senthilingam (2014). The italics are mine.

101 Tagliazucchi et al. (2014).

102 Alford (2014). The italics are mine.

103 Tagliazucchi et al. (2014), p. 5443. The italics are mine.

104 Tagliazucchi et al. (2014), p. 5452. The italics are mine.

105 Tagliazucchi et al. (2014), p. 5448. The italics are mine.

106 Technically, to calculate the 'spectral power' one must first
     derive the so-called Fourier Transform of the brain activity
     signal. By doing so, the original time-domain signal is
     moved onto the frequency domain and broken down into
     its many frequency components (the so-called 'frequency
     spectrum'). The 'spectral power' is calculated by squaring
     the amplitude of those frequency components. One then
     knows how much 'power' each component contributes to the
     original time-domain signal. But because phase information
     is discarded in the calculation, one doesn't know whether
     the contribution of each component is constructive or
     destructive. In other words, one doesn't know whether a

component interferes constructively or destructively with the others. Often the total spectral power is huge but, because the components interfere mostly destructively with each other, the time-domain signal is puny. In contrast, low total spectral power often corresponds to a significant time-domain signal, because the component frequencies are in phase and interfere constructively with each other, adding up their respective contributions.

107 Dresler et al. (2011).

108 Carhart-Harris (2014). The italics are mine.

109 Ibid.

110 Feltman (2014). The italics are mine.

111 Email sent on 17 November 2014, at 10:52am Central European Time (CET). This is its key part: 'In your 2012 PNAS paper you explicitly say that psilocybin decreases brain activity mostly in the DMN [Default Mode Network, a brain area associated with the ego] and doesn't increase it anywhere in the brain. In your new HBM [*Human Brain Mapping,* a neuroscience journal] study you talk of an increase in variability and spectral power of activity in dream-associated areas. Naturally, an increase in variability is not necessarily an increase in activity. Similarly, an increase in spectral [power] is also not necessarily an increase in activity, since phase information is ignored. I've concluded then that your new study in no way contradicts your earlier findings: psilocybin has NOT been found to increase sheer brain activity ... in dream-associated areas, even though the media seems to have described the study that way. I've attributed the inaccuracy to journalists. Yet, in your own [*The Conversation*] write-up you wrote 'that psilocybin increased the amplitude ... of activity in regions of the brain that are reliably activated during dream sleep and form part of the brain's ancient emotion system.' You also wrote of 'the principle that the psychedelic state rests

on disorganised activity in the ego system permitting disinhibited activity in the emotion system.' Both statements are at least highly suggestive of a direct increase in brain activity ... even though no indication of this seems to be found in your technical papers ... I wonder if you could help me understand the discrepancy. Have you ever found that psilocybin increases sheer brain activity ... anywhere in the brain?'

112 Tagliazucchi's email reply to me on 18 November 2014, 2:57pm CET.

113 Ibid.

114 Upon my original inquiry of 17-Nov-2014 at 10:52am CET and several follow-up email messages from me, I've received the following email replies. From Carhart-Harris: 18-Nov-2014 at 12:12pm and 2:09pm CET; 28-Nov-2014 at 12:15pm, 1:38pm and 1:43pm CET. From Enzo Tagliazucchi: 18-Nov-2014 at 2:57pm and 7:24pm CET.

115 Laughlin and Pines (2000), p. 28. The italics are mine.

116 See, for instance: Kelly and Kelly (2009), Chapter 6, and Lommel (2011).

117 Kuhn (1996), Chapter 10.

118 Kuhn (1996).

119 The results are available online at: http://noosphere. princeton.edu/results.html (Accessed 22 December 2014).

120 See, for instance: CBS 2 news report on the Global Consciousness Project, aired on 3 May 2005, with journalist Brandon Keefe interviewing Jeff Scargle, research astrophysicist at NASA.

121 The American Institute of Physics estimated the odds against chance of the discovery of the 'top quark' – a subatomic particle – to be about a million to one. Their 1995 bulletin stated: 'THE TOP QUARK AT LAST! ... [researchers] announced yesterday that they had indeed discovered the top quark. ... [they] are now confident that their inventory

of top quark events ... represents a true signal and not just a spurious effect due to some background phenomenon. ... *the overall possibility of the observed top quark events being purely due to some background phenomenon is less than one part in a million.'* (Schewe and Stein 1995) The italics are mine.

122 Kastrup (2013).
123 Tsakiris (2014).
124 Rosenberg (2011).
125 See, for instance: Pigliucci (2014).
126 See, for instance: Shavinina (2003), pp. 440-441.
127 Rice and Hostert (1993).
128 See, for instance: Rosenberg (2011).
129 Rosenberg, for instance, speaks of the 'illusion of purposes' (Rosenberg 2011, Chapter 9).
130 Ohno (1972).
131 Doolittle and Sapienza (1980).
132 See, for instance: Marsaglia and Tsang (2002).
133 See, for instance: Bub (2014).
134 Shermer (2014).
135 See, for instance: Vergano (2006).
136 See, for instance: Shavinina (2003), pp. 440-441.
137 Kuhn (1996), p. 117.
138 Steadman (2014).
139 Bucke (2009).
140 Borde, Guth and Vilenkin (2003).
141 After all, science can only causally explain one thing in terms of another, previously existing thing (Russell 2007).
142 In Kim et al. (2000), it is shown that observation not only determines the reality observed at present, but also retroactively changes the history of what is observed accordingly. This is entirely consistent with the notion that reality is fundamentally a story playing itself out in mind. In Gröblacher et al. (2007), it is shown that reality is either entirely in consciousness or we must abandon our

most basic intuitions about what strong-objectivity means. In Lapkiewicz et al. (2011), it is shown that, unlike what one would expect if reality were independent of mind, the properties of a quantum system do not exist prior to observation. In Ma et al. (2013), it is again shown that no naively objective view of reality can be true, which is consistent with the notion that reality is fundamentally subjective.

143 Aczel (2014).
144 Sheils (2011).
145 See, for instance: Economist (2014).
146 See, for instance: Breggin (2007).
147 See, for instance: Leeming (2010).
148 See, for instance, the academic philosophers featured in the 2010 documentary film *Being in the World,* directed by Tao Ruspoli.
149 Mack (1999), p. 6.
150 See, for instance: Jung and Segal (1998).
151 Prescott (2012).
152 Bunzel (2014).
153 Kuhn (1996).
154 See, for instance: Kelly and Kelly (2009), Nagel (2012) and Kastrup (2014), chapters 1, 2 and 3.
155 Gladwell (2002).
156 Bucke (2009).
157 Huxley (2009).
158 See, for instance: Strassman et al. (2008).
159 This is a more strict definition of NDE than that used by researchers like Pim van Lommel (Lommel 2011, p. 7).
160. As cited in Lommel (2011), pp. 11-12.
161 Alexander (2012).
162 Harris (2012a).
163 Tononi (2004).
164 Dresler et al. (2011).

165 As quoted in: Harris (2012a).

166 Harris (2012b).

167 Ibid.

168 Ibid.

169 See, for instance: Treffert (n.d.) and Piore (2013).

170 Urgesi et al. (2010).

171 Kastrup (2014), Chapter 2.

172 Jung (1979).

173 Vallée (1990), p. 105.

174 Crick (1981).

175 Lucas (1961).

176 Tallis (2010).

177 Jung (1991).

178 Franz (2001).

179 Jung (1972), p. 169.

180 See, for instance: Vergano (2006).

181 Thomas et al. (2000), p. 344.

182 See, for instance: Silberman (2009).

183 See, for instance: Okasha (2002), Chapter 4.

184 See, for instance: Davies and Alexander (2005).

185 Keats (1899), p. 277. The italics are mine.

186 See, for instance, the short documentary film *Farm to Fridge – The Truth Behind Meat Production,* widely available for free online viewing on the Internet.

187 Martel (2015), p. xx.

188 See, for instance: Marsh and Onof (2008).

189 See, for instance: Bonabeau (1999).

Bibliography

Aczel, A. (2014). Pseudophysics: The New High Priesthood. *Huffington Post,* 6 March 2014. [Online]. Available from: http://www.huffingtonpost.com/amir-aczel/pseudophysics-the-new-high-priesthood_b_5340183.html [Accessed 23 December 2014].

Alexander, E. (2012). Proof of Heaven: A Doctor's Experience With the Afterlife. *Newsweek Magazine,* 8 October 2012. [Online]. Available from: http://www.newsweek.com/proof-heaven-doctors-experience-afterlife-65327 [Accessed 23 December 2014].

Alford, J. (2014). *Your Brain On Magic Mushrooms.* IFL Science, 3 July 2014. [Online]. Available from: http://www.iflscience.com/brain/your-brain-magic-mushrooms [Accessed 21 December 2014].

Bacciagaluppi, G. (2012). The Role of Decoherence in Quantum Mechanics. In: Zalta, E. N. ed. *The Stanford Encyclopedia of Philosophy* (Winter 2012 Edition). [Online]. Available from: http://plato.stanford.edu/archives/win2012/entries/qm-decoherence/ [Accessed 18 December 2014].

Barbour, J. (1999). *The End of Time: The Next Revolution in Our Understanding of the Universe.* London, UK: Weindenfeld & Nicolson.

Beauregard, O. C. de (1963). *Le Second Principe de la Science du Temps: Entropie, Information, Irréversibilité.* Paris, France: Éditions du Seuil.

Blackmore, S. J. (1993). *Dying to Live: Near-Death Experiences.* Buffalo, NY: Prometheus Books.

Blackmore, S. J. (2002). The grand illusion: Why consciousness exists only when you look for it. *New Scientist,* 174(2348), pp. 26-29.

Bohm, D. (1980). *Wholeness and the Implicate Order.* London, UK: Routledge.

Bonabeau, E. (1999). Editor's Introduction: Stigmergy. *Artificial Life,* 5(2), pp. 95-96.

Borde, A., Guth, A. and Vilenkin, A. (2003). Inflationary space-times are incomplete in past directions. *Physical Review Letters,* 90(15), 151301.

Breggin, P. R. (2007). *Brain Disabling Treatments in Psychiatry: Drugs, Electroshock, and the Psychopharmaceutical Complex.* New York, NY: Springer.

Bub, J. (2014). Quantum Entanglement and Information. In: Zalta, E. N. ed. *The Stanford Encyclopedia of Philosophy* (Fall 2014 Edition). [Online]. Available from: http://plato.stanford.edu/archives/fall2014/entries/qt-entangle/ [Accessed 22 December 2014].

Bucke, R. M. (2009). *Cosmic Consciousness: A Study in the Evolution of the Human Mind.* Mineola, NY: Dover Publications.

Bunzel, T. (2014). The Book That Shows That The World Cannot Be Properly Understood Through Just The Mind. *Collective Evolution,* 27 February 2014. [Online]. Available from: http://www.collective-evolution.com/2014/02/27/book-review-why-materialism-is-baloney-by-bernardo-kastrup-2/ [Accessed 23 December 2014].

Carhart-Harris, R. L. et al. (2012). Neural correlates of the psychedelic state as determined by fMRI studies with psilocybin. *Proceedings of the National Academy of Sciences of the United States of America,* 109(6), pp. 2138–2143.

Carhart-Harris, R. L. (2014). Magic mushrooms expand your mind and amplify your brain's dreaming areas – here's how. *The Conversation,* 3 July 2014. [Online]. Available from: http://theconversation.com/magic-mushrooms-expand-your-mind-and-amplify-your-brains-dreaming-areas-heres-how-28754 [Accessed 22 December 2014].

Castro, J. (2013). The Era of Memory Engineering Has Arrived: How neuroscientists can call up and change a memory. *Scientific American,* 30 July 2013. [Online]. Available from: http://www.scientificamerican.com/article/era-memory-engineering-has-arrived/ [Accessed 21 December 2014].

Cedars-Sinai. (2013). Q+A with Keith L. Black, MD: Setting His Sights on Alzheimer's Disease. *Discoveries Magazine, Winter 2013.* [Online]. Available from: http://www.discoveriesmagazine.org/ qa-with-keith-l-black-md/ [Accessed 21 December 2014].

Center for Consciousness Studies University of Arizona, Anesthesiology. (2012). Scientists claim brain memory code cracked. *ScienceDaily.* [Online]. Available from: www. sciencedaily.com/releases/2012/03/120309103701.htm [Accessed 19 December 2014].

Chalmers, D. (2003). Consciousness and its Place in Nature. In: Stich, S. and Warfield, F. eds. *Blackwell Guide to the Philosophy of Mind.* Malden, MA: Blackwell, pp. 102-142.

Cheetham, T. (2012). *All the World an Icon: Henry Corbin and the angelic function of beings.* Berkeley, CA: North Atlantic Books.

Cheu, E. Y. et al. (2012). Synaptic conditions for auto-associative memory storage and pattern completion in Jensen et al.'s model of hippocampal area CA3. *Journal of Computational Neuroscience,* 33(3), pp. 435-447.

Churchland, P. S. (1989). *Neurophilosophy: Toward a Unified Science of the Mind-Brain.* Cambridge, MA: A Bradford Book.

Corbin, H. (2010). *Cyclical Time and Ismaili Gnosis.* London, UK: Routledge.

Coyne, J. (2014a). John Dickson at the ABC: Theology is so sophisticated that it doesn't need a subject. *Why Evolution Is True,* 9 September 2014. [Online]. Available from: http:// whyevolutionistrue.wordpress.com/2014/09/09/john-dickson-at-the-abc-theology-is-so-sophisticiated-that-it-doesnt-need-a-subject/ [Accessed 18 December 2014].

Coyne, J. (2014b). A new proof of God: The argument from The Matrix. *Why Evolution Is True,* 15 September 2014. [Online]. Available from: http://whyevolutionistrue.wordpress.com/201 4/09/15/a-new-proof-of-god-the-argument-from-the-matrix/ [Accessed 17 December 2014].

Craddock, T. J. A., Tuszynski, J. A. and Hameroff, S. (2012). Cytoskeletal Signaling: Is Memory Encoded in Microtubule Lattices by CaMKII Phosphorylation? *PLoS Computational Biology,* 8(3): e1002421.

Crick, F. (1981). *Life Itself: Its Origin and Nature.* New York, NY: Simon and Schuster.

Davies, J. L. and Alexander, C. N. (2005). Alleviating political violence through reducing collective tension: Impact assessment analyses of the Lebanon war. *Journal of Social Behavior and Personality,* 17(1), pp. 285–338.

Dennett, D. (1991). *Consciousness Explained.* London: Penguin Books.

Dennett, D. (2003). The Illusion of Consciousness. *TED2003.* [Online]. Available from: http://www.ted.com/talks/dan_dennett_on_our_consciousness [Accessed 19 December 2014].

Doolittle, W. F. and Sapienza, C. (1980). Selfish genes, the phenotype paradigm and genome evolution. *Nature,* 284, pp. 601–603.

Dresler, M. et al. (2011). Dreamed Movement Elicits Activation in the Sensorimotor Cortex. *Current Biology,* 21(21), pp. 1833–1837.

Expanding the shrinks. *The Economist* (British Edition), 11 October 2014. [Online]. Available from: http://www.economist.com/news/britain/21623773-popularity-cbt-freezing-out-more-traditional-forms-therapy-expanding-shrinks [Accessed 23 December 2014].

Faye, J. (2014). Copenhagen Interpretation of Quantum Mechanics. In: Zalta, E. N. ed. *The Stanford Encyclopedia of Philosophy* (Fall 2014 Edition). [Online]. Available from: http://plato.stanford.edu/archives/fall2014/entries/qm-copenhagen/ [Accessed 18 December 2014].

Feltman, R. (2014). Psychedelic mushrooms put your brain in a 'waking dream,' study finds. *The Washington Post,* 3 July 2014. [Online]. Available from: http://www.washingtonpost.com/news/to-your-health/wp/2014/07/03/psychedelic-drugs-put-your-brain-in-a-waking-dream-study-finds/ [Accessed 22 December 2014].

Fogelin, R. (2001). *Routledge Philosophy Guidebook to Berkeley and the Principles of Human Knowledge.* London, UK: Routledge.

Franz, M.-L. von (2001). *Psyche and Matter.* Boston, MA: Shambhala.

Gelbard-Sagiv, H. et al. (2008). Internally Generated Reactivation of Single Neurons in Human Hippocampus During Free Recall. *Science,* 322(5898), pp. 96-101.

Gladwell, M. (2002). *The Tipping Point: How Little Things Can Make a Big Difference.* New York, NY: Back Bay Books.

Goethe, J. W. (author) and Bernays, L. J. (translator) (1839). *Goethe's Faust, Part II.* London: Sampson Low.

Graziano, M. (2013). *Consciousness and the Social Brain.* Oxford, UK: Oxford University Press.

Graziano, M. (2014). Are We Really Conscious? *New York Times,* 10 October 2014. [Online]. Available from: http://www.nytimes.com/2014/10/12/opinion/sunday/are-we-really-conscious.html [Accessed 18 December 2014].

Greene, B. (2003). *The Elegant Universe: Superstrings, Hidden Dimensions, and the Quest for the Ultimate Theory.* New York, NY: W. W. Norton & Company.

Griffiths, D. J. (2004). *Introduction to Quantum Mechanics, Second Edition.* Harlow, UK: Pearson.

Gröblacher, S. et al. (2007). An experimental test of non-local realism. *Nature,* 446, pp. 871-875.

Harris, S. (2012a). This Must Be Heaven. *Sam Harris: The Blog,* 12 October 2012. [Online]. Available from: http://www.samharris.org/blog/item/this-must-be-heaven [Accessed 23 December 2014].

Harris, S. (2012b). Science on the Brink of Death. *Sam Harris: The Blog,* 11 November 2012. [Online]. Available from: http://www.samharris.org/blog/item/science-on-the-brink-of-death [Accessed 23 December 2014].

Hendricks, M. (2009). *Reducing memory to a molecule: A researcher explores the molecular essence of memory.* Johns Hopkins Medicine, Institute for Basic Biomedical Sciences. [Online].

Available from: http://www.hopkinsmedicine.org/institute_
basic_biomedical_sciences/news_events/articles_and_stories/
learning_memory/200906_reducing_memory_molecule.htm
[Accessed 21 December 2014].

Humphrey, N. (2011). *Soul Dust: The Magic of Consciousness.*
Princeton, NJ: Princeton University Press.

Humphrey, N. (2014). *The magic of consciousness.* Ri Channel.
[Online]. Available from: http://richannel.org/the-magic-of-
consciousness [Accessed 19 December 2014].

Huxley, A. (2009). *The Perennial Philosophy.* New York, NY:
HarperPerennial.

Huxley, A. (2011). *The Doors of Perception: includes Heaven & Hell.*
London, UK: Thinking Ink Limited.

Ilachinski, A. (2001). *Cellular Automata: A Discrete Universe.*
Singapore: World Scientific.

Journal of Transpersonal Psychology. Palo Alto, CA: Association for
Transpersonal Psychology.

Jung, C. G. (1969). *Aion: Researches into the Phenomenology of the Self,
Second Edition.* Princeton, NJ: Princeton University Press.

Jung, C. G. (1972). *The Structure and Dynamics of the Psyche, Second
Edition (The Collected Works of C. G. Jung, Vol. 8).* Princeton, NJ:
Princeton University Press.

Jung, C. G. (1979). *Flying Saucers: A Modern Myth of Things Seen in
the Skies.* Princeton, NJ: Princeton University Press.

Jung, C. G. (1991). *The Archetypes and the Collective Unconscious.*
London, UK: Routledge.

Jung, C. G. (author) and Segal, R. A. (editor) (1998). *Jung on
Mythology.* London, UK: Routledge.

Jung, C. G. (2002). *Answer to Job.* London, UK: Routledge.

Kastrup, B. (2011). *Rationalist Spirituality: An exploration of the meaning
of life and existence informed by logic and science.* Winchester, UK:
O-Books.

Kastrup, B. (2013). The Fairytale of Materialism: How
'Fundamentalists' Hijacked Science. *New Dawn Magazine,*

Special Issue, 7(5), 26 September 2013. [Online]. Available from: http://www.newdawnmagazine.com/articles/the-fairytale-of-materialism-how-fundamentalists-hijacked-science [Accessed 22 December 2014].

Kastrup, B. (2014). *Why Materialism Is Baloney: How True Skeptics Know There Is No Death and Fathom Answers to life, the Universe, and Everything.* Winchester, UK: Iff-Books.

Keats, J. (1899). *The Complete Poetical Works and Letters of John Keats, Cambridge Edition.* Boston, MA: Houghton, Mifflin and Company.

Kelly, E. and Kelly, E. W. (2009). *Irreducible Mind: Toward a Psychology for the 21st Century.* Lanham, MD: Rowman & Littlefield.

Kim, Y.-H. et al. (2000). A Delayed Choice Quantum Eraser. *Physical Review Letters,* 84, pp. 1–5.

Koch, C. (2004). *The quest for consciousness: a neurobiological approach.* Englewood, CO: Roberts & Company Publishers.

Krioukov, D. et al. (2012). Network Cosmology. *Scientific Reports,* 2(793). [Online]. Available from: http://www.nature.com/srep/2012/121113/srep00793/pdf/srep00793.pdf [Accessed 18 December 2014].

Kuhn, T. S. (1996). *The Structure of Scientific Revolutions, Third Edition.* Chicago, IL: The University of Chicago Press.

LaBerge, S. and Rheingold, H. (1991). *Exploring the World of Lucid Dreaming.* New York, NY: Ballantine Books.

Lapkiewicz, R. et al. (2011). Experimental non-classicality of an indivisible quantum system. *Nature,* 474, pp. 490–493.

Lashley, K. S. (1950). In search of the engram. *Society for Experimental Biology Symposium No. 4: Physiological Mechanisms in Animal Behaviour,* pp. 454-483. Crambridge, UK: Cambridge University Press.

Laughlin, R. B. and Pines, D. (2000). The Theory of Everything. *Proceedings of the National Academy of Sciences of the USA,* 97(1), pp. 28-31.

Leeming, D. A. (2010). *Creation Myths of the World: An Encyclopedia,*

Second Edition. Santa Barbara, CA: ABC-CLIO.

Lehar, S. (1999). Gestalt isomorphism and the quantification of spatial perception. *Gestalt Theory,* 21(2), pp. 122-139.

Lessing, D. M. (1999). *The Golden Notebook.* New York, NY: HarperPerennial.

Levine, J. (1999). Conceivability, Identity, and the Explanatory Gap. In: Hameroff, S., Kaszniak, A., and Chalmers, D. eds. *Toward a Science of Consciousness III, The Third Tucson Discussions and Debates.* Cambridge, MA: The MIT Press, pp. 3-12.

Libet, B. (1985). Unconscious cerebral initiative and the role of conscious will in voluntary action. *The Behavioral and Brain Sciences,* 8, pp. 529–566.

Lloyd, S. (2006). *Programming the Universe: A Quantum Computer Scientist Takes on the Cosmos.* New York, NY: Alfred A. Knopf.

Lommel, P. van (2011). *Consciousness Beyond Life: The Science of the Near-Death Experience.* New York, NY: HarperCollins.

Lucas, J. R. (1961). Minds, Machines and Gödel. *Philosophy XXXVI,* pp. 112-127.

Ma, X.-S. et al. (2013). Quantum erasure with causally disconnected choice. *Proc. Natl. Acad. Sci. USA,* 110, pp. 1221-1226.

Mack, J. E. (1999). *Passport to the Cosmos.* New York, NY: Three Rivers Press.

Marsaglia, G. and Tsang, W. W. (2002). Some Difficult-to-Pass Tests of Randomness. *Journal of Statistical Software,* 7(3), pp. 1-8.

Marsh, L. and Onof, C. (2008). Stigmergic epistemology, stigmergic cognition. *Cognitive Systems Research,* 9(1-2), pp. 136-149.

Martel, J. F. (2015). *Reclaiming Art in the Age of Artifice: A Treatise, Critique, and Call to Action.* Berkeley, CA: North Atlantic Books.

Miller, G. (2005). What Is the Biological Basis of Consciousness? *Science,* 309(5731), p. 79.

Mobbs, D. and Watt, C. (2011). There is nothing paranormal about near-death experiences: how neuroscience can explain seeing bright lights, meeting the dead, or being convinced you are one of them. *Trends in Cognitive Sciences,* 15(10), pp. 447-449.

Mosley, M. (2011). *'I took magic mushroom drug psilocybin in clinical trial.'* BBC News Health, 6 January 2011. [Online]. Available from: http://www.bbc.co.uk/news/health-12122409 [Accessed 21 December 2014].

Nagel, T. (2012). *Mind and Cosmos: Why the Materialist Neo-Darwinian Conception of Nature is Almost Certainly False.* Oxford, UK: Oxford University Press.

Novella, S. (2014). After the Afterlife Debate. *NeuroLogica Blog,* 8 May 2014 [Online]. Available from: http://theness.com/neurologicablog/index.php/after-the-afterlife-debate/#more-6561 [Accessed 22 December 2014].

Ohno, S. (1972). So much 'junk' DNA in our genome. In: Smith, H. H. ed. *Evolution of Genetic Systems: Brookhaven Symposium in Biology,* No. 23, pp. 366–370. New York, NY: Gordon and Breach.

Okasha, S. (2002). *Philosophy of Science: A Very Short Introduction.* Oxford, UK: Oxford University Press.

Paller, A. and Suzuki, S. (2014). The source of consciousness. *Trends in Cognitive Sciences,* 18(8), pp. 387-389.

Pearsall, P., Schwartz, G. E. and Russek, L. G. (2005). Organs Transplants & Cellular Memories. *Nexus Magazine,* 12(3).

Petrucelli, J. ed. (2010). *Knowing, Not-knowing and Sort-of-knowing: Psychoanalysis and the Experience of Uncertainty.* London, UK: Karnac Books.

Pigliucci, M. (2014). Neil deGrasse Tyson and the Value of Philosophy. *The Huffington Post,* 16 May 2014. [Online]. Available from: http://www.huffingtonpost.com/massimo-pigliucci/neil-degrasse-tyson-and-the-value-of-philosophy_b_5330216.html [Accessed 22 December 2014].

Piore, A. (2013). When Brain Damage Unlocks the Genius Within. *Popular Science,* 19 February 2013. [Online]. Available from: http://www.popsci.com/science/article/2013-02/when-brain-damage-unlocks-genius-within [Accessed 23 December 2014].

Plato (author) and Zeyl, D. J. (translator) (2000). *Timaeus.* Indianapolis, In: Hackett.

Popper, K. (2005). *The Logic of Scientific Discovery*. London, UK: Routledge.

Prescott, M. (2012). Pep Talk. *Michael Prescott's Blog: Occasional thoughts on matters of life and death*, 22 April 2012. [Online]. Available from: http://michaelprescott.typepad.com/michael_prescotts_blog/2012/04/pep-talk.html [Accessed 23 December 2014].

Pribram, K. H., Nuwer, M. and Baron, R. J. (1974). The Holographic Hypothesis of Memory Structure in Brain Function and Perception. In: Atkinson, R. C. et al. eds. *Contemporary developments in mathematical psychology, Vol. II*. San Francisco, CA: W. H. Freeman.

Ramirez, S. et al. (2013). Creating a False Memory in the Hippocampus. *Science*, 341(6144), pp. 387-391.

Ramsey, W. (2013). Eliminative Materialism. In: Zalta, E. N. ed. *The Stanford Encyclopedia of Philosophy* (Summer 2013 Edition). [Online]. Available from: http://plato.stanford.edu/archives/sum2013/entries/materialism-eliminative/ [Accessed 18 December 2014].

Rice, W. R. and Hostert, E. E. (1993). Laboratory experiments on speciation: what have we learned in 40 years. *Evolution*, 47(6), pp. 1637–1653.

Rosenberg, A. (2011). *The Atheist's Guide to Reality: Enjoying Life without Illusions*. New York, NY: W. W. Norton & Company.

Rothschild, B. (2000). *The Body Remembers: The Psychophysiology of Trauma and Trauma Treatment*. New York, NY: W. W. Norton & Company.

Russell, B. (2007). *The Analysis of Matter*. Nottingham, UK: Spokesman Books.

Schewe, P. F. and Stein, B. (1995). *Physics News Update: A digest of physics news items*, No. 216, 3 March 1995. College Park, MD: The American Institute of Physics.

Searle, J. R. (1980). Minds, brains, and programs. *Behavioral and Brain Sciences*, 3(3), pp. 417-457.

Senthilingam, M. (2014). *How 'magic mushroom' chemical could free the mind of depression, addictions.* CNN Vital Signs, 17 September 2014. [Online]. Available from: http://edition.cnn.com/2014/09/17/health/magic-mushroom-chemical-depression [Accessed 21 December 2014].

Shavinina, L. V. (2003). *The International Handbook on Innovation.* Oxford, UK: Elsevier Science.

Sheils, J. (2011). Double Twit Experiment – What Brian Cox Gets Wrong. *Field Lines: The writings of James Sheils,* 23 December 2011. [Online]. Available from: http://fieldlines.org/2011/12/23/double-twit-experiment-what-brian-cox-gets-wrong/ [Accessed 23 December 2014].

Shermer, M. (2014). Anomalous Events That Can Shake One's Skepticism to the Core: I just witnessed an event so mysterious that it shook my skepticism. *Scientific American,* 311(4), 16 September 2014. [Online]. Available from: http://www.scientificamerican.com/article/anomalous-events-that-can-shake-one-s-skepticism-to-the-core/ [Accessed 22 December 2014].

Shomrat, T. and Levin, M. (2013). An automated training paradigm reveals long-term memory in planarians and its persistence through head regeneration. *The Journal of Experimental Biology,* 216, pp. 3799-3810.

Silberman, S. (2009). Placebos Are Getting More Effective. Drugmakers Are Desperate to Know Why. *Wired Magazine,* 17.09, 24 August 2009. [Online]. Available from: http://archive.wired.com/medtech/drugs/magazine/17-09/ff_placebo_effect [Accessed 23 December 2014].

Smolin, L. (2013). *Time Reborn: From the Crisis in Physics to the Future of the Universe.* Boston, MA: Houghton Mifflin Harcourt.

Steadman, I. (2014). Deepak Chopra doesn't understand quantum physics, so Brian Cox wants $1,000,000 from him. *New Statesman,* 7 July 2014. [Online]. Available from: http://www.newstatesman.com/future-proof/2014/07/deepak-chopra-doesnt-understand-quantum-physics-so-brian-cox-wants-1000000-him   [Accessed 22 December 2014].

Strassman, R. et al. (2008). *Inner Paths to Outer Space: Journeys to Alien Worlds Through Psychedelics and Other Spiritual Technologies.* Rochester, VT: Park Street Press.

Strawson, G. (2005). Intentionality and Experience: Terminological Preliminaries. In: Smith, D. and Thomasson, A. eds. *Phenomenology and Philosophy of Mind.* Oxford, UK: Oxford University Press, pp. 41-66.

Strawson, G. (2006). Realistic Monism: Why Physicalism Entails Panpsychism. *Journal of Consciousness Studies,* 13, pp. 3-31.

Tagliazucchi, E. et al. (2014). Enhanced repertoire of brain dynamical states during the psychedelic experience. *Human Brain Mapping,* 35(11), pp. 5442–5456.

Tallis, R. (2010). How Can I Possibly Be Free? *The New Atlantis,* Summer 2010, pp. 28-47. [Online]. Available from: http://www.thenewatlantis.com/docLib/20100914_TNA28Tallis.pdf [Accessed 23 December 2014].

Tanenbaum, A. (1992). *Modern Operating Systems.* Upper Saddle River, NJ: Prentice Hall.

Tegmark, M. (2014). *Our Mathematical Universe: My Quest for the Ultimate Nature of Reality.* New York, NY: Alfred A. Knopf.

Thomas, S. P. et al. (2000). Anger and cancer: an analysis of the linkages. *Cancer Nursing,* 23(5), pp. 344-349.

Tononi, G. (2004). An information integration theory of consciousness. *BMC Neuroscience,* 5(42). [Online]. Available from: http://www.biomedcentral.com/1471-2202/5/42 [Accessed 23 December 2014].

Treffert, D. A. (n.d.). *The 'Acquired' Savant – 'Accidental' Genius: Could such dormant potential exist within us all?* Wisconsin Medical Society. [Online]. Available from: https://www.wisconsinmedicalsociety.org/professional/savant-syndrome/resources/articles/the-acquired-savant-accidental-genius/ [Accessed 23 December 2014].

Tsakiris, A. and Koch, C. (2012). Dr. Christof Koch on Human Consciousness and Near Death Experience Research. *Skeptiko Podcast,* episode 160, 7 February 2012. [Online]. Available from: http://www.skeptiko.com/160-christof-koch-consciousness-and-near-death-experience-research/ [Accessed 21 December 2014].

Tsakiris, A. and Kastrup, B. (2012). Bernardo Kastrup's Controversial View of Consciousness Research. *Skeptiko Podcast,* episode 158, 17 January 2012. [Online]. Available from: http://www.skeptiko.com/bernardo-kastrup-consciousness-research/ [Accessed 21 December 2014].

Tsakiris, A. (2014). *Why Science Is Wrong... About Almost Everything.* San Antonio, TX: Anomalist Books.

Unger, R. M. (author) and Cui, Z. (editor) (1997). *Politics: The Central Texts, Theory Against Fate.* London, UK: Verso.

Urgesi, C. et al. (2010). The Spiritual Brain: Selective Cortical Lesions Modulate Human Self-Transcendence. *Neuron,* 65(3), pp. 309-319.

Vaidman, L. (2014). Many-Worlds Interpretation of Quantum Mechanics. In: Zalta, E. N. ed. *The Stanford Encyclopedia of Philosophy* (Winter 2014 Edition). [Online]. Available from: http://plato.stanford.edu/archives/win2014/entries/qm-manyworlds/ [Accessed 18 December 2014].

Vallée, J. (1990). Five Arguments Against the Extraterrestrial Origin of Unidentified Flying Objects. *Journal of Scientific Exploration,* 4(1), pp. 105-117.

Vergano, D. (2006). 'Spaghetti Monster' is noodling around with faith. *USA Today,* 27 March 2006. [Online]. Available from: http://usatoday30.usatoday.com/tech/science/2006-03-26-spaghetti-monster_x.htm [Accessed 17 December 2014].

Wheeler, M. (2008). How memories are made, and recalled: UCLA, Israeli researchers record single cells as they call up memories. *UCLA Newsroom,* 10 September 2008. [Online]. Available from: http://newsroom.ucla.edu/releases/how-memories-are-made-

and-recalled-62588 [Accessed 19 December 2014].

Zandonella, C. (2012). Princeton scientists identify neural activity sequences that help form memory, decision-making. *News at Princeton,* 14 March 2012. [Online]. Available from: http://www. princeton.edu/main/news/archive/S33/17/36M20/ [Accessed 19 December 2014].

Zee, A. (2010). *Quantum Field Theory in a Nutshell, 2nd Edition.* Princeton, NJ: Princeton University Press.

BOOKS

ACADEMIC AND SPECIALIST

Iff Books publishes non-fiction. It aims to work with authors and titles that augment our understanding of the human condition, society and civilisation, and the world or universe in which we live.
If you have enjoyed this book, why not tell other readers by posting a review on your preferred book site.

Recent bestsellers from Iff Books are:

Why Materialism Is Baloney
How True Skeptics Know There is no Death and Fathom Answers
to Life, the Universe, and Everything
Bernardo Kastrup
A hard-nosed, logical, and skeptic non-materialist metaphysics,
according to which the body is in mind, not mind in the body.
Paperback: 978-1-78279-362-5 ebook: 978-1-78279-361-8

The Fall
Steve Taylor
The Fall discusses human achievement versus the issues of war,
patriarchy and social inequality.
Paperback: 978-1-90504-720-8 ebook: 978-184694-633-2

Framespotting
Changing How You Look at Things Changes How
You See Them
Laurence & Alison Matthews
A punchy, upbeat guide to framespotting. Spot deceptions and
hidden assumptions; swap growth for growing up. See and be free.
Paperback: 978-1-78279-689-3 ebook: 978-1-78279-822-4

Is There an Afterlife?
David Fontana
Is there an Afterlife? If so what is it like? How do Western ideas
of the afterlife compare with Eastern? David Fontana presents
the historical and contemporary evidence for survival of physical
death.
Paperback: 978-1-90381-690-5

Nothing Matters
A Book About Nothing
Ronald Green
Thinking about Nothing opens the world to everything by illuminating new angles to old problems and stimulating new ways of thinking.
Paperback: 978-1-84694-707-0 ebook: 978-1-78099-016-3

Panpsychism
The Philosophy of the Sensuous Cosmos
Peter Ells
Are free will and mind chimeras? This book, anti-materialistic but respecting science, answers: No! Mind is foundational to all existence.
Paperback: 978-1-84694-505-2 ebook: 978-1-78099-018-7

Punk Science
Inside the Mind of God
Manjir Samanta-Laughton
Many have experienced unexplainable phenomena; God, psychic abilities, extraordinary healing and angelic encounters. Can cutting-edge science actually explain phenomena previously thought of as 'paranormal'?
Paperback: 978-1-90504-793-2

The Vagabond Spirit of Poetry
Edward Clarke
Spend time with the wisest poets of the modern age and of the past, and let Edward Clarke remind you of the importance of poetry in our industrialized world.
Paperback: 978-1-78279-370-0 ebook: 978-1-78279-369-4

Readers of ebooks can buy or view any of these bestsellers by clicking on the live link in the title. Most titles are published in paperback and as an ebook. Paperbacks are available in traditional bookshops. Both print and ebook formats are available online.

Find more titles and sign up to our readers' newsletter at
http://www.johnhuntpublishing.com/non-fiction

Follow us on Facebook at
https://www.facebook.com/JHPNonFiction
and Twitter at https://twitter.com/JHPNonFiction